A Well-Trained Wife

A Well-Trained Wife

Wife

My Escape from Christian Patriarchy

TIA LEVINGS

ST. MARTIN'S PRESS
NEW YORK

First published in the United States by St. Martin's Press,
an imprint of St. Martin's Publishing Group

A WELL-TRAINED WIFE. Copyright © 2024 by Tia Levings.
All rights reserved. Printed in the United States of America.
For information, address St. Martin's Publishing Group,
120 Broadway, New York, NY 10271.

www.stmartins.com

Library of Congress Cataloging-in-Publication Data

Names: Levings, Tia, author.
Title: A well-trained wife : my escape from Christian patriarchy / Tia Levings.
Description: First edition. | New York : St. Martin's Press, [2024]
Identifiers: LCCN 2024003514 | ISBN 9781250288288 (hardcover) |
  ISBN 9781250288295 (ebook)
Subjects: LCSH: Levings, Tia. | Abused wives—United States—
  Biography. | Christian biography. | Psychology, Religious. |
  Fundamentalism—Psychological aspects. | Wife abuse. | Authority—
  Religious aspects—Christianity.
Classification: LCC BR1725.L43526 A3 2024 | DDC 286.092 [B]—
  dc23/eng/20240220
LC record available at https://lccn.loc.gov/2024003514

Our books may be purchased in bulk for promotional, educational,
or business use. Please contact your local bookseller or the Macmillan
Corporate and Premium Sales Department at 1-800-221-7945,
extension 5442, or by email at
MacmillanSpecialMarkets@macmillan.com.

First Edition: 2024

10 9 8 7 6 5 4 3 2 1

For ACCWR.
You are my heart.

Train up a child in the way they should go, and when they are old, they will not depart from it.

—*Proverbs 22:6*

A wild patience has taken me this far.

—*Adrienne Rich*

Contents

Preface

IN ORDER TO WRITE THIS BOOK, I RELIED ON MY OWN MEMORIES, journals, reference materials, interviews, The Way Back Machine (Internet Archive), and the contributing stories of others. There are composite characters, and some names and identifying details have been changed.

While this story is my own memoir, the situations in these pages are far from unique. With me stands a choir of invisible fundamentalist women, too silenced to tell their stories themselves.

A Well-Trained Wife

Prologue

THIS WAS MY FAULT. I CHASED HIM UP THE STAIRS.

At the top of the landing, I caught his right sleeve. When he spun around, his forearm cuffed my cheek. The force knocked me to the wood floor, shocked and dizzy. The bedroom door slammed behind him.

Like a wounded reptile, I crawled over the threshold and lay on the cold vinyl, kicking the door shut.

Out of breath, I remembered: the death of our family happened in so many layers. I couldn't cry anymore, even though my cheekbone throbbed. I let the cold concrete of reality settle in my blood. Allan was right—I was a shit wife, a shit housekeeper, and a shit mother.

All along, I thought I was protecting the kids. Shielding them from realities behind closed doors. Sacrificing to maintain a two-parent Christian home. Making hard, better choices for their faith, family, and education than I made for myself, trying to safeguard them from pain.

But they saw. That was obvious now. And staying meant raising sons who hit women. Staying meant raising a daughter who stayed with the man who hit her. And that would be my fault. I'd be the one who taught them life like this was okay. I didn't just let erratic violence continue happening—I helped by refusing to leave. Good mothers don't let this happen to their kids.

I swallowed. How does a nothing woman, a failure, make it out of here with them alive?

I was a thirty-three-year-old hag, wrinkled, sallow-cheeked, and plain.

So much older than my years. I didn't have an education or a real job. I'd convinced everyone our lives were picture-perfect. Not even my parents knew the truth. So, where the hell could I turn, now that I realized our survival was tangled in lies?

How could I mother and support four children alone? What if something happened to them while I tried? And the pets? Who takes in a woman with four kids, three chickens, two dogs, and too many cats to count?

What about school? Would I have a job and make it home in time to ask them about their days? Would I even still be their mom? I cringed at the thought of a judge denying me custody.

The floor creaked beneath me—footsteps in the hall. I held my breath and watched the crack beneath the door. When the sounds descended the stairs, I exhaled.

Our church had moved us to Lutherville in the Cumberland Mountains a year ago, to a hundred-year-old home we called the Blue House. Lutherville was named for Martin Luther, the greatest Reformer of them all. Lutherville had two stoplights, a courthouse, a pizza joint, and a Hardee's—an old coal town in a line of coal towns, an hour from Knoxville.

Almost idyllic on the outside, the Blue House had a wide front porch, white columns, and a white picket fence. A stately red maple tree shaded the front yard and a steep hill rose behind it. Across the street was an old country church with a dignified steeple and wooden stairs. Our corner looked like a photo for a jigsaw puzzle, a charming image of life out in the country, but no one knew the secrets inside.

Allan screamed every night at the demons in the walls. He clutched at my neck as often as he tore his hair seeing those fiery red eyes. He swore he'd kill me. Or he'd take the kids "forever." Finally, I begged him to see a doctor. I called him "unwell," too afraid to call it insanity.

The church called Allan's demons spiritual warfare. Seeing demons pointed to spiritual truth, not illness. Allan didn't need medicine—I needed correction. They told me to submit more. Go to church more. And anyway, Allan refused doctors. That settled that.

And I was supposed to turn the other cheek. Divorce wasn't allowed any more than doctors. Now, my long hair hid the scars resulting from my vows to love, honor, and obey. "Till death do us part" could mean by his hand, but who cared?

I curled onto my side, hugging my knees to my chest. Here's what I knew for sure:

The church sanctioned my suffering.

They were on his side.

The churches didn't care about our safety as long as the threat was from inside our home. Because, based on what I'd been taught, it was possible some of the men I turned to did this to their wives as well. Before every submissive woman I knew stood a patriarch who'd learned to hold the line. No one wanted their secrets exposed. When your cup runneth over, sometimes it's not with blessing. Sometimes your cup's full of crap.

As much as I wanted to be a woman who found comfort in her faith, my faith continued to hurt me and hold me here. This airlessness was more than my marriage. It was more than my fault. More than his, even. He needed help too.

So, I grounded myself in time: *today is Sunday, October 28, 2007.*

Like a reflex, I counted the good. My babies' faces. The years. Changing leaves and new-teeth smiles. The sound of Katie's laugh. My boys with flowers from the yard. The flow of milk. Sounding out words, the colors of crayons. Fresh bread. Lullabies by moonlight. A layer of snow. The scent of their heads. The way they looked at me with such love and trust when I took their picture. The hush of a house at midnight. The moon and stars as I rocked in the chair and watched everyone sleep.

Could I risk all that?

In birth, the midwives said the only way out is through. I swallowed and braced myself.

Today it hit me when he hit me, blood shaking in my brain. Maybe there wasn't a savior coming. Maybe it was up to me to save me.

There was only one way out of here.

I pushed my hands flat to the floor and rose to get the kids.

Part One

GROOM

Belong

Three days. Two parents in their mid-twenties, two daughters, one elderly cal-
ico cat named Piddles. A Dodge sedan and an old UPS truck painted gold and
Kelly green. A hand-painted sign that read SHERWOOD FOREST BUILDERS.
Jackson's "Thriller" on the radio. Both vehicles packed tight and out of gas
on this April day in 1984. This was how we arrived in Jacksonville, Florida,
sweaty and bewildered. I was sure I'd just landed in hell.

Before the move from Michigan, the dominoes of our lives began to fall.
The domino of my parents buying eighty acres more than they could afford.
The domino of my falling in love with that farm and those trees. The domino
of meeting God in the woods. The blizzard dominoes, so close together and
cutting the power, the roads, the food supply. The Michigan economy and
union strike dominoes. The domino of bankruptcy. The domino of the job
offers in Florida. The domino of two months to sell everything you own, including the dog. The domino of no time to say goodbye.

These truths happened and led to one another. The fatal finger from the
sky knocked those dominoes down, down, down.

But while my parents came to Jacksonville relieved, I came crying.

Because I'd spent my first ten years on wild acreage in the Michigan woods.
I knew solitude. Resilience. Creativity and freedom. I'd met God in the trees,
not at church. Sweet witches and fairies too. I read often and wrote stories of my
own. I loved Fred Rogers, Bob Ross, and Laura Ingalls Wilder. I daydreamed

of motherhood and authorship—of making my mark on the world in unique and vibrant ways. I'd be an artist mother writer hiker friend.

My second ten years happened in Florida. I came with all that I knew, and what I knew wasn't useful here.

We had pizza at the apartment pool on our first day in *Jack-son-ville*. I ground the hard consonants of this new town in my head. We'd come from vowel sounds. *Es-ca-na-ba*. Nothing would ever be the same again.

The dominoes kept on falling.

The domino of an apartment in a blistering hot Southern city, full of foreign sounds, colors, and crowds. The dominos of air-conditioning and cable TV: endless reruns of *Perry Mason, Little House on the Prairie*, and *Trapper John, M.D.* I kept a blanket over my head, afraid to go outside. I cried, stopped eating until my stomach ached, and sat in the dark.

A year later, I was eleven, watching R-rated *Silkwood* and Stephen King's *Cat's Eye* on HBO in the apartments of kids whose mothers weren't home. I avoided the heat, stayed angry at the world, and started to find my words. I screamed often. My body popped sudden boobs and pimples, like a carnival sprouting in a parking lot. Anger is a stage of grief, but no one told me that, and no one called it grief anyway. They called it adolescence, and it was a problem to solve.

And so, there was the domino of my bad attitude. The domino of my rapid changes. The domino of my parents' efforts to resettle in a new city. The domino of us all feeling so overwhelmed. The domino of a glistening megachurch in the heart of downtown Jacksonville, shining like a beacon on TV, offering hope and belonging. The domino of my dad's resistance against the domino of my mom's persistence. The domino of the magic words from the pastor's lips.

We were sitting in our living room around the TV—Dad, Mom, me, and my younger sister, Monica. My mom wanted us to go to church like when she grew up. She said it would help us settle in better, adjust to Florida. The church promises to comfort the vulnerable and soothe the grieving.

The camera panned the audience—more people than I'd ever seen all together. A bald man with sharp features and a Hollywood suit stood at the wooden pulpit. "That's Dr. Vines," Mom said. "They have two pastors at First Baptist."

Dad sipped his coffee in his recliner. "That place is huge," he muttered.

First Baptist in the mid-eighties was majestic. Mom said they owned the largest pipe organ in the South, and the walls behind the choir and orchestra held pipes like tin soldiers. A replica of a mountain waterfall cascaded down fake rocks and real plants between the pipes. I'd never seen a church with a waterfall before.

"They have two services too," Mom said. "The building seats over thirty-five hundred people. Two choirs, two orchestras. I'd love to sing in a choir like that." She beamed. In Michigan, she'd directed the choir and sang solos. I knew she missed music.

The pastor paced and waved his hands. "You need to get plugged in to a good church," he urged. "Children need to be raised in a *good* Christian family. Their eternity depends on it!!"

It was as if this man reached through the screen to speak directly to our family. He leaned over the podium, begging. "Brothers and sisters, we need the hearts of your young people. Adolescents still have a pliable mind. We must get ahold of children while they're still young."

I didn't want an old man in a suit to get ahold of me. But "adolescence" was a big word that meant dangerous territory. In adolescence, kids either went right, or they went wrong—against what God wanted. I rolled my eyes. I still played with dolls, hated dresses, and wanted to move back home to the trees. Nothing wrong with that.

But I could tell First Baptist was the cool place to be. Mom wanted this for her new life—singing onstage, pretty clothes, friendly faces. At First Baptist, the women didn't have to roll up their sleeves and work like men on farms. Men wore suits, women wore perfume, children smiled and walked in line. First Baptist was as opposite from where we came from as possible, and I'm sure she found that reassuring. The fatal finger from the sky tipped the dominoes ever so slightly. It was just enough to trigger a visit for a "New Members Tour," an orientation session designed to help visitors find their bearings.

The following Sunday afternoon, we crossed one of seven bridges over the sapphire ribbon of the St. Johns River to get to "the big church downtown." Instead of trees, Jacksonville had billboards. All over town, little frames around license plates read FOLLOW ME TO FIRST BAPTIST, so we did.

A short man polished like a game show host greeted us. "Howdy there, folks. My name is Tom. I'm a deacon here at First Baptist and your guide for the afternoon. It's a big place—we cover eleven city blocks! And we're built for expansion. But don't worry a bit. If you get lost either on the campus or in life, First Baptist hands out maps!" He winked and Monica shuffled behind me. Neither one of us wanted his attention. "You must be here for our children's ministry," he said to our parents. "We have the very best youth program in all of Jacksonville. Some say in the entire country."

Tom passed out brochures to our tour group. Four other families walked with us through the halls. "Dr. Vines sure can preach a good sermon, can't he?" Tom said. "Really knows how to reel 'em in."

The tour progressed through a series of restored retail and office buildings converted to Sunday School rooms. "These were built when people drove downtown to shop, in those big cars they had in the 1950s. That was before the suburbs. Over here's our library and bookstore. Those are the Sunday School buildings—every age level gets their own floor."

Our group walked past nurseries full of glistening brass baby cribs. "Folks, kids here meet their spouses at church, raise their families here, and graduate to our senior citizens building. You can attend cradle to grave, six days a week, and never have to leave."

Tom strutted like a turkey in the Macy's Thanksgiving Day parade, I thought. He told us the history of the church, and how the stone-and-stained-glass Hobson Auditorium was built after the Great Fire. The "sister churches" in the inner city—the Bethel Baptist temples and the Holy Congregations and the Fellowships of the Shekinah Glory of God—came through segregation. "As Dr. Lindsay says," Tom told us, "everyone is just happier with their own kind."

"Didn't segregation end twenty years ago?" Dad muttered. I wished Tom had overheard him. I wished Dad would say we could leave and go get ice cream.

Tom motioned for us to follow him. "Every one of these buildings is owned outright, including our new auditorium across the street! We don't believe in debt. We're headed over there now. And we don't even have to watch for cars! Would you believe it, God has blessed us with covered crosswalks? Don't that just make you want to say, Amen?"

"She has a stomachache every Sunday!" Mom yelled at Dad in their bedroom several weeks later, pressuring him to pressure me to get my butt out of bed so we could make it to church by 8:45. I scrunched into a ball under my covers. I couldn't eat when I was unhappy, and not eating made my stomach hurt.

A soft knock sounded on my door. "Can I come in?" he asked. When I nodded he sat on the edge of my bed.

"I don't want to go," I said.

"Yeah . . . but if you do, we'll go out to dinner after. Sound good?" Sunday was the only day of the week Dad took off from woodwork and concrete, so offering dinner was high-stakes family time. If I got up, we'd have a good day. If I rebelled and refused to get dressed, he'd spend the day in the woodshop working, and she'd spend it bent over her sewing machine.

"I don't have any friends, Dad," I said. This was true. I'd been unable to make friends with anyone at school or church. Sunday School made it worse because the whole time they were talking about love and God and how great the youth group was for lifelong friendships, while I sat there feeling ugly and alone.

"You've got me," he said. He looked at me hopefully, Michigan-solid to his bones. I'd lost the solace of the trees, but Dad was still here. Wood dust. Structure. Unbending loyalty.

"Oh, *okay*," I said. I swung my legs over the side of the bed and sat up, irritated and comforted at the same time. He closed the door and I got up, went to the closet, and reached for one of the ruffled dresses Mom had made. When I came out of my room she said, "I'm glad you decided to cooperate." The four of us headed to the car, my parents dressed up and smiling.

I tucked the lesson away, into a mental folder I kept inside myself for things I needed to know. Church made Mom happy. Mom happy made Dad happy. Parents happy made Monica happy. The power to make them *all* happy was mine, and I could wield it by swallowing it down and cooperating. Smiling children who got in line made parents, and God, happy.

As I walked into Sunday School, I tried to ignore the stares of shiny rich children wearing mall clothes. Most of these kids had been friends since the baby nursery. They had common names like Jennifer and Lisa, Jimmy and John. None of them knew what to do with a redheaded pimply new kid named Tia in homemade clothes.

Supposedly, God loved us all the same, but how did that work? We weren't all the same. Some were rich, some poor, some good, some ugly. If church was a glimpse of heaven, then God played favorites.

I sat down in a wooden chair off to the side. The seat next to me usually sat empty as the rows filled with the pretty girls. But instead, a girl sat down. I looked at her flowered dress and recognized the pattern from Cloth World. She had a home perm and barrettes in her hair too. *Like me,* I thought.

"Hi, I'm Hannah," she said. "What's your name?"

"Tia," I said, and she smiled.

"What a nice and unusual name. Do you have any brothers and sisters? I have four sisters, three older and one younger. Their names are April, Charity, Jo, and Laura. We're like *Little Women* plus one," she laughed.

She sounded like a little adult, but she'd just said more words to me than any person my age all year. I loved her immediately. The teacher stood up and rapped on her podium for our attention.

"Now girls, we have a new member. Please welcome Hannah. And girls, let's ask God for a miracle for her mother, who has cancer."

We all gasped in collective "Oh no's" of empathy. My stomach clenched. I knew from *Trapper John, M.D.* that cancer was very bad.

The teacher went on. "Hannah, we'll be praying for your mother and also your dad, who must be very worried, having five daughters."

"Thank you, Mrs. Thompson," Hannah said. I wondered if her father would be less worried if he had sons. Was cancer something only women got?

"Cancer is a consequence of sin in the world, girls," said Mrs. Thompson. "Hard things like cancer are never God's will, unless He brings you hardship to teach you a lesson. The Lord disciplines those He loves. We must submit to His good and perfect will. Now girls, I want you to hold hands and let's ask Jesus to give Hannah's mother a miracle—if it's His will."

We stood in a circle and took one another's hands. Hannah's was cold. Some of the girls started crying. I felt desperate to reassure her—miracles were our superpower. Christians had a golden ticket out of our problems because the Bible was a book of miracles. Like, the one where Abraham didn't kill Isaac. And the one where God didn't let the lions kill Daniel. God was all about miracle rescues. This was part of our doctrine.

To get a miracle, the Bible said we just had to believe that God could do the big thing we asked. And then, because my own "big thing" sat like a rock in my heart, I weighed why my prayers to go back to Michigan hadn't worked.

We were what Mom called "headstrong." We didn't submit enough in Michigan. We didn't pray as a family or have devotions or go to church enough, so going back wasn't God's will. Like it or not, we had to stay in Jacksonville to be disciplined into becoming better Christians. The Bible said even people in hell could pray, although it might not do them any good.

God didn't kill mothers though, I reasoned. Hannah's mother would be fine.

Over the next few months, we prayed every Sunday for Hannah's mother and her miracle. I squeezed Hannah's hand as we prayed, so she'd know I was believing extra-hard God could and would do the big thing we asked.

As the weeks passed, Hannah's homemade dresses faded, and her permed hair straightened. Then one Sunday, she didn't come.

"Girls," Mrs. Thompson said, smiling, "Hannah's mother is with Jesus now. She's gone to heaven and Hannah will see her again someday. Let's not be sad. To die a Christian is to be with your Lord and Savior. To God be the glory!"

The fatal finger in the sky knocked over the single domino of my friend because Hannah didn't come back. And, God did kill mothers. He was in control, not us. If I didn't submit, he'd teach me a lesson too. I knew now God could take anyone, at any time, and I didn't want to lose my family.

A year later, I didn't have stomachaches only on Sundays—I had them every day. Mom took me to a doctor who kept photos of his pretty equestrian daughter on the wall. He pressed sausage fingers into my abdomen and told me to stick out my tongue. He asked me about my grades and how often I pooped. Then he declared, "These stomachaches are all in her head. Sometimes emotional distress leads to what we call chronic dyspepsia."

"Well, what about allergies? Or her hormones?" Mom asked. "Her father has high acid."

He gruffed, more dad than doctor, "Your daughter doesn't need medication—she needs friends."

My parents gave his diagnosis to the Lord in prayer, which was stronger than medicine. They'd already decided on a new school: the heat was on at church to enroll in private academies.

As it happened, the rise of private schools in the South was the result of someone else's dominoes. The domino of civil rights. The domino of de-segregation. The glitch in the chain when Jacksonville's neighborhoods didn't organically diversify. The mandate from the Supreme Court to use bussing to mix us up. The threat religious leaders felt with inner-city Black kids from the hood coming to the suburbs. The rise of private Christian academies as an alternative. The pressure from the pulpit to help parents decide.

"Don't let the government teach your children about feminism! Abortion! Sex education!" The preachers' faces reddened with anger. "Beloveds! Put your children in schools where they can freely pray to God! Prayer belongs in schools! And all God's people said . . ."

The congregation clapped and answered, ". . . AMEN!"

So my parents pinched their pennies and placed me in Grace Christian Academy, a small school of a few hundred white kids. I was excited to hear the news. A new school meant a second chance at getting Florida right. Maybe Grace was my rescue from hell.

Mom drove me to a redbrick building that squatted behind massive old oak trees and bright pink azaleas. The brown paneled classrooms seemed dark at first but with wide windows that faced the woods. My schedule said I was in Mrs. Duvall's class. Today my stomach buzzed with happy nerves, the good kind of fear.

I found my desk and sat down. The other kids high-fived and laughed. A girl a few rows up turned and smiled at me. I smiled back—so happy to meet my new Hannah.

"Oh my gosh, you're right. She's *hideous.*" The girl laughed. "Her teeth are *disgusting.*" The boy next to her said, "See? I told you." The whole cluster of them laughed and pointed at me.

I felt on fire, burning with a sudden fever of humiliation. My teeth *were* gross. They were right. As a baby, I'd fallen off a balcony, and my adult teeth came in crooked and brown. Michigan kids only went to dentists sometimes, when something hurt. In Florida, ugly teeth were a problem, but my parents couldn't afford to fix them and pay for private school tuition.

Kelly did not become my new Hannah. Every day she came to school in her Colors of Benetton sweaters and gleaming white Keds with her giant Le Bag. She said, "Hey there, Hideous." And Paul, the boy who sat next to her, would add, "*Iguana*. It's, hey there, Hideous Iguana." This joke never got old, even months later. I hated them.

Our parents thought private school provided a superior education. Our three most important lessons at Grace:

- Get saved so you don't burn in hell.
- Jesus is coming to steal you like a thief in the night.
- Abortion is evil business and probably contagious.

Getting saved was a bookmark in a Christian's life, as important as birth, marriage, death. A person gets saved by praying the Sinner's Prayer, by inviting Jesus inside their heart. Without him, my heart was wicked and disgusting. But Jesus came in and cleaned things up. He's a professional, like how you'd want a cleaner to help dissolve a body if you killed someone. I saw that once on Cinemax.

I'd already prayed the Sinner's Prayer as a six-year-old, after my Sunday School teacher showed me a picture of people in hell, a sea of flailing arms and screaming faces drowning in flames. Getting saved was Hell Insurance and I wasn't supposed to worry anymore. But I worried all the time.

Because Jesus was coming to steal us like a thief in the night—a robber who'd grab us out of bed. The rapture was the end of second chances. If you weren't a good enough Christian on that night, it sucks to be you—you're going to hell. But first you'll suffer the Great Tribulation, a seven-year period of extreme worldwide pain that ends in total apocalypse. Drought. Heat waves. Famine. War. The Works. You'd better hope he comes and steals you.

We watched marathon showings of *A Thief in the Night*, *Image of the Beast*, and *The Prodigal Planet*. These films depicted life after the rapture. Mrs. Duvall said they should "scare us straight."

In the movies, UNITE (the government police force) arrested girls who didn't get saved in time. The officers dressed the sobbing girls in white baptismal robes and beheaded them. We heard the icky thump of their severed heads fall into a bucket beneath the slice of the guillotine blade.

The lesson was that these girls died because they only *pretended* to believe in Christ. They secretly preferred their rock music and immodest clothing to repentance and salvation, and we'd better not be like them.

But keeping your head wasn't any better. The Anti-Christ would rise and force everyone to accept the Mark of the Beast. The 666 barcode tattooed on their forehead or hand would help left-behind sinners buy gas and food. No mark? Well, you starve. Judgment Day was coming no matter what. Time's up, suckers.

We had to learn to watch out now. The UN and the one-world government would put their plan in place ahead of the rapture. The wrong president was a sign. Our doctrine must be spread because Jesus was only waiting for us to tell enough people He was coming.

We had a mission to take dominion, because lost people without Jesus kill babies. The next movie day included trash cans full of ground-up baby body parts—piles of tiny infant hands reaching out for life and half-formed skulls with the brains drained out. It was way worse than anything I'd seen on cable.

"This is what the liberals want," they said. "This is what will happen if we don't reverse *Roe v. Wade*." We pledged to vote Right for Life when we were old enough because nothing mattered more than saving the unborn and leading them to Christ.

The *Challenger* explosion became a lesson too. Mrs. Duvall cried as the clouds billowed with disintegrated astronauts on TV. But then she said, "Such arrogance. People die when scientists play God."

Fear was our vaccine against hell, science, and abortion. So, along with stomachaches, I now had nightmares. Sweaty dreams that ended in choking screams over what I was learning in school. Guillotine blades and severed baby heads and empty houses where no one's home, ever again.

One morning I woke up with blood between my legs. I'd read about periods in *Are You There God? It's Me, Margaret.*, but how did I know a period from a painful God-lesson? What if the blood was a sign of death or the end times? I got up and went to school as usual, sure I'd find out I'd been left behind, but I wasn't.

"These are end times," our principal said in chapel. "There will be wars and rumors of war. Disease. Pestilence. Look around, kids. The world is already headed for hell."

When I walked to the front of the class, Kelly whispered loudly, "Ew, she has her period." Everyone laughed. I scrubbed my pink pants in the bathroom, crying and hating Kelly, angry over feeling scared and stupid all the time, and wanting to punch her in the face.

What if the cross was just a really gross way to die? How could blood shed two thousand years ago mean anything for the sins I committed last week? Like, when I snooped through the drawers of the family I babysat for, or fought with Monica over chores?

Jesus heard me griping because the next day in chapel, the principal said, "Do you have the sin of hatred in your hearts? The sin of your hatred killed Jesus."

I looked over at Kelly and Paul. Could I be sorry for hating them if it helped me keep my head? Fear was supposed to be good for me. What did it mean if I prayed the prayer before, as a little kid, but hated people now? Did I undo my salvation?

Some families were doing rapture drills, to scare their kids to Jesus. I didn't want my parents to find out and think an empty house was a good idea. I didn't want to be left alone, ever, and sometimes I cried like a baby and begged not to go anywhere. Mom said, "Tia, you're too big to be acting like this. You're a young woman now. Get up and get ready for church."

I decided fear and power were friends. My church had an eleven-blocks-in-the-city kind of power. We had the biggest-money and oldest-families-in-Jacksonville sort of power. We had TV power. That many powerful people had to be right. So, I decided in my head to agree with them. Belief is a choice. Feelings lie. I could choose my way to Jesus.

I prayed the Sinner's Prayer at every altar call, car ride, and anytime I thought I might die. Repetition didn't help my stomach, but it helped me in my head. Prayer convinced me this was my doctrine too.

Sometimes, God gives you a chance to go your own way and see what happens. It's called free will—a test to see what you'll choose. My free will was named Marci.

Marci's parents sent her to Grace when they caught her having sex. No one would talk to a promiscuous rebel who meant trouble, so I decided to be her friend. With Marci, my second year at Grace was better than the first.

Marci wasn't afraid of hell, the rapture, or anything else, and she lived within walking distance of my new house. Marci liked boys—and since she was tall with bouncing boobs but walked with confident power, boys liked Marci too. We listened to Debbie Gibson and Fleetwood Mac records in her bedroom. *Tell me sweet little lies.* Or made mixed tapes from the radio. Often, we'd sneak up to the mall and bum quarters off old men who were waiting for their wives to finish shopping.

"Excuse me, sir, do you have a spare quarter so I can call my mom?" After a few of them, we'd have enough quarters to buy a bag of candy. Even when we hit the same men twice, the old men seemed to enjoy turning their quarters over to Marci and her tight purple T-shirts with the low necklines. "It's the power of our pretty boobs, Tia," she said. "But you need to wear something other than that old Garfield T-shirt."

I liked hiding under my baggy clothes. And Marci was patient with me. She didn't seem to mind that I was a hideous iguana with broken teeth and zits. She said, "You're funny, Tia," and laughed at my jokes. With Marci, I could be sarcastic and bold. I used dirty words fluently—*shit, fuck, bitch, cunt*— and walked tall to her house. With Marci, I felt like I might even have some fucking power of my own. Maybe it was okay to go my own fucking way. Perhaps I didn't need to worry so much about sin and God and the rapture. When I was with Marci, my stomach didn't hurt.

Besides the mall, Marci and I often went to the library, especially once school let out for the summer. I devoured *Flowers in the Attic, The Diary of a Young Girl, Wuthering Heights,* and *Fried Green Tomatoes at the Whistle Stop Cafe.* The girls in the books I loved had voices and opinions. They were brave on the inside and behaved only enough on the outside—they didn't pretend. Marci and the heroines made the rapture feel like fiction, and I loved our rebel hearts. Maybe I was wrong about wanting to blend in and belong. Maybe being the heroine of my own fucking story was better.

Some days we didn't go to the library or the mall, because Marci wanted to see a boy. My role was to stand guard outside their houses in the summer heat while Marci gave out blow jobs. Later, she coached me on her deep throat tricks with a banana, which made me gag. "When it's over, make sure you spit it out," she said. I didn't want to ask what "it" was.

Bored in her role as teacher, Marci decided the best way to fix our inequality was to get me a boyfriend. "Then we can hang out together," she said.

"Shit, Marci. I didn't know we might not," I said. She laughed but I didn't. With Marci, I belonged. I didn't want to get kicked out and lose my only friend.

Marci knew an older boy already in high school who might take me, and she arranged for him to meet us at the school pool. Troy was sixteen, doughy with thin brown hair. When he saw me in my pink-and-black swimsuit, he crossed his arms with his hands in his armpits and said, "I like your boobs."

He told Marci I was okay. Excited I'd passed his inspection, she planned the next step. It felt good to be wanted by a mysterious stranger and I giggled with nervous excitement. The big event of my first boyfriend was happening right now—this would be how my romantic life began. Troy might be the man God wanted me to marry (sorry, God, for so much cussing). Troy might be my Gilbert Blythe, my Almanzo Wilder, my 007. Maybe he'd wear cologne. My favorite was Eternity for Men, and I always got a sample at the mall.

The instructions were to go to Troy's house tomorrow afternoon. His parents weren't home then, and he'd be my boyfriend. That seemed easy enough.

I spent lots of time getting dressed up, stealing Monica's new shirt, and using *Teen* magazine advice to put on makeup. I rode my bike the mile to his house and knocked on the front door. He pulled back an angry German shepherd and told me to go around back to their camper.

I swallowed my nerves, eager to show him I was mature enough to be someone's girlfriend.

The dilapidated camper smelled dank and stale from being closed up without electricity. Troy stomped up the metal stairs and told me to take off my shirt.

"Show me your tits," he said. Then, he started kissing all over my face and neck with a meaty salamander tongue that tasted sour, like bad morning breath. I didn't want to remember this taste as my first kiss. Within seconds, he'd painted me in sweat and slime, my pale skin red and irritated as if I were allergic.

"I've never seen pink titties before," he said.

I felt embarrassed about a difference in my body I hadn't known existed. What color were they supposed to be?

He unbuttoned my pants, and I pulled his hands away.

"Stop," I gasped, hoping I sounded shocked but still sweet, like the girls on TV.

"It's what you're here for, bitch," he said, hands groping, pulling, and tearing at my clothes.

"Stop it," I said again. "I'm not ready for that. You're going too fast." I batted his hands away and tried to walk around him toward the door.

Troy grabbed my wrists. "You'd better let me. Or I'll sic my dog on you."

The camper shrank, so hot, brown, and gold. Summer-sour and rotting. Troy pulled his pants down and pressed something hard on my leg. I pulled away and screamed this time, which startled him.

I grabbed Monica's shirt and broke for the door, falling forward and missing the steps completely. I landed hard on my knees and palms and dug my fingers into the dirt to push myself up. I ran.

The dog chased me as I fled, half-dressed, across Troy's neighbors' yards, and he scratched angry red lines down the length of my pale back with his filthy claws. I ran straight into an old man's gut. "Honey, honey, are you okay?" He held my shaking arms. I was crying.

Troy saw the man and called off his dog.

The man walked me over to my bike. I didn't want him to look at me, and I tried wrapping my shirt around myself tighter, wishing I had more clothes.

On the humiliating bike ride home, the torn white blouse streamed behind me like a flag of surrender. *This* was the danger of adolescence. This was how teenagers went wrong instead of right. This was what I did with my free will: I sent myself to hell.

I took a shower, which washed off the blood, sweat, and spit, feeling dirty enough inside to shave off my skin. Afterward, I sat on the floor in my room and inventoried my wicked heart.

Profanity. Reading dark books. Telling lies. The feel of a boy's hands on my body. Letting the dog destroy Monica's shirt. Throwing the shirt away. Using the power of pretty boobs to do bad things, like steal from old men. Letting my body put me in danger. Not being careful with what boys want.

I apologized to God and promised to pray without ceasing. I'd stop complaining about church. I'd be the very best Christian my parents had ever seen. This time, *I* took a domino away.

When Marci called, I told Mom I couldn't come to the phone. And a week later, I told Marci I couldn't come over anymore because I belonged to Jesus.

"Some friend you are," she seethed before slamming down the receiver.

My parents said they were taking me out of private school to fix my teeth and send me to summer camp. I thanked God for His faithfulness. I saw how fearing the Lord was a good thing that paid off with earthly blessing and eternal security. Obedience would make me and everyone else happy. And I'd never have to worry about boys like Troy or hell ever again.

Lines

WE MEASURED TIME IN SUNDAYS AND A YEAR LATER, DAD AND I sat in the balcony for the morning worship service together as a habit. We were part of the audience now, the ones folks at home might see on TV.

Life is a lot easier when you play along, but I wanted more assurance. There had to be a secret for happiness and heaven because prayer didn't feel like enough, no matter how hard I tried.

Everyone around me was super-sure they were going to heaven when they died. They "knew that they knew that they knew" they were saved. And they didn't just say it—they lived it by following rules. It was more than the Ten Commandments or the Golden Rule to do unto others as you'd have them do unto you. It was more than magic prayer. I knew I was still too close to going to hell with decapitated liars and baby killers because I hadn't discovered the secret rules that no one said out loud. So, Sundays became a chance to study and be observant.

Mom sang in the choir. *"What a day that will be, when my Jesus I shall see."* The orchestra played on each side of the marble podium, with the pastors, orchestra conductor, and Minister of Music in the middle. We usually sang two blood hymns and a heaven. Hymns like prayers that taught our doctrine of the Lamb's Book of Life and how we made sure our names were in it.

The sermons were rinse and repeat. Get saved. Tell people about "Jee-zuz." Preach the gospel and don't get left behind. Take up your cross and follow Him. Spread the Good News and pray for America. Get ready to see Jesus in Glory. It starts with who you marry.

At fourteen, my job was to prepare to be a Christian wife and mother. Sold-out Christian girls wore modest clothing, protected their purity, and sat like ladies. They didn't care about where "the line" was because good Christian girls crossed legs, not lines. Rules helped us keep our feelings in. *Smile now.* And then one day God would bring your holy prince. This was better than a fairy tale—it was our God-given destiny as girls.

Sunday after Sunday, I sat in the pew, crossed my legs at the ankle, and opened my Bible, leaning into the convenience of wanting what they wanted for me. Christian or not, I wanted that destiny. Whereas some girls held on to dreams of becoming a doctor, lawyer, or world traveler and would have to box up those dreams in order to do God's will, I did not. Modesty protected my shyness, purity protected me from the Troys, and I knew I wanted babies.

The music minister, with his glossy Welcome to Disney World smile and hair, announced it was time to shake hands and greet our neighbors. The congregation roiled in a sea of hugs, handshakes, and "Hi, how are you?" Charismatic love surged like a wave, rock-concert loud.

Pastor Homer G. Lindsay Jr. braced his long arms on the pulpit. The lights glinted off his shiny forehead and square glasses. We sat down as he said, "Turn your Bibles to Ephesians chapter one."

A big man, Dr. Lindsay was beloved at First Baptist. He was a fat and fancy grandpa, with a straightforward view of the world and a pocket full of peppermints. Dr. Lindsay screamed, but somehow, he didn't seem as angry as some of the other pastors, and his zeal only made him more endearing. He had a "heart for families."

For some reason, I felt compelled to look toward the left of the sanctuary. And I couldn't believe it! Hannah's dad was here! With his family!

I counted their names like numbers: April, Charity, Jo, Hannah, and Laura. Next to Mr. Miller was a flowery woman holding a ruffled baby—and she looked pregnant too. Remarried and two more babies, wow—he'd moved fast.

Seeing such a big family reminded me: dominion hastened the return of Christ. We had to stand out from the world and its national average, and China, with its communist infanticide of girls. Women weren't supposed to work outside the home because lady-jobs interfered with the biblical mandate to bring forth and multiply. Also, big families were a witness for Christ. They showed off our superior family values and willingness to trust and follow God.

I noted the new rule in my head. Having more babies advanced a mothering career—the highest calling a woman had. And if having lots of kids made you poor, then you needed to get creative to make it work. As long as you continued to tithe 10 percent of your income to the church, God could bless you in your poverty.

I smiled to myself, knowing I was ahead in the game. I was made for this, and good at being creative. Tithe + Creative. Got it. Another rule for a happy life.

My dad nudged me to quit daydreaming and offered a peppermint. Eyes forward, Bible in lap, I'd learned from example. Mere seconds later, Dr. Lindsay was on fire.

This frothiness was likely to happen anytime he got going on heaven—or ranted about being born again, the possibility of cathead biscuits and fried chicken in Glory, or *SEX-U-AL* immorality. Most Sundays, Dr. Lindsay was on fire. This Sunday he got lost in memories of meeting Shirley and the familiar story of how older men sometimes married barely legal girls after very brief engagements.

The congregation collectively sat back and settled into story time.

"Before I met Shirley, I'd been praying for a wife for over a year. I was twenty-five and in seminary and I began to get desperate! I even bought an engagement ring and wedding band with cash! I'd look at it now and then and say, 'Lord, where is she?' I was looking hard, but nobody looked back. Brothers and sisters, it takes *two* looks."

The congregation laughed. I noticed the TV cameras panned the audience for a close-up of sweet, huggable Shirley, who beamed as Homer told their love story. Dr. Lindsay paced the stage, microphone clipped to his lapel. In the pauses, I could hear the trickle of the fountain in the baptistry.

"When I came home from Texas, I picked my dad up in Jacksonville and we headed for the Southern Baptist Convention. 'There's a girl in the glee club I want you to meet,' he said. She was the cutest thing, just a hundred and ten pounds and everything in the right place! I mean, my heart fluttered. I was ready! I said, 'Where can I meet you?' But she wasn't out of school yet, and I had to go down to Deland the following week to see her. By the time she got out of school, I'd been down three times, and the third time, I asked her to marry me. I'd known her for three weeks! It's a good thing the Lord doesn't make mistakes, isn't it?"

The congregation laughed again but I swallowed hard. He always skipped over her answer. I mean, clearly, she said yes. It was fifty years and four children later, and a host of grandchildren. But she married a man she'd only known for three weeks. What if she wanted to say "wait," or even "no"? And God . . . well sometimes He *did* do things that some considered a mistake.

Dr. Lindsay moved on to raising teenagers—a topic that sometimes led to rules I didn't like.

"Father should maintain control of the television. You don't give up control just because he's entered junior high. And make sure you send them to camp! Your young people *need* camp. You want them to be serious about Jesus! And movies are out! There aren't any decent movies! Walt Disney is dead! The movies they're producing are for degenerates—they're filthy, ungodly, and nasty!"

The only time my dad controlled the TV was on Sunday afternoons when he wanted to nap to NFL football.

He'd watch a play or two and then snore, and we all knew not to turn it off. He wasn't mean about it. But if we woke him, he'd have a look of misery come over him and head out to the shop for more work. If we let him nap, he might wake up rested, buy a bag of crinkle cuts for family fry night, and put on a movie.

I loved our movie nights—*Jaws, E.T., Grease, The Princess Bride.* I didn't think they were filthy and nasty.

The first quiet piano notes of the altar call began, followed by the violins and Dr. Lindsay's pleas for repentance. Now was the time to twist the screw. "If all you did was join the church and become a Baptist without Jesus in your heart, you're going to hell! You need a miracle! You've got to be ready for the second coming of the Lord!"

Despite my new devotion, fear carbonated in my belly and a chill passed over my skin. If Jesus came right this minute, he'd catch me doodling in my Bible. *He could've caught you with Troy.*

I tasted the sharp tang of acid in my throat and my armpits felt wet. Maybe I should repent again for Troy and all that led to him. I closed my eyes and focused on my Rapture Drill.

Go to the church kitchen and secure a food supply.

Find the secret rooms—there are tons of nooks in a church this size.

Stay hidden.

I could live inside the church for a long time before the Anti-Christ's henchmen found me. This way, I could put off hell a little bit longer.

First Baptist made good on their promise to solve adolescence. Throughout middle and high school, they kept us busy serving God and having fun. Our parents loved it.

The process began with summer camp. Camp offered leadership our undivided attention and set the tone for the year ahead. Every August, I packed dresses for chapel, a one-piece bathing suit, Rave hair spray, a hot pink Kit-and-Caboodle of natural-looking makeup, my Bible, my flute, and colored pens. We loaded onto eight yellow school buses and headed to Lake Yale.

Alexa, Hannah's worldlier cousin, sat next to me with her blue paisley Bible cover and explained why Hannah wouldn't be there.

"Homeschoolers don't do youth group. Not Gothard homeschoolers anyway," Alexa said. "We're a bad influence on them."

"What are Gothard homeschoolers?" I wondered.

"They're special Christians," she said. "Like saints. And they have tons of extra rules."

My ears perked up. Ha! Special rules, I knew it! I needed to know more because there was way more to happiness and heaven than just a magic prayer.

"They're super-strict," Alexa said. "It's run by Bill Gothard. He's like their pastor. His seminars are like Billy Graham's—held in stadiums all over the country. I don't know though—my parents got the red textbook. They say the institute is crazy and life is already hard enough."

She rolled her eyes and looked out at the longleaf pine forests, while I wondered how to find out more about this Mr. Gothard and his textbook of rules.

I needed to Nancy Drew it and find out, but we were here. The buses pulled into the dirt driveway at the camp.

Concrete buildings called "cabins" squatted beneath sprawling, moss-draped oak trees. The cabins were like houses and had AC, making modest clothing a lot easier in August. Church camp was nothing like real camping; camp meant classes, chapel, and choir rehearsal.

The first year, I tucked my chin, found my bunk, and hoped my bunkmate was more Hannah than Kelly. But every year after that I had friends. I saw Mary and Ruth Ellen every day at school and church. And Kyle, Tim, Tammy, and Michael in orchestra too.

On the first chapel night, Reverend Richards paced the stage next to a record player on a cart.

"Young people! You're getting ready to LEARN!" he screamed. "I'm going to teach you the TRUTH! Satanic Panic! Back-masked devil music! Demonic rituals, sexual perversion, abortion, and the fiery flames of HELL!"

The AC blew so cold that condensation streamed down the windows like rain. Kamikaze bugs slammed into the glass, drawn by the chapel's bright light.

Rev. Richards put a record on the player and cranked the volume up. The window glass rattled from the evil beats of rock music we weren't allowed to listen to in real life.

John Lennon sang, "Turn me on, dead man, turn me on." The whole room sat stunned that songs really did have hidden messages.

"These beats are SEXUAL! They will drive you to sin, young people!" He screamed, beet red and livid. Spit foamed around his mouth and I saw a plump vein in his temple bulge. He looked like a stuffed tick ready to pop purple blood on us. "The lyrics are blasphemous and nasty! They're meditations on bad love and broken hearts, not about life and Jesus. I beg you! Don't listen to this garbage!"

When the music grew too terrifying and angry, I looked down at the margins of my Bible. Instead of doodling and daydreaming, I now wrote meaningful quotes to train my mind toward God.

"Life is too short to learn everything from experience."—Dr. Lindsay
"God can do anything but fail."—Dr. Jerry Vines

"You can't have God's love without fear."—Dr. Lindsay
"Whenever you find a contradiction with the Bible, the problem is with you—not the book."—Dr. Vines

My stomach clenched as Richards yelled. Dad used rock music to stay awake on the road. I didn't want rock music to be a rule.

As we got ready for bed, I asked Mary, "If rock music sometimes does good things for people, like makes them happy or keeps them safe, how can it be bad?"

"Because of what's in it. Didn't you listen? All you need is a good substitute," she said.

Mary was smart and made me feel safe. "What kind of substitute?" I asked. Classical or gospel would've landed Dad in a ditch.

"Contemporary Christian music," she said. "Carman instead of Michael Jackson and Sandi Patty instead of Whitney Houston. And if you like metal, there's Stryper. It's like rock, but better, because it glorifies God. The more you get into Christian alternatives, the less you'll struggle with the temptations of this world. Problem solved."

"Lights out, girls," our counselor yelled. The room went black immediately. I kept my eyes open as long as I could, thanking God for Christian friends. Safety was in the answers.

We had training sessions during the day. Girls learned about purity and modesty. Boys learned how to control their thoughts and keep their hands off body parts—ours and their own.

Charity Miller was our teacher. While Hannah wasn't allowed to come to camp, her sisters April and Charity served as counselors. *Gothard Christians can be leaders then,* I noted.

"Genuine modesty is more than covering your private parts at the beach, girls," she said. "Modesty is an attitude that shows in your clothes. It even shows in private."

My cheeks burned. How did Charity know the immodest things I did in private?

I looked at her closely. She covered her collarbone. Her dress reached her ankles. I bet she was even modest in the shower. How was she not sweating?

Even with AC, the rest of us got sweaty walking between buildings. Marci would've said she had a bad case of swamp-ass, but I pushed her voice away and told God I was sorry for my thoughts.

"Women aren't sexual," Charity said. "Sex is about pleasing your husband and you girls are *far* away from that." She laughed. "I, however, am betrothed."

Our eyes widened. "What's that?" someone asked.

"Betrothal is a biblical form of engagement. It's part of courtship. I'm promised to a man my father chose for me. When he finishes college and can support a wife, he'll ask me to marry him, and I'll say yes. Then we'll be engaged. This is my promise to my father."

She held up her left hand and showed us a delicate band of gold with a cross and a little chip of a diamond in the center. We gawked with envy.

I opened my Bible to my notes. At the top: COURTSHIP IS A RULE.

"Men like it when you leave a little mystery."
"Give them something to imagine."
"You want a boy to see you as a future wife—not a fun five minutes in the backseat of his car."

"Girls," she said, "you have *no idea* how sexy men will find your ankles if that's the only part you show!"

I wrote that down too and bit my lip against the memory of how much men liked pretty boobs.

The sex lessons intensified in the morning chapel. Rev. Richards lathered up quick, screaming that we needed to avoid HOMOSEXUALITY at all costs.

We'd heard this word before. Dr. Lindsay often preached about Jezebels and ladies of the night. The dangers of premarital SEX included pregnancy and GONGA-RHEA.

I guessed Gonga-rhea was some kind of genital diarrhea that happened when you fornicated against God. But homosexuals were a certain kind of sinner, and lesbians were the worst, because what kind of woman turned down a man? Hussies and Jezebels, that's who.

When Rev. Richards launched into the Dangers of Being Gay, I figured he'd repeat Dr. Lindsay's points. But his sweaty violet face signaled more.

"The world is showing you it's okay to be a HOMO. The world wants you to believe these people are normal." He paced and snorted like a bull locked in a pen. "They're. NOT. NORMAL!"

The air in the room had changed. I looked at the doors, at the exits. Did our parents know this is what they were teaching us? I imagined my dad walking in and telling Rev. Richards to shut it.

"These queers *choose* against the nature of their bodies, against God's design. They hump and grind in ways that God did not intend! It's not sex—it's *mutual masturbation*! They have orgies and golden showers and generate diseases like AIDS that will come and kill us all!"

The room hung dead-still as he screamed words we weren't allowed to say. I didn't know some of them. I'd heard of AIDS. I'd seen Princess Diana in *People* magazine, being kind to sick men in hospital beds. The men looked more like concentration camp victims than dangerous perverts out to get us. But I didn't know what golden showers and orgies were, and it seemed important to avoid them. So, I decided to ask.

After chapel, as Rev. Richards walked ahead of me on the gravel path, I ran to catch up.

"Hey, Reverend Richards, can I ask you a question about today's sermon?"

He didn't stop walking right away. I could see him weighing a response: spiritual need versus wild-card weird.

"Sure, Tia," he said. "Ask away."

I brushed aside an impressed feeling that he knew my name. "What are orgies and golden showers?"

His feet ground into the gravel as he hit a dead stop. I wondered if I'd said something wrong—or funny. Had I made a mistake?

He swallowed before answering and I watched his Adam's apple ripple up his neck. "A golden shower is where a bunch of men pee on each other while having sex. An orgy is group sex."

"Oh," I said. Hot acid burned my throat and I felt my face and neck turn red.

Hours later in the blackness of lights out, I replayed it in my mind. I could smell Troy's rancid camper when Rev. Richards spoke, and taste Troy's sour kiss. Somehow, for listening and asking, I was less innocent than when I came here. *This is why you don't ask questions,* I thought. *Being quiet is a rule.*

The next day, Charity's class resulted in more nuggets for my Bible's end pages.

"If you save yourself for marriage, your sexual relationship will be perfect and blessed by God."
"If you have sex with someone, it's the same as having sex with everyone they had sex with."
"Sex within the bonds of marriage is an act of sacred worship to God."
"Let Jesus be your lover."

And in chapel, Rev. Richards wanted to talk about porn.

"Looking at porn is as bad as cheating on your future mate!" he screamed. "Do you know what porn is, young people? It's naked people having SEX!"

Every time I heard the word "porn," I had the same dirty flashback, and wondered why my prayers to feel clean hadn't worked.

When I was seven, I saw a magazine in my uncle's welding shop. I remembered the cover of *Penthouse* clearly: the yellow Hollywood hair and smear of red lipstick, the scene with the man in the elevator. I'd never seen a naked man before or heard the word "sex," and at seven, I didn't know what to make of their pained expressions. I was confused by the images and also by my embarrassment for having looked at this magazine. I knew I wasn't supposed to tell anyone I'd seen it. But I didn't know why.

Now, seven years later at church camp, I knew this was porn, and by looking at it, I'd already cheated on my future husband. When they asked us to raise our hands if we'd ever seen porn, I had to raise mine or I'd be a liar. I also had to repent for tempting men with Marci in the mall, because now I knew I'd used my boobs to make them sin. Their arousal was my fault.

During the altar call, I joined the majority of kids who went forward for forgiveness. Then we signed pledges to carry our Bibles to school, never do drugs, listen to rock music, or have sex outside of marriage. Lots of kids went home promising to burn their rock music collections.

But our repentance had one more step. When we got home to our Sunday

School room, there was a large wooden cross. We had to crucify Jesus with our sins.

As the pianist played "Turn Your Eyes Upon Jesus," we paraded to the front to nail our pledge cards to the cross. And that's when I realized what the rules were all about.

By following the rules, we didn't sin as much. We weren't as guilty as the other people re-crucifying Jesus. That's why He'd keep and bless us. He could see we were good—special and worth saving, worth blessing. The rules *were* salvation.

Secret unlocked, I couldn't wait to get on with life. Being less of a sinner meant my dreams could come true. Except not everything I wanted was at church. How could I be loved and go to heaven if I wanted what was *out there,* in the world?

Choose

THE PROBLEM WAS THAT THERE'S MORE TO LIFE THAN CHURCH, and outsiders didn't understand Christian priorities and God-rules. So, I started learning how to live two lives. This way, I could still fit in at church and also hold on to what I loved outside of it: art, school, and Michael. My senior year, I got good at keeping my two worlds, and two kinds of Tia, separate.

Unlike rock music or porn or weird sex, these pieces I held to myself couldn't be outlawed. School, where I painted and danced in the color guard, fell under a legal requirement. My attendance was literally mandated. No one thought twice about my love of art because everyone needs a hobby. And Michael, whom I'd met five years earlier at camp, went to church. Church friends who crossed worlds were safest of all, because they were splitting two versions of themselves too.

I knew co-ed friendships were short-lived—tolerated in childhood but decidedly cut upon graduation. Deep inside, I knew I'd lose all three of them in June. No more art, school, or Michael. But for now, I could pretend and believe this was my ordinary life.

At church, our new youth pastor, Reverend Spencer, loved object lessons with sharp punch lines, like how having sex made you chewed gum. Or, if twelve people share a toothbrush and spit into the same cup and then drink it . . .

"You're disgusting! When you have sex with someone who isn't a virgin, you're having sex with everyone they've ever had sex with. Girls, guys . . . all of it. It's DISGUSTING and it makes you filthy before God."

His lessons made me wonder: What made sex, *sex*? Where was the line between not having it and having it? Did it mean fingers in your pants? Saliva on your chest? Did sex have to be the whole thing until you bled? What if you didn't bleed? Did putting things inside mean you weren't a virgin?

Like tampons. I'd tried once, when I wanted to go swimming, and Ruth Ellen freaked out. "Maybe you can be re-virgined," she said, crying.

"What's that?" I asked.

She explained. To be a "born-again virgin," I had to promise not to put anything else inside, ever, until marriage. The tampon didn't go in far anyway because I had no idea how to use it. *Virginity saved by stupidity.* The words came in Marci's voice and I sucked in a laugh.

Now, Reverend Spencer paced, as sweaty and red as pastors got. "You've got to say no to what you want so you can say yes to God!"

No to what I wanted. No to college, art, and boys who couldn't be husbands. Time was ticking.

I thought about ways to make Michael be my husband. I meditated on his teal eyes and impossibly long chestnut lashes. But he didn't like me "that way." He said he thought Ruth Ellen was pretty and that he'd like to date her.

Dating meant sitting next to each other in Sunday School and holding hands during prayer. It was sideways glances and asking God to be the Lord of your relationship, so you stayed pure. Dating looked like regular attendance, except now you were a couple. In high school, couples got together because we spent six days a week together. That's a lot of dating.

Every Saturday we canvased Jacksonville's neighborhoods for Discipleship. We split into teams of two, with eight school buses dropping us off in groups.

Knock, knock.

Who's there?

"If you were to die tonight, do you know where you'd go?"

I learned slammed doors meant they wanted to go to hell.

Lunch at the mall, then back to church. Two hours of choir and orchestra rehearsal. An hour of gospel training. A book full of daily devotions and verses to write in our hearts. It was a lot on top of homework and marching band, but it was worth it for the free ski trip to New York. First Baptist promised parents they'd make submission easy. "Give us the hearts of your young people and we'll reward you with soldiers for God. Your young people will not go wrong if you give them to us." Snow skiing in exchange for witnessing and Scripture memory? It was a no-brainer.

Michael decided he wanted to ask Ruth Ellen on a real date—they'd go to a youth group activity, but he'd pick her up in his car. Chaperoned dates kept kids pure. So, swallowing the tang of not being chosen first, I agreed to become a third wheel and sit in the backseat, a shadowy conscience to prevent kissing and line crossing. At least I was on the team.

Ruth Ellen came over and did her hair in my bathroom. She used hot rollers and hair spray to tease it up real big. "We've decided we want to have four children," she said. "We're going to choose their names on the bus to New York." She said it with the earnest seriousness we were used to, as if it were totally normal for seventeen-year-olds to choose their future children's names. For us, it was.

Third-wheeling turned out to be a lot of fun. Pretty soon Michael was picking me up before Ruth Ellen, and we were talking about more than church. We liked the same movies, candy, jokes, marching band stories, and orchestra. Michael and I clicked like a good three-legged race. Like siblings. We never talked about how many kids we'd have or how Ruth Ellen felt her future husband should go to seminary.

Pick me, I prayed. *I'm the fun one.*

Our church world had no word for co-ed friendships that weren't romantic. And I was bound to lose him because he was going to regular college. The only clock Michael felt ticking was how soon he could get out of high school and on with his life.

I looked down and away when the lesson sunk in, embarrassed it took me so long. Men got to keep what they wanted. College *and* heaven. Not one or the other.

But I felt will rise inside me, like a wildcat who wanted to roar, the way it had with Marci. I wanted what Michael had. But I also wanted love. I paced back and forth. Choosing the open wilderness of my own way meant the dominoes would fall. I'd lose, like my parents lost the farm, and then I'd burn in hell with baby killers and pornographers. Temptation to be like Michael and dream of going to art college tore at me to turn away from my calling. The pastors called it "forgetting my first love."

So, I kept it a secret and tried to convince myself I loved Jesus more than art and words. At school, the teachers homed in on students with potential. While I sucked at math and science, I had honors English and art.

I felt a surge of hope the day a SCAD scout came to class. Savannah College of Art and Design sounded as close to a heavenly kingdom as anything I could imagine. City blocks paved with art supplies, not gold. The slight man with ink stains on calloused fingers walked past our tables and evaluated our portfolios.

"You've got a great eye for composition," he said, stopping at mine.

I smiled and said thanks, awed to be chosen.

"Talk to your guidance counselor. She can walk you through the process of coming to SCAD. See you in the fall of '92." Like the devil holding bread before a starving girl, he winked. All I had to do was take it.

Daydreams I got lost in began immediately. Instead of quotes in the margins of my Bible, I made lists of art supplies on the back of the Sunday bulletin. I searched the library for scholarships. I started bouncing on my toes when I walked. I had a dream, a goal, and a future. Senior year was suddenly fun—the launch of things instead of the end of them.

I didn't know why I hadn't seen it before—the answer was that I'd simply *use my art for God*. The way Christian rock stars used music for God. And how Jo Miller was going to be a midwife to catch babies for Gothard women.

I could *totally* be an artsy wife and mother. I could write and illustrate books that led children to Jesus! This was using my talents, like it said in the Parable of the Talents: "For to everyone who has will more be given, and he will have an abundance. But from the one who has not, even what he has will be taken away," Matthew 25:29.

I was so proud of myself for learning this lesson that I shared it in a testimony in Sunday School.

"God is the Master artist," said Rev. Spencer, indulging me. "Just be sure you never create art that doesn't glorify your creator," he said.

Jesus homework paid off. God felt like my best friend. God was going to work miracles in my life—I just had to believe He could do the big thing I asked. I'd have an amazing husband and a house full of beautiful children, just like *Anne of Ingleside*. But first I'd go to the best art school in the country and become a star illustrator. My paintings and illustrations would win awards. My teachers would be sad to hear that I was stepping away to raise a family, but secretly, they'd be so proud of me and my holy priorities that they'd all become Christians.

One night from the orchestra stage, I looked up from my margin sketches and noticed a large family sitting down front.

I recognized their special Gothard hallmarks. Enough kids to fill an entire row. The parents were thin and stern, like *American Gothic Goes to Church*. They'd look out of place in any school, hospital, or youth group because while we were modest, we weren't 1890s modest.

Gothard Christianity had increased at FBC. I could tell by how many women dressed like prairie wives, always pregnant and holding a baby.

I looked at the wife. The midwife Jo apprenticed with delivered this woman's babies at home. What kind of job did the fathers have? I knew Mr. Miller did something for a bank but I didn't know what it was. What kind of job should my future husband have?

And what was terrible about schools, hospitals, and youth groups? My mind spun through a flip chart of questions. What kind of car did they drive? How did they get their little kids to sit still? Why didn't they use birth control and space their babies out more?

I squinted into the bright TV lights to gaze at the family. Birth control was a sore subject. Asking about it meant planning to have sex. But it made sense to me that a newlywed couple might want some time alone before adding kids. Otherwise, they might have a baby a year like this family. Was it okay to use birth control in marriage? I didn't know who to ask.

I decided to try Ruth Ellen on the way home from school. She'd broken up with Michael right after the ski trip, because she said she felt like she was cheating on her future husband by dating. She wanted her father to choose her husband. She talked about marriage all the time, so maybe she knew about birth control. We had two miles in the February sun to talk it out.

She wanted to hear some of my qualifications for a husband first—something we were working on in Sunday School. My list had over a hundred so far and I listed a few of my most important:

- Gentle
- Good relationship with his parents
- Wants a family
- Goes slow physically
- Wants to move out of Florida
- Forgives my past
- Understands I won't always want to have sex

She stopped so fast she almost tripped on the sidewalk. "What? You can't tell him no, Tia. You're his *wife*." Her eyes were as wide as dinner plates.

"Yes, I can. A wife is not a *slave*, Ruth Ellen. She can say no. She can be not in the mood." I'd heard Mom say that sometimes. *"Honey, I'm not in the mood."* I wanted to be able to decide for myself when something came inside my body. I knew there'd be times when I didn't want it to.

Ruth Ellen clutched her books to her chest and turned red. "Wives belong to their husbands. It's your duty to be available to him at all times, not just the times you feel like it."

"But forcing sex on someone is rape," I said. My eyes burned from cold air and horror.

"Don't be ridiculous, Tia. There's no such thing as rape in marriage."

"Of course there is! Rape is being forced to have sex! Are you saying husbands don't sometimes force their wives?"

"I'm not saying that, silly goose. I'm saying if he has to force her, she's disobeying. He's not raping her." She turned to keep walking.

"That makes no sense." I resented her trying to make this lighter. My angry words stammered. The thought of sharing a bed with someone who could force his way in whenever he wanted made me want to forget marriage altogether.

"It makes perfect sense, Tia," she said. "It's biblical marriage."

I hated how she kept saying my name as if she were teaching me a lesson. I shook my head, dead-sure of her wrongness and leaning harder than ever toward SCAD. My chin was set, my face red as I fumed and squinted angrily at the sky.

"Besides," she continued, "I'm learning about courtship. When my parents meet a boy they think will be a good match for me, they'll decide if he can date me. At the wedding, authority over me will transfer from my father to my husband. He'll know he can never rape me, and I'll know I'm supposed to obey."

"*Obey?* Arranged marriage? Are you nuts?"

"Why are you so surprised, Tia? Courtship is a safer way to date. I don't want boyfriends. I want to save myself for marriage. Charity Miller is right— dating goes wrong. Dating breaks your heart."

I clutched my books harder as if holding the words themselves could dam the coming flood.

What was breaking my heart most was the empty space I needed money to fill. I didn't have the GPA for scholarships. My parents didn't have the money for tuition. SCAD was expensive and when I asked for a miracle in Sunday School, my teacher said, "Sometimes God tells us no by shutting all the doors." But if the Bible was full of provided fishes and loaves and vessels of oil, why couldn't my modern miracle be paid tuition?

Michael was the only one who said I should keep trying. The ticking clock had returned, and I held on to our movie nights with a tightly gripped fist. I called it seizing the day, like in *Dead Poets Society,* but it felt more like white-knuckled fear. Happiness had a bottom. It ran out.

Three nights a week he pulled up in his black Grand Am blasting the B-52's. We howled, "Fifteen miles to the loooooooove shack!" Michael wore Eternity cologne, used good manners, and had great taste. We talked for hours about design, clothes, stories, music, and life. I never had to choose against myself when I was with Michael—he just accepted all the parts of me. After he dropped me off at home, I'd journal about the movie we saw and what we talked about at dinner. One night, after *Philadelphia,* I wrote down one of my deepest worries—that Michael might be gay.

My hand trembled when I wrote the word, my mind flashing back to camp and Princess Diana and skeletal men ruined by AIDS. Would he still be a Christian? We knew men at church that seemed gay and never married. You couldn't say you were gay and stay.

I closed my journal, sorry I'd written the words. I could be wrong. I decided I was.

Next, I drew a circle with a line through it on my journal page.

In one half of the pie, I had band friends, SCAD, movies, rock music, and dreams of hiking. In the other half, I had purity and modesty, soul-winning, and being a godly wife and mother. The two sides were in opposition—and so were the two Tias.

"Narrow is the way to salvation," they taught us. So, I scrapped the circle and drew two parallel lines instead.

I put all the Jesus stuff in between the lines, straight railroad tracks. *Husband wife mother God.* A path snapped into place clearly, priorities on the page.

I stared at the words. It was easy to see who and what didn't fit. God's rules were salvation. If I wanted to be happy and loved, I needed to say no to what I wanted, and yes to God. If the money wasn't coming, I had God's answer.

The rest of senior year felt like tying off a sweater I'd spent years knitting.

Mrs. Kidder tried to get me to reconsider a few times. "You write well," she said. "Don't waste your gifts."

Mr. Legge reminded me of SCAD. "That's a great piece for your portfolio," he said.

But outsiders didn't understand Christian priorities. I packed my notebooks and portfolios away.

High school ended in a bright glare of sun showers and graduation events at both school and church. At our cap and gown service, Dr. Lindsay spoke, and we sat in our tasseled caps for a sermon dedicated to us.

"Now, young people," Dr. Lindsay preached, "when I watched you walk in here, I had tears in my eyes. I've been praying for you since you were little! Every day! And now you're ready to be adults! And you determine who you are going to be. Who are you going to marry? What do you want in life? You do not have the wisdom to make these decisions on your own. You *need* God. You *need* your parents."

I scanned our graduating class. A soloist sang Michael W. Smith's "Friends." We'd stay friends forever "if the Lord's the Lord of them." As long as we stayed Christians, we'd stay friends.

But what about Michael? And what if no one wanted me? As "Pomp and Circumstance" played, sound waves bouncing off the vaulted ceiling, I felt like I was evaporating out of high school. An unprepared, unskilled, childlike future bride who didn't know what she didn't know, fading into mist.

As Dad said, "Failing to plan is planning to fail." It was Dad quoting Zig Ziglar quoting Ben Franklin. The domino of my parents' Amway years cast a long shadow. But waiting for God to see and notice you have needs is boring.

"Hey, God!" I wanted to scream. "Remember what I gave up for you?! Send me a man! And make sure he smells good!"

I got a job as a daycare worker to show potential husbands I was good with kids. And then I had an idea: Bible college.

Word of Life Bible Institute (WOLBI) in upstate New York offered a one-year program and a potential scholarship to Liberty University in Lynchburg. It would be crawling with eligible young men who loved the woods and God. So I could hike, study the Bible, and find love—all at once.

I went to Dad's woodshop to tell him I hadn't failed to plan—sure he'd be happy enough to help with tuition.

But he wanted me to learn a lady-trade, like sewing or cooking.

"What's a year of Bible college going to get you?" he asked from his sawdust-covered workbench. "The Bible won't pay your bills."

"I told you. A scholarship to another school," I said. I squared my shoulders so he could see my confidence.

"To do what? Going up there without a goal is a bad idea." He continued the steady peel of his hand-planer. A ribbon of wood curled and fell on the floor.

I took a deep breath. I couldn't say I was looking for a man or a walk in the woods. "I'm going on faith, Dad. I know this is the next step, and I don't have to know all the steps that come after it for it to be right." I left the shop with a slouch. Failing to sell a dreamer a vision is a bad sign.

Without my parents' help, my next option was church. First Baptist had a reputation of sending the cream of the crop to Liberty, and as a friend of Jerry Falwell, Dr. Vines was well-connected. I scheduled an appointment, confident he'd be proud of my hunger to study the Bible. I went on a Wednesday night before church.

A Southern Baptist Convention president, Dr. Vine had an office that was lined with books on doctrine. He rose from his large wooden desk and greeted me with a pale handshake.

"How are you, Tia? Thank you for coming to see me," he said. He held out a plate of fancy chocolates. "Would you like one?"

The beautiful gourmet candies were the prettiest I'd ever seen. I reached for one, and he laughed. "Oops! They're glass! I keep them here to see who looks like they might want one. My little joke." He smiled. "What can I do for you tonight, dear?"

Burning with red-faced embarrassment, I muttered about WOLBI and a partial scholarship, stammering and without any of the confidence I'd tried with Dad.

"Well, young lady, we use our precious dollars to assist men called into the ministry. We don't spare that money for girls."

I threw up when I got home. Boys got what they wanted. Girls gave it up for God.

Dad bought me a white hatchback I called Gladys (because she made me glad) and said I needed to figure out my plan.

"You're in thirteenth grade," he said. "You can't stay at home forever, you know."

I knew. I drove around town blaring the Cranberries and Alanis Morissette, rebelling against Christian radio because all the songs sounded like cheap knockoffs. I didn't even skip the cuss word when Alanis yelled *fuck*. I still went to church six days a week because that's where God would send my husband. I needed to be swimming in the right water if I hoped to get caught, but I felt like I was wandering in a desert between two lives: childhood and an adulthood out of reach.

"If I'm supposed to be a wife and mother, God, why won't you send someone who loves me?" I prayed.

Dr. Lindsay preached on evil Murphy Brown, who led women astray on TV with her feminism. "That hussy wants you to vote for Bill Clinton! And his wife is even worse!" Then he'd veer off into the evils of Blockbuster Video and how lost people might see us there and assume we were renting R-rated movies.

But Michael worked at Blockbuster and we still went to movies. We saw *Point of No Return* twenty-one times in the theater. We couldn't get enough of Bridget Fonda's transformation from drug-addled sinner to badass assassin.

And we fell in love with Nina Simone's raw, deep rage and passion on the soundtrack. Her sound felt like words I couldn't find.

"I think I'm going to be an actor in New York," Michael said one day while we waited for the show to start. He passed me the popcorn.

I cringed that he'd be gone soon and took a handful, wiping buttery fingers on my napkin. "I read an article about the boundary waters in Minnesota. They need guides. Do you think I could be a backpacker?"

His smile gleamed. "Of course. You can do anything you want," he said.

Anything I want said no Christian kid ever. But post–high school, Michael almost never came to church anymore.

A rash of forgettable weddings took place—short engagements and ceremonies using the same candelabras with different-colored ribbons. First Baptist churned out newlywed couples like manufactured candy on a conveyor belt. But I had nothing to show for the year. My worthlessness piled up.

Instead of college, I spent my earnings on clothes and movies.

Instead of dating, I spent all my free time with Michael, my secretly gay best friend.

Instead of a career, I wiped butts.

Limbo stole my appetite, but it led to a discovery. When I couldn't control anything else in my life, controlling my food felt good.

Buttery popcorn, fried mushrooms, and candy had made me soft. But skipping meals made my body feel as small and weightless as my spirit. Like Dr. Vine's glass candies, satisfaction was an illusion. Hunger felt real. Like when I was a kid, not eating made my stomach hurt, but now it was a pain I trusted. And like modesty rules, food rules helped keep the feelings down.

So, I ate half a plain bagel in the morning, some lettuce in the afternoon, and a bowl of Mini-Wheats at night after a long run. If I went out with friends, I ordered what they ordered and allowed myself two bites with unlimited Diet Cherry Cokes.

Ten pounds slid off, then ten more. As I walked through the halls of FBC, I felt fresh eyes on my body.

The new attention offered me three chances to get married.

First, Brad, stationed on the *Saratoga,* an aircraft carrier at Mayport.

"Dating" Brad meant talking about everything we had in common—hiking and canoeing dreams, favorite songs, favorite movies. We went soul-winning and sat next to each other in church. He was twenty-two. There weren't any fireworks between us but maybe there didn't need to be.

One Wednesday night after service, he held my hand. "I'm heading out to jump school in California. I'm not ready to get married yet, Tia, so let's take a break, okay?"

I wanted to scream at God. I finally get a real boyfriend, and he gets stationed somewhere else? "Will you write to me?" I asked.

"If I get time." He shrugged and took his hand back. "This is Navy life. It happens."

Two weeks later, I walked through the crowded aisle of the sanctuary. I looked over to my left, and there was Brad! Sitting with a giraffe of a girl I'd never seen before, with her arm linked into his. He hopped up to greet me, followed by the giraffe.

"Hi, Tia! Meet Lisa, my fiancée. She came down while I'm on leave."

I felt like I'd fallen off a balance beam—then turned around to see there was no beam at all. Maybe I'd imagined it. I buckled my belt in another notch and bought small shirts instead of mediums.

Next, Scott.

Tall and talented, Scott was a graphic artist in the Navy who smelled like graphite and sandalwood. I checked "smells good" off my husband list. He cooked for me in his apartment and tried not to touch me because he was a new Christian trying to do this right. We didn't have much to talk about, so we sat next to each other and awkwardly smiled at the TV until it was time to leave.

Scott broke up with me because he was four years older and his friends said we had nothing in common.

Ruth Ellen rolled her eyes when I told her, snot crying and confused. "This is the problem with dating, Tia. If you give part of your heart away every time, you won't have anything to offer your husband."

Marci Michael SCAD "You Oughta Know" Troy Zombie. I only cried harder.

Fatigue is a side effect of extreme diets and broken hearts. So is depression. So, by late fall of 1993, all I wanted was to stay in bed and sleep.

I turned Mary and Ruth Ellen down for a solid month of events. Michael was busy with his new acting friends. I marveled at how easy it was to check out and retreat. People moved on.

But by the time the Christmas hayride rolled around, Ruth Ellen wasn't having it. She showed up in my bedroom, probably sent there by my frustrated mother. "You can't be this tired all the time, Tia. Get up. You're going."

"It's not cold enough for a hayride," I said. And I knew I was right: Florida has humid, swamp-ass winters. Even the dirt would be damp.

But if I gave her this event, I could cross "did something social" off the expectation list. Everyone would get off my back about being sad. So we drove out to Hilliard, and I put on my fake-smile game face.

That's when I met Allan.

"Jingle Bells" jangled on the loudspeaker. As I stuck to my girlfriends, laughing and singing, playing foosball, and eating red-and-white candy canes, I loosened up. I joined a table of speed chess games where partners rotated quickly, feeling pepperminty, competitive, and happy.

A particular sailor kept landing on my board. I noticed his arms first—a skull tattoo with demon eyes.

"It's called Psycho Eyes," he said. "My Navy nickname. We all have one." He laughed and moved his knight.

I looked up into eyes as blue as the ocean, sparkling pools of deep shadow and want. Six-foot, wavy blond hair clipped regulation short, military posture. I felt a jolt of electric recognition move through me. He *was* somebody.

"Checkmate," he said. He'd taken my queen in five quick moves.

"What's your real name?" I asked.

As absent as Allan Brown was from my life until the day I met him, he was just as present as soon as I did.

Allan attended every social function for the three weeks leading up to Christmas, using his deployment leave instead of going home for the holiday. He got my number, and if it wasn't a church night, we were on the phone.

He loved Steely Dan and Italy. He shared his dreams for life after the Navy. "I want to build a wooden boat and sail with an adventurous girl who loves the mountains and nature. Then, I'll settle down and have a family."

Even as he said the words, I saw myself on the bow of his boat, on the trail in the woods, the mother of his children.

But even so, I wanted to play it cool, stay fun, stay casual. Allan wasn't from here and he wasn't staying here either. He shined, smelled good, and when I got home, I wrote in my journal I'd found magic. I reread what I wrote, surprised the words themselves didn't sparkle.

Allan lived with five other sailors in a rented house—happy souls high on Jesus and the freedom of their lives. When I showed up for game night, they urged me to get serious with Allan. Scot and Dave seemed to be on a mission to convince me.

I shrugged. "Sailors leave. You'll all get stationed somewhere else," I said.

"He's getting out," they said. "He's staying in Jax."

"Why though?" I said. "His family is in Arkansas. Why not go home?"

"Oh, you know," Dave said. "Good church and all."

"Hint, hint," Scot said, winking. "You're the 'and all' part."

They laughed, and when Allan came in, he gave me a hug and asked, "What's funny?"

"Our secret," said Scot.

Allan smiled and shook his head. "Roomies," he said.

But it felt good when friends approved.

On Christmas Day, Michael came over to exchange gifts. We sat on the couch and I caught him up on the last few weeks.

"Have fun," he said. "That's what I'm doing."

I cocked an eyebrow. "Yeah?"

"Dating different . . . people," he said. "First Baptist is a fishbowl. It's good to get out a little."

I wondered if Michael and Allan could be friends.

"I got a part," he said. "In *Joseph and the Amazing Technicolor Dreamcoat*. You're coming, right?"

"Wouldn't miss it," I said, unable to shake the feeling we were each floating farther and farther away.

On Sunday after church, Allan called to see if I'd go on a drive, and it became our first date. He picked me up in a shiny new Mitsubishi Galant. "Named like a white knight," I joked.

"Yep. *Your* white knight." He smiled, holding my door open. I sat on the leather seat and looked through the sunroof to the beautiful day.

As we drove, the wind that blew through my hair felt as much from the answered prayers as from the open windows. He got on the new highway bypass, shifting the gears smoothly, driving fast, moving fast. With a finger, I brushed a tendril of windblown hair off my face.

"You're the girl I've been waiting for, Tia. You're better than the other girls. You're different."

His turbo words laid it out. I blinked. We'd only just met.

"You should know . . . I don't believe in divorce," he said. "I want one wife for life. I want a solid marriage and an unshakeable family. And I'd like to consider you for the job." He winked and shifted into a higher gear. I reached for the hand grip.

I wondered if we were pre-engaged now. Promised, as Charity described all those years ago. And fast, like Shirley and Dr. Lindsay. I couldn't say no, when there hadn't even been a question. I stuck my head out the window far enough to let the wind sweep my hair behind me, waving in the sun like a flag.

Dating Allan felt like a plan I was falling into, rather than one I developed. Allan led the way, always a step faster than I expected. My emotions struggled to catch up, always a step behind. But I knew from nine years of lessons that what mattered was what happened—not how I felt about it.

Within a week, we'd been out to dinner three times and onto the *Spruance* for a tour of the ship. As we stood on the bow next to the giant gun, we watched the portlights and saw two falling stars.

"Here's another first," he said, tipping my chin up to his. His kiss was a soft petal on my lips, and a bloom of warmth spread down my neck and across my shoulders. He wrapped his arms around me and breathed into my hair.

I felt my bones collapse like those little skeleton toys. Allan held me up.

Now I knew this was my first kiss. What happened with Troy didn't count because of how it felt. I'd re-virgined myself with repentance. Sweet kisses in the starlight were God's reward.

The next day I brought him to Sunday dinner at Houlihan's to meet my family. He used his military manners on Mom and Grandma, who actually swooned from the attention. "I sure do like your man in uniform, Tia," Gran said. "I hope there's not a girl in every port," she laughed.

Dad interrogated him on what he knew how to fix. But Allan wasn't handy, and the questions made him uncomfortable. "What are you, a putz?" Dad laughed. Allan didn't.

In the car on the way home, I could tell Allan's energy had shifted. He was so quiet. When we got to my house, I invited him in.

"Not with your dad there," he said.

"Well, let's hang in the garage. There's a couch and AC. They'll leave us alone," I said. "We can talk."

But as soon as we sat down, Allan moved to kiss me. Expecting the feelings I'd had on the ship, I didn't resist. This time, though, was different. His hands groped my body as his mouth gulped my breath, my skin, my neck.

I put my hands on his and tried to hold them. But he pulled them free and buried his fingers in my hair, clutching it hard. "I can't get enough of you, Tia. It's like you're my very own cookie jar."

He tugged at my shirt buttons and the zipper on my jeans. Heart pounding, I moved his hands again to my arms and neck, debating the line between passion and chewed gum. The garage suddenly smelled mildewed, like a camper. Allan's skin was clammy, like Troy's. I twisted to get away, reaching for anything to help me escape. "My dad could come in," I whimpered.

It worked. Allan sat back and took a breath. He wiped his mouth with the back of his hand.

I ground into the date. *January 2, 1994.* I tucked my shirt back into my pants and willed the redness of my skin to fade, trying to slow my breath, reminding myself there was no dog, no old man asking, "Honey, are you okay?" I felt like a crumbled broken cookie—the pieces no one wants.

When Allan left, I grabbed my journal and didn't write what happened. *I can imagine marrying him someday,* I wrote. *But I'm afraid to say I love you because it's too soon.* I flipped back to the night of the hayride. December 3, 1993. We'd only known each other for a month.

A week later, he told me dating was expensive. "I like being in the car with you anyway," he said. "So, it's better if we have a short engagement, as Dr. Lindsay says. That way, we can get right to the good parts."

I counted breaths and pulse beats—1, 2, 3. Maybe I needed an engagement plan the same way I needed a rapture plan—steps to make the overwhelming manageable. I started to ask questions about his home and why he didn't go back for a visit after deployment.

"I left on bad terms," he said while we shared French fries from the Krystal's drive-thru. "My dad's a mean cuss, and he decided at the last minute not to pay for my college. So, we got into a fight, and I punched him. Then I joined the Navy."

Punching your parents? Didn't only terrible kids do that? Total rebels? Right away, I thought about his poor mother and her heartbreak.

He raised his eyebrows at my silent reaction. "Trust me. I was sadder than whatever you were thinking. He had it coming. He punched me too."

My eyes widened at his ability to read my thoughts, but I couldn't think of anything to say. Maybe it was my job to fix him. God could heal him through my love—this was a wife's highest calling.

Allan told me about enduring years of verbal abuse. "You can see it in my baby pictures. I was a happy kid. A fat kid, but happy. Smiling. And then, one day, it stopped."

He took out his wallet and showed me a photo of a little golden boy in a red shirt. He looked happier and lighter than the shadowed man next to me, but the blue eyes were the same. My heart broke to see how badly he craved love. "You were a little boy who lost his laugh," I said.

"You're right," he agreed. "But someday, I'm going to be a better father. With the right wife, I'm going to be happy."

The *right* wife. I saw the challenge and took a deep breath. The girl who makes the *right* wife is chosen. She isn't like the other girls. Our union explained the friendless years, the dateless high school experience, and how it felt to be a hideous iguana. All of it prepared me to complete the right man.

I reached for Allan's hand and looked into his blue eyes. I saw the little boy in him. "I love you," I said. And then I said, as much to God as to Allan, "I choose you too."

Happiness and heaven were on the way.

Pure

NOW THAT I'D ACCEPTED GOD'S PLAN INSTEAD OF DEVISING MY own, I wondered how best to help Allan. I'd started practicing my new signature and retrofitted his face onto Gilbert Blythe and whipped out my wife and mother homework. I rehearsed how to love the man God brought me, understanding now that Shirley must've done the same for Dr. Lindsay. Love isn't lightning—and like a hiker walking in a different altitude, I needed time to acclimate.

Dates would help, I reasoned. That week, Allan wanted to go to Mickler Beach, even though a nor'easter was hitting Jacksonville. "Oh, come on, we'll be alone," he said. He was right. No one else was on the beach during a storm. We walked while the frigid wind churned up the dunes and tossed sand in our faces. The water was bone-cold, white-capped, and violent.

But he wouldn't hold my hand. I felt more than physical distance between us, and it worried me. Any good church girl knows that when there's distance, it's her sin that's to blame. I felt acid rise in my throat, wondering what I'd done.

Then he turned. "What did you think about my roommates?" His blue eyes stood out against the darkening sky. "That night . . . I came in and you all were laughing."

The night with Scot and Dave? Allan had laughed too. Why was he mad about that now?

"Answer me," he demanded.

"Well . . . at first, I liked you all the same—which wasn't very much. I didn't go to the hayride looking for a boyfriend." I hoped I sounded cheerful. Light.

"But you played chess with me."

"So?"

Allan's posture hardened. "I guess this is your habit," he said. "Spending time alone with single men, leading them on."

"What are you talking about?" I swallowed, my mouth wet and sour. Jagged wind sliced through me like a blade.

"Maybe you're a slut. Your best friend is a single man. You spent time alone with me before we were even dating. What about when I'm out to sea?"

My eyes widened. "I was playing speed chess with strangers! You were nobody!"

Like a storm surge, his forearm slammed into my neck and spun me around.

I grasped my throat, choking. I hadn't seen his hand move—I hadn't even flinched. I pulled at my turtleneck and reached for air, surprised he'd missed my face. Had he *meant* to hit me in the windpipe?

Allan walked off, disappearing into the sand-blown darkness. I felt disoriented and faint, afraid to be here alone.

There was only enough light to see the shadow of the boardwalk to the parking lot.

I pressed my feet into the sand mounds and forced myself forward. I'd solve this a step at a time. There was a gas station a mile up the road. I'd get there, call my dad, say we broke up. Ask him to come get me.

But in the parking lot, two red lights flared like eyes. Allan spun the car around, and his white high beams caught me. I stood still as a deer, eyes wide with terror. He accelerated toward me, and I jumped back into the palmettos, afraid he would hit me with the car.

The Galant skidded to a stop, and the passenger door flew open. "Get in."

I debated if I should turn and run back toward the water.

"Don't be stupid," he said, reading my mind. "Get in."

We passed streets lined with sleeping houses, the windows like eyes staring at my shame. I was screwing up God's plan and upsetting the man He wanted me to marry. Even if we broke up now, I needed to make it right.

"Allan, I'm sorry if I hurt your feelings," I said. My fingers clenched hard on the hand grip. He was going 70 mph in a 45 zone.

He sniffed, and I realized he was crying. "Yeah? Well, you did. You're my everything, Tia. I want to marry you—and you called me a nobody."

"I meant I didn't know you yet."

His hand draped on the steering wheel at the wrist. "Don't spin this. We both know full well what you meant."

I begged God to lighten Allan's foot on the pedal. "I'm sorry. You're right. Please forgive me."

He sniffed and kept his eyes straight forward on the empty streets.

Thank God no one else was out in the storm. With my thumb, I stroked the leather seat over and over. "Are we okay?" I asked.

"Huh," he said, and the rest of the drive was silent.

Allan parked the car in front of our neighbor's house, out of the sight line of my parents' bedroom window. Of all nights not to have a curfew.

Ruth Ellen had one. Her father had come around to the idea of courtship. So, at nineteen, Ruth Ellen couldn't be out with boys and had to be in by ten every night. Ruth Ellen was not getting hit in the throat on the beach.

"Let's take a walk," he said. He didn't open my car door. Instead, he walked on ahead, knowing I'd follow.

Once outside the pool of streetlight, he pulled me down into the bushes. He pressed his entire body on top of me with rough and urgent kisses. He writhed, grinding his hips and hardness against me, moaning into my neck, "Let me do it."

My fingers clutched at cold grass. I tried to kiss him back, reaching up to touch his hair. But he squeezed my wrists and pressed my fingers to his belt buckle. "Take it off," he said.

I pulled my hands away. He grabbed them harder and put them back on his belt. Sand and sticks ground into the back of my hair.

"I have to go home," I said, trying to sit up. "I have to wait for marriage."

He panted, and then his whole body stiffened. I wondered if he was having a seizure. He gasped, then released, and rolled off me.

"So, go home," he said, out of breath.

I sat up and clasped my bra, tucked in my shirt, smoothed my hair. Allan walked on ahead. I got up and followed, pulling my turtleneck higher, grateful that modesty would help me hide.

The next day he sent flowers. The card read, *I'm sorry we argued. Love, Allan.*
I took the card and flowers and leaned against the doorframe of Mom's
sewing room. I wanted to ask her if love was like this. I wanted a hug. But I
tucked it down and stayed where I was.

Her head was bent over the machine, matching up a seam and tucking
it under the needle. Her foot pumped the pedal, and the engine hummed.
"What was that about?" she asked.

I watched her sew. Mom kept her art because she'd found out how to make
it glorify God. She was loved *and,* not loved *or.* This wasn't love's fault or God's
fault—it was mine. Men didn't get upset for nothing.

"Oh, we just got our wires crossed," I said with a shrug.

"Well, you've gotta love a man who knows how to apologize well," she said.
"Still head over heels for this guy, Tia? Things seem to be moving a little fast."

God's plan, I remembered. I tucked the florist's card back into the bouquet
and said "Yep" as I walked to my room.

In the weeks that followed, a quietness like early flu settled into me. Getting flowers, dating, kissing—none of this felt as good as I'd always imagined it would. I wanted to tell Michael about the beach, but I knew he'd say
to walk away. I was afraid that if I took anyone's advice, Allan would feel hurt
and angry. Besides, there wasn't even time.

Allan started coming to orchestra rehearsal, walking in near the end to sit
in the back, waiting for us to finish. Then he'd walk me to my car to make
sure I got home okay. He said he didn't like to think of me walking through an
empty parking garage alone, even though the church posted security guards.
I stopped hanging out with the singles after church or going out with Mary
and Ruth Ellen, because Allan said he didn't like feeling chaperoned.

It's hard to ask friends for advice when there's not a chance to see your friends.

One day I came in from work, sweaty and tired from an afternoon of toddlers, and went to the sewing room to tell Mom I was home.

"Your sweetie called," she said. "Mind your p's and q's with this one, honey.
It sounds like he could be the one." She smiled playfully. I remembered happy
mom meant happy family. The power to make them all happy was mine. I
just had to choose what they wanted.

I went to my room and took out my journal. I scanned the list of husband qualifications—number fifty-eight: *Not too possessive.* Number sixty: *Isn't jealous.* This Sunday School teacher–approved list now seemed inordinately long. Allan didn't match several items.

But did he have the same potential as them? Were these seeds that could grow if God and I helped? The men's ensemble sang a song about how God grew potential into substance. "Little Is Much When God Is in It."

I got up and walked down the hall to the kitchen phone. I dialed Ruth Ellen's number and wound the coiled cord around my fingers as the line rang, relieved when she answered.

"Can you come over? It's urgent," I said.

An hour later, the two of us sat across from each other, cross-legged, on my bedroom floor, my Bible and journals open between us.

Confession felt like pouring a little liquid from an overly full cup. I told her what I dared but left out the bruises. "What should I do?" I moaned.

She pursed her lips and gave me a stern look. "Tia. You asked God to bring you someone, and He did. And now your faith is being tested. Did you think God wouldn't be faithful?"

I sighed. "But how do I know if he's the one or not?"

"Has he asked to be?" She crossed her arms.

"Pretty much," I said. "We're engaged in private. But he's going to make it real tonight, I'm sure of it," I said.

"That's great!" she said. "Tia! You're *engaged*! Of course he's the one!"

When I didn't say anything, she said, "Look. Everything is fixable. Don't worry about not knowing anything. Books can help. My mom just gave me *Fascinating Womanhood*. It's great for learning how to be a good wife, even to a man who has a temper. He's justified in wanting you all to himself. Seriously, Tia. You should be grateful to be so desired. It takes practice to be a submissive wife."

Sometimes friends knew us better than we knew ourselves. "Thanks, Ruth Ellen," I said, hugging her. "Thanks for being a faithful friend."

Later that night, I picked at my salad with jittery hands and ordered refills of Diet Cherry Cokes.

Allan pushed his plate aside and leaned in across the table. "I told my parents about you last night," he said. "My mom is going to call you when

I'm on deployment to check on you." Weirdly, I'd meet my mother-in-law on the phone.

"I love you, Tia," he said. "I want to marry you. I've never wanted anyone the way I want you. You're my good thing. My cookie jar and I want you in my world forever."

His blue eyes pleaded. I could tell this wasn't easy for him. Only a very mean person would refuse. The seconds ticked by, the space of my silence pooling between us.

"I want that too," I said. The words felt honest. I knew I could learn to love God's plan.

But he needed something else. "You can only see Michael with a chaperone now."

I held my fork mid-stab and stared at him, my mouth wet like I might throw up.

"He's not your brother. He's not your family. And my wife doesn't hang out with fags."

The word "fag" hit me as hard as his hand and I sat back, setting my fork on the table. No one talked about Michael's gayness. Everyone at church understood that a suspicion like that was an "unspoken prayer request." We'd never even talked about it. Was this part of Allan's proposal? What would happen if I left right now?

"He's no threat to you," I said. The room spun. *Don't do this, God,* I prayed.

"Don't be an idiot," he said. "You're under his influence."

I swallowed and Allan reached over the table to take my hand. "Remember, you're my good thing."

This is how it felt to be caught. I let my hand go limp.

When Michael called a movie night, I took a deep breath and said, "I can't see you anymore." I clutched the phone receiver so hard my fingernails dug into my palm. The pain helped me keep going. "We can't go out alone without a chaperone, and I know we can't do that either."

I heard him inhale. "What are you talking about?" he said, his voice breaking. "It's been almost eight years. What the hell are you talking about?"

"I'm sorry. I'm so sorry," I said, trying not to cry.

"Don't be sorry," he said. "Just tell me what's going on."

And there it was. Michael saw through me. He saw through the bullshit around me too. He'd always know in a glance that I wasn't as happy as I pretended to be.

Tears burned and hung on my lashes. "We're getting married. I can't go out with other men anymore. That's how it is. We both knew this couldn't go on forever," I said.

"I didn't," he said. "I didn't think there'd ever be a reason we wouldn't be friends. This is unbelievable. Whatever. I gotta go."

The line silenced. The tears spilled, two hot wet streaks down my face.

Mom called from the sewing room. "Everything okay, honey?"

Seconds passed. And then, a new routine came, one that helped me tuck myself inside.

I squared my shoulders back and swallowed.

Took a breath.

Wiped my cheeks.

I tipped my chin and lied.

"It's fine," I said. "Everything is fine."

The ring provided evidence of adulthood. Suddenly women who worried I'd come to no good now cared what color towels I wanted in my bathroom. What kind of dishes I'd stack in the cupboard. Tia was getting married. Adolescence was over.

We chose a date, and it became a deadline for the end of being aimlessly single. My choice made so many people happy. By saying yes to Allan and God, I'd confirmed my value.

I decided to focus on our love story. I wanted the little boy to find his laugh. If he was happy, we'd be happy.

So, I took over planning our dates.

I taught Allan how to pack a charcuterie picnic for the park, and we spent lazy autumn afternoons nuzzling under the oak trees. Then I taught him how to carve a pumpkin because he'd never done one. On sunny days we tossed a football or laid back and watched the clouds, dreaming of the names of our future children. I took pictures and started a scrapbook. *This is how our life started,* I'd say to our children someday, smiling with tears in my eyes.

Allan was calmer and tenderer now. He held me in his arms and called the dip between his muscular shoulder and neck my spot. We found an apartment in the historic district, on a tree-lined street one block from the old stone library. He moved in ahead of the wedding, away from the roommates. We danced in the moonlight at Memorial Park to music only we could hear, watching the starshine sparkle on the St. Johns River. There were many starlight kisses.

This is belonging, I thought, softening my guard. *This is the happiness of choosing God's plan.*

Everything else, I kept secret.

The day he threatened to behead me by driving us under a semitruck. And begging to have sex before the wedding. The night he promised to drive us off the Acosta Bridge. And the way the back of my head hurt because he so often pulled my hair. I kept secrets like black rose petals, a bridal bouquet of shadows.

Dedicated to my new life, I packed up my childhood bedroom. I threw away the letters and pictures of life before Allan. My real life was to be a submissive and servant-hearted wife. My real life began with the wedding.

But the domino of my changed mind hovered, waiting like a comma in the air, and as firmly as I was determined to choose Allan, windows kept opening so I could fly away. This only made the ground feel uncertain, like a bounce house where no matter what I did, I'd wobble and fall. I'd expected obeying God and falling in love with the one He sent to feel safer, like an item to cross off the to-do list.

Florida required premarital counseling for a wedding license to become effective at the ceremony. Without it, we'd have a three-day window for regrets and annulments. Churches pressed to offer faith-based, divorce-adverse advice. So, I signed us up to check the box for the wedding coordinator, hoping sticking to the plan would solidify the ground and walls around me.

"Oh good," she said. "Without that counseling requirement, you'll be having sex for three days without really being married."

Allan hated having to pay for it. "If it's a state requirement, the state should pay," he said. His foot pressed down on the gas pedal and I gripped the handle. "We hear enough sermons as it is."

Sermons were a hack for counseling, according to Allan. And understanding Allan's thriftiness was my responsibility. He parked in the garage and opened my door. Nervously, we checked into the counseling center and Reverend Brewer's office.

Rev. Brewer was a kind man, with a thick silver grandpa mustache, who'd gone to this church for a long time. He was friends with my parents. I wondered if my secrets were safe with him or if he'd report what I said in our session.

He greeted us with a meaty handshake. "Howdy, folks. Great to see you today."

Allan turned on his shiny manners and smiled. He shook the reverend's hand and said, "Cordial office you have here, Reverend."

"Yes, thanks . . . well, let's start with these, shall we?" He handed us both a packet with a questionnaire and personality test and led us each to small, private rooms.

I filled in the bubbles with my pencil perfectly. The questions were about how I handled problems, spent my free time, felt when I was alone—easy questions with straightforward, honest answers. I turned it in and sat next to Allan while we waited for Rev. Brewer to grade our tests.

We watched as he shuffled the paperwork. Then he cleared his throat and looked at me, staring hard. I blinked away, wondering if I'd answered wrong.

"I often see couples like you . . . with differences," said the reverend. "I can assist with some of those issues."

Allan stiffened. "With all due respect, sir, I'm quite capable of seeing our differences on my own. I don't need to pay for counseling to find that out."

"Well, Allan," said Rev. Brewer, "that might be true. You're very astute. However, it's a requirement, not an option. And your tests were quite revealing."

My breath came thin and silent. *What did I answer wrong?*

"Revealing how?" Allan demanded.

I kept my eyes straight ahead. I didn't need to look to know his pupils were black and shining. The room felt stifling hot and small, the air pulsing me into waves of green nausea. I reached my hand up to pull on my turtleneck, hoping for cool air.

Rev. Brewer pursed his lips, which made his mustache twitch. "I'm afraid you failed the compatibility test," he said. "You are two very different people. Your personality types clash. The test predicts that should you marry, one of you will dwarf the other. There's no way for two lights to shine in this union."

Allan laughed. "Well, duh . . ." He looked over at me and gestured like, *get a load of this joker.* "Of course, there aren't two lights in a sacramental union. What kind of cockamamie counseling is this?"

"It's my professional recommendation that you two do not get married. Marriage to one another isn't a healthy option for your individual growth." He raised one eyebrow and bore his words into me like a laser. "At the very least, you should postpone the wedding and get counseling."

"Oh, there it is!" Allan cackled. "The sales pitch! How convenient. And if we stay single, we'll eventually be back here with someone else, and you'll collect twice."

"This is not about my counseling fee."

"The heck it isn't!" Several seconds passed. Allan fumed, nostrils flaring, caged.

Reverend Brewer sat calmly, his face unreadable. He turned to me. "How are you taking this, Tia?"

My mouth felt clay dry. Pressure hung on my shoulders like a horse collar—four hundred embossed invitations. Gifts already arriving in the mail. The bedroom boxes sitting at the curb for the trash pickup. The consequences of being alone with Allan when we left this room.

I spotted the lifeguard throwing me a line. It was just too far for me to swim. *Little is much when God is in it.* I squared my shoulders back. Took a breath. Folded my hands. I tipped my chin and found my voice. "Well . . . can't we do all things through Christ, who strengthens us?" Years of memorized Scripture paid off when my own words failed.

The reverend sighed.

Footsteps were the only sounds on the way back to the car. Once we were inside the Galant, Allan pounded the steering wheel with rage. "This always happens! Every time something good comes, someone takes it away. Every. Damn. Time."

He listed examples, most of which I'd never heard before.

"My father's drunk parents died when he was a kid and his cruel older sisters raised him. So he didn't think I needed my mama and he made her go back to work when I was just a baby. When I was winning tennis but had acne, he scrubbed the skin off my nose with a pumice stone, and I had to quit. When I was headed to college, that fucker refused to pay. So, I had to join the damn Navy. When I wanted to dive, the Navy said I had to learn fucking Morse code instead." Allan pounded the steering wheel again. "Fuck you, Jessica!"

Jessica. The first fiancée in Massachusetts. "Her fucking parents made us break up because of the way we argued. And NOW. Just as I'm about to take a wife again, the fucking counselor dooms the union!"

I stared at the blue dashboard. I hadn't known they'd been forced to break up. *We grew apart while I was overseas,* he'd said once.

If my parents had seen the beach, they'd have done the same thing. Reverend Brewer saw. Somehow, he knew. I tried digesting this information. What did it change? Who can argue with God?

He cried into his hands, but I couldn't access any feelings. What were these tears? Was he afraid of losing me? He hadn't said that, exactly. It made him angry to be criticized.

"You're always trying to outshine me," Allan said, sniffing.

"I don't mean to," I said. "I'm trying to do better. I'm reading *Fascinating Womanhood.* I'm sure I'll learn. You'll be the leader, Allan, I promise."

"Oh, you'll learn alright. I'll train you," he said.

I looked out at the concrete columns of the garage. The sky felt distant and judgmental. "We have God," I said. "And we have the wedding. Planning will help."

Planning did help. It helped me protect our appearance—and this, I'd quickly learned, is a Christian woman's job.

Mom designed my dress, and we traveled out of town for ivory fabric embroidered with gold, and midnight-blue velvet, also embroidered with gold, for the bridesmaids. We'd look like Christmas princesses.

Over the following months we tasted cakes, registered for dishes, and read books about Christian marriage. Little girls I nannied were my flower girls. Sunday School teachers threw four showers. Allan wanted bagpipes and his tartan plaid incorporated, so we ordered it from Scotland and found a piper. Mom ordered sheet music from Mannheim Steamroller—a trumpet solo written by Chip Davis. I tried not to feel disappointed when over half of our guests RSVP'd no because the Gator Bowl game was scheduled for the same day.

That fall, I removed the domino of a changed mind. On December 30, 1994, the domino of our wedding took its place in line. We were nineteen and twenty-one.

The sanctuary sparkled with twinkle lights and candelabras. Evergreen boughs hung from every pew and in arches over the doors. The organ pipes resounded with *Canon in D* and *Jesu, Joy of Man's Desiring*. A white runner covered the red carpet.

Michael came and sat on the bride's side.

As Ace and Chuck played the first clear notes of "Lo, How a Rose E'er Blooming" on the trumpet and organ, Dad and I waited at the back of the church.

"Are you sure you want to do this?" he said.

My eyes widened. What?

I turned and looked down at the corridor that led to the door and the street.

Where would I go?

Where did a runaway bride go once she stopped running?

Who could run from God?

I tucked in, using my routine. "Help me with my veil." As we flipped my veil over my face in the dim candlelight, I realized we'd never rehearsed with the veil down. "Dad, I can't see!"

My heart pounded, my chest flushing red from the pressure. I *had* to walk with a veil. A veilless bride signaled impurity. The only option was to walk the aisle blind.

"You've got me," Dad said.

I walked through shadowed candlelight. At the stage, the minister said, "Who gives this woman?"

Dad lifted my veil, kissed my cheek, and laid my hand inside Allan's.

Allan's hand was unsteady, and I stumbled as I grasped the weight of my wedding dress to climb the stairs. The fingernail on my ring finger tore off at the quick. Pain surged as crimson blood beaded on my nail bed.

Breathe.

I squared my shoulders, tipped my chin, and smiled. Only the minister saw my recalibration. I vowed to love, honor, and obey Allan until death do us part. He kissed his bride.

The rest of the wedding went by in a happy blur of laughter, cake, and congratulations. Michael said he was moving to New York, and then he left.

A few hours later, Mom draped a velvet cape around my shoulders, and Allan and I climbed into a horse-drawn carriage that delivered us to the threshold of our future.

My second ten years had groomed me for the life ahead.

Part Two

A WIFE

Threshold

ONE REDBRICK FOURPLEX BUILT IN 1917. FOUR CONCRETE STEPS. One wooden door with two glass side panels. Twenty-four wooden switchback stairs with a worn landing in between. Two metal house keys, one for each of us. I bounded into my first home with Allan with candy-store excitement on my face. *We were married!*

I'd make Allan an excellent wife and embrace every duty with joy. And we'd have what Elisabeth Elliot wrote in *Passion and Purity*: the reward for following God's plan. Confident joy reverberated through me like a happy string concerto.

I set the basket of reception leftovers on the counter and stood in my kitchen. My very own Magic Kingdom. I wanted to sing!

"Let's get you out of that dress," Allan said.

"I'll need help with the buttons," I said. "Mom sent a crochet hook."

Allan tugged on 104 buttons, careful not to tear my gown. The bodice released, and birdseed fell from my bra. I giggled as it sprinkled onto the floor.

Allan led me to the bed. Deep inside I was pleasedonthurtme nervous, but I hoped he couldn't tell. *Sing! Smile! You made it!* Tonight would be magic.

"Relax," he said. "I know what I'm doing."

Jessica. Four others whose names he couldn't remember. He knew where he wanted to put his hands and where he wanted me to put mine. I wondered if someone taught men, or if they just knew.

I shrugged the thought away and raised my mouth, ready for kisses as the chosen one.

But this night, unlike every other, Allan didn't spend time kissing or groping. Instead, he tore into me like long-awaited mail, shocking me with dry,
hard stabs and strokes. I gasped from searing pain as my skin broke, and then
my body went numb.

"It hurts," I said, crying. "Please stop."

His body stiffened, and he grabbed my hair in two fists.

I felt him release.

He rolled off me. "It's better to get it over with fast," he said.

After a little while, I heard him snoring. I moved words around in my
mind. *Sacred. Holy. Passion. Better to get it over with.* I stared at the ceiling. Shadows from the streetlights made the long fingers of bare trees
dance as the wind blew outside. I curled onto my side and tried to sleep,
glad it was over.

Hands woke me, turning my body over onto my stomach.

He spread my legs with his hand and got on top of me, tearing me open
again. I buried cries into the pillow. This time "please" and "stop" and "that
hurts" constricted in my throat. I tried to hold my breath. Submerge into
darkness. But my jagged exhale came with sound, a cry I knew didn't sound
like pleasure.

Behind closed eyes, I saw home. My old bedroom with its twin bed and
locked door. I tried to go there, in my mind, but it didn't work.

Plaster ceiling.

Tree shadows.

Wind.

Time.

He finished and rolled off, dragging a wet slug across my leg. I wiped it away
with the bedsheet. My body, rigid and braced, refused sleep, and I watched
the tree-fingers instead.

When

he

pressed

into

me

a third time,

I detached and left my body. I watched in silence from the shadowed corner across the room, small and very sorry for that poor girl.

The drive to Gatlinburg, Tennessee, took eleven hours. I sat with my feet pressed into the floorboards, trying to keep the pressure off my burning, inflamed bottom. I stared at the mountains that lay like a woman beneath a rumpled wool blanket and at dreary winter skies. Ribbons of slate smoke rose from hidden chimneys. What did it mean to have a husband?

A Christian wife is responsible for the peace and happiness of her home. She has to meet his needs. Why had no one told me what that really meant? In *Intended for Pleasure,* the Christian sex book we'd been given as a gift, it said the marriage bed was a holy place in the sight of God. I was supposed to be one with Allan now, and look at him with such reverence that he'd become a "king among men." Our marriage was now a "private little kingdom, secluded from view." Dr. Wheat had cautioned that gray mornings would come, because emotions never sustain a marriage. I guess that included Day One.

I thought of tree hollows—cavities formed in the trunk of a living tree. An injury like lightning creates an opening through the bark, exposing the sapwood. Bacteria eat its heart out.

I wanted to go home.

When we arrived at the cabin, I took in the wraparound porch, rocking chairs, and fireplace. We visited an orchard for apples and a small grocer for food. I bought popcorn and hot chocolate. There was only one VHS tape in the cabinet, so we watched *So I Married an Axe Murderer* on repeat. We didn't talk much. Allan seemed less interested now that we'd crossed the threshold into marriage.

On the fourth day, I woke up with a high fever and stabbing, intense belly pain. I cried every time I went to the bathroom. Allan called a small-town clinic that took walk-ins.

The grandfatherly doc had one small examination room. He told Allan to wait outside. Then, he handed me a cloth gown. "You can change behind that green curtain," he said.

I heard the clink of metal things on a tray and my nose burned with the sharp scent of antiseptic. I came out and sat on the table.

"Have you ever had a pelvic exam before?" he asked. "Lie back and put your feet together. Let your knees drop like a frog's." He had one hand on my leg. "I promise to be gentle. I just need to take a look."

I flinched when his cold, gloved hand touched my bruised labia.

"I see signs here of significant trauma, honey," he said.

I stared at the ceiling tiles with tiny holes in them like the constellations. "It's . . . I'm on my honeymoon," I stammered.

"Were you a virgin?"

"Yes, sir."

He sighed and pulled his hand away. "Well, honey, I don't have to look inside to know what's going on here. You've got an infection and it's a doozy. Plus, bruising. Your body can't handle that much battering."

Bat-ter-ing. My eyes blinked fast at the flickering fluorescent light in the ceiling.

"I'll talk to your husband. You're getting this week off." He patted my leg. "Are you on birth control?"

"Pills," I answered.

After I dressed, he handed me a prescription. "Fill it at the grocery store up yonder. Get some diaper cream to help your tissues heal. Why don't you wait outside?"

He called for Allan to follow him. I sat in the car with my arms over my belly, which still hurt plenty. Nothing we'd done yet had given me any relief. And now I'd have to face whatever Allan handed me when he came out of that room.

But he was quiet and meek when the doctor opened the door, and we left. We didn't discuss it at all. He filled my prescription and bought apple juice to help me stay hydrated with the fever. My tissues and I got the week off.

When we got home and went to church, everyone asked how the trip went. I squared my shoulders and smiled. *The local apples were amazing. So were the waterfalls.*

But in service, I looked at the women. *Is this what marriage is like? Will it always hurt this much?* I'd spent my whole life preparing to be a virgin bride. I didn't know anything about how to be a submissive wife.

In the sea of women, no one stood out. We dressed alike, sat alike, and turned the pages of our Bibles alike. Legs crossed the same way, at the same time. Yawns stifled. Smiles plastered uniformly. Peppermint for our breath, perfume for our scent, paint for our face. Our movement flowed in unison: sit, stand, sing, pray. Even our silence harmonized. Maybe it was the same at home, too.

Allan repented. He said his mood swings weren't healthy or holy and that he'd found the solution. What we needed—us and America—were proper gender roles. If I learned how to be a woman, he'd be free to be a man. To learn his part, he studied R. C. Sproul Jr., John F. MacArthur, and John Piper.

"It's called *Recovering Biblical Manhood and Womanhood*. Complementarianism. Men and women are different according to gender, and our roles complement one another. Godly harmony is the result and this country would be a lot better if women understood their place. My job is to lead you, Tia. Yours is to serve."

So, I curled with the cat on the couch, studying how to recover my feminine role in the pages of *Fascinating Womanhood*.

Helen B. Andelin said a woman should dress in soft, feminine fabrics only. She should not talk with her hands or move them too much when she walks. She should not walk aggressively. A submissive wife practiced listening to her husband talk. She didn't offer him advice because suggestions implied self-sufficiency. Men needed to feel needed. Serious consequences happen when a wife refuses to need or obey.

Knowing something about serious consequences, I kept reading.

According to Helen, I needed to become a domestic goddess. But I didn't know how to cook five meals in a row or meal-plan. I couldn't shop on a budget or clean with a routine. I knew how to do these specific, individual things but not all together. So, I threw myself into learning how.

I started with dinner. After a shift as a nanny, I came home to Martha Stewart 101 and got to work. Homekeeping led to harmony; I was sure of it.

As I cooked, I counted my blessings. Like when Allan and I read in bed with the cat between us. The sound of the metal key turning in the lock of our first home. The scent of roast chicken with garlic and lemon in the cavity.

"You *whore!*" Allan seethed. Then, he walked over and grabbed me by the hair. "You're a fucking whore."

Stunned, I tried to pull away, which only made his grip tighter. *What happened?*

Reflexively, I twisted around and slapped him across the face, like Scarlett slapped Rhett Butler. "*Never* call me that word," I said through gritted teeth. "Don't call me names."

We stood frozen. Panting. With horror, I realized I'd uncaged a starving lion. I ran.

He chased me down the hallway to our bedroom and grabbed me, my long hair in his quick grasp a natural rope. He dragged me down the hall to the kitchen and slammed my head into the doorframe, pressing my face against the floor, and sat his full weight on my head until my body stilled. Then he told me what I did wrong.

"Look at this damn floor! You said you scrubbed it today, you lying bitch."

"I did, Allan. I mopped it with—"

"Don't lie to me, cunt. This floor is disgusting!" He smeared my cheek across the green linoleum. "You think I don't check your work? You're going to get on your knees and scrub this until *I* say it's done."

He gave my head a thrust and got up. I sat on the floor and tried to breathe. He kicked the mop bucket toward me, dirty water sloshing. Then he left the room.

Slowly, I got on my hands and knees and dipped the scrub brush into the cold disinfectant water, murky from the morning's mop. Back and forth. Circles. The shape of a square tile. The black seam between tiles.

I dug the corner of the brush into the baseboard edge where the floor met the wall. I could see where I'd missed spots by only mopping. Allan was right. He was the man of the house, doing his job by making sure I did mine.

The next morning, he said, "I'm sorry for our fight, Tia. I never thought marriage would mean fighting. You have such a redheaded temper."

I took a breath, tipped my chin, and apologized. "I'm sorry I slapped you."

"I'm glad to hear that. Slapping is abuse. But I forgive you. I want you to think about what you've done."

He left the room. I sat down on the edge of the bed and looked over at the

Fascinating hot pink paperback on the nightstand. I turned to the chapter on "Housekeeping, a Matter of Character."

Poor housekeeping revealed self-centeredness. "Lack of order is a serious fault" because God created a masterpiece of organization that I abused through negligence. Helen allowed the newly married might suffer from a lack of knowledge, but it was my God-given responsibility to learn.

I was to focus on Allan at all times to anticipate his needs. Scrubbing in the corners mattered because Allan said it did. If I thought about what mattered to him ahead of housework, not only would I do a good job, but I could prevent his anger.

I wondered about his sexual needs.

Elisabeth Elliot taught that married sex was hot and frequent. But he hadn't touched me since Tennessee.

"I'm healed," I told him six weeks after the honeymoon. "We can try again. Maybe more slowly."

He ignored me.

I turned to Helen for help. A good wife possessed a feminine manner, a childlike playfulness, and a dependency on her man that made him feel strong. He needed to see me be small.

Valentine's Day was our first holiday as a married couple. I wanted it to be special, like a second-chance honeymoon. I started prepping a week ahead of time, following Helen's recipe.

A clean house:

I spent the weekend scrubbing the apartment from top to bottom, polishing the floors, and disinfecting the corners.

Next, a clean spirit.

I carefully moderated my voice for tone and volume and avoided arguments.

Third, a clean body.

Helen had rules for radiant health. I drank water, slept well, ate fruits and vegetables, and took walks. On Valentine's Day, I showered, shaved, did my hair and makeup. I'd even bought a red negligee from Frederick's of Hollywood with some wedding savings.

Then, I prepared the apartment for an indoor picnic. I laid out a spread of candles, bread, brownies, grapes, and cheese. I got a massage oil that could also serve as a lubricant. I sat on the blanket posed like a Frederick's model, legs partly open, arm draped over my hips, hoping I looked like a hot Christian wife.

When I heard his key in the lock, I smiled and said, "Happy Valentine's Day, baby!"

"What's this?" he said.

I got up to take his bag. My neck reddened with blood pressure because he wasn't smiling, but I kept going. "How was your day? Would you like a massage? I bet you're hungry. I am too. We can take our time. I have everything right here."

He tried to adjust the pillows I'd stacked for him to recline against and fidgeted. He wouldn't look at me.

I tried kissing him, first down the side of his face and then toward his mouth. He pulled away. Regrouping, I said, "Let me make you a plate."

"I don't want to eat with my hands," he said.

I giggled, hoping it sounded childlike because Helen said men loved that.

He stood up. "I'm not doing this made-up holiday. I'm tired. And you smell like a period. You're disgusting." He bent down and blew out the candles on the coffee table.

I sat alone in the living room watching dusk fall. Without the sun, the room grew cold with winter shadows.

He'd come home empty-handed. No roses. No chocolates. No plan of his own for Valentine's Day. Why hadn't I been able to anticipate that better?

Allan wasn't a Hallmark holiday kind of guy. I should've known. I sniffed my armpit. I could change soaps. I could've added perfume. I was sure it was overwhelming to come home to all this. How stupid of me not to hint a little this morning.

I gathered the food and threw it in the trash.

Weeks passed. I started to wonder if I had options. Every now and then, marriages at First Baptist didn't "take."

Sex ruled out an annulment. Divorce wasn't allowed. The people who got one left the church. Marriage is till death do you part. I had to lie in the bed I had made.

I wanted to talk to my friends, but there wasn't anyone left to tell. Monica had left for college on a music scholarship. My high school friends were gone. Ruth Ellen was betrothed.

The other wives wouldn't crack. We skirted the point in Sunday School. No one talked about sex. As far as I knew, these wives all knew how to do it and their husbands wanted it all the time. Our teacher encouraged us to learn to love our husbands. We could decide to, especially if the feeling didn't come naturally.

I didn't want someone to read my journal and call me suicidal because good Christians don't kill themselves. So, I kept up appearances even on those pages and imagined shattered glassbonesmetalblood in my dreams. I could use the car.

Finally, after a desperate four months, I committed to Helen's assignments. I'd skipped the homework.

"*Fascinating Womanhood* teaches women to be happy in marriage." It's written to women who are "disillusioned, disappointed, and unhappy . . . because they feel neglected, unappreciated, and unloved. When a man doesn't love his wife with his heart and soul, it's the wife's fault."

My fault.

The lessons showed I'd failed to appreciate the pressure Allan faced. My new husband had a stupid wife. I used Helen's "Love Booklet" to record what I learned.

#1: *Write your husband a note. "I'm glad you're the man you are. I can see I haven't understood you in the past and have made many mistakes. I'm glad you haven't allowed me to change you."* I taped this to the bathroom mirror.

#2: *Ask him for help opening a jar. Show him you recognize and appeal to his masculine strength.* I asked Allan to open a new jar of peanut butter.

The next assignment was big and took me several weeks.

#3: *Organize your household so that even if you get up in the middle of the night, you can find anything you need without turning on the light.*

Several assignments required behavior modification.

Use a gentle, feminine voice that's clear and variable, like a song . . .
Learn to laugh without deep tones, opening your mouth wide, throwing
*   your head back, slapping your thighs, or roaring at coarse and vulgar*
*   humor. Make your laugh acceptable. . . .*

Words seemed to jump off the page:
Coo.
Purr.
Try not to be too much.
Oof. I'd been too much for as long as I could remember. I was a hard
worker. Athletic. As comfortable in the woodshop as I was in the kitchen. I
didn't know how to purr.
Express childlike anger. Stomp your foot, lift your chin high, and toss your
curls. Put your hands on your hips, wide-eyed. Beat on his chest with your fists.
Valentine's Day memories flooded in. Best keep my hands to myself.
Call him a big hairy brute. Call him stubborn. Stick out a pouty lip like a child.
One night just before summer, he came inside me when I was half-asleep,
without kissing or talking. He finished in a couple of thrusts. He said he
needed relief.
When he fell asleep, I took out my love booklet and recorded this victory.
I understood now: marriage takes work.
The shadows on the ceiling danced with new spring leaves.
The thing about tree hollows is that sometimes, they become homes.
Allan got up early every morning and sat in a puddle of lamplight turn-
ing the pages of his Bible, feverishly praying and begging God for wisdom.
Where I'd checked off Scripture for ski trips, Allan did it for passion. He said
God would make him a better man.
I lay in bed while he prayed, careful not to disturb him. I liked that he
prayed this hard, like King David after adultery, like Jesus before crucifixion.
Passion. These devoted hours would help him become gentle.
One morning, I peed in a cup and stuck an e.p.t wand in it.
Two lines to explain my queasy stomach and missed period, even though

I'd never forgotten a pill. Now, I'd learn to be a wife and mother at the same time. Dreams came true too quickly.

The next time we had orchestra, I sat on the stage with my flute watching the homeschooling, home-birthing Gothard families and had an idea. Jo Miller caught babies for her sisters; April and Charity both already had four. I'd heard Hannah was pregnant too. I decided to give Jo a call.

That afternoon, she offered words I'd cling to for years: "Babies come when they're supposed to."

Choosing home birth wasn't just cheaper; it appealed to Allan's goal to thumb his nose at the government. He was out of the Navy now and working in a warehouse. He said we needed to step out of culture and be different on purpose.

But the intelligent midwives and my instant comfort in them pissed him off.

Jo apprenticed under Tina, a jolly, comforting hippie who lived near the Bridge of Lions in St. Augustine. Tina's house smelled of patchouli and garlic, and there was a fat Buddha in the yard. Allan sniffed in judgment.

The first thing Tina did was pull me into her soft chest and squeeze her arms around me. "How are you, my love?" And I melted into her warmth, holding back tears, aching for a kind touch.

"We need to teach you to eat more," she said.

As the months passed, Tina reviewed every bite I recorded and heard every fear and anxiety. Tina spent hours tending my pregnancy, mothering me as my body mothered. I rested on the chenille bedspread in her office and let my bones relax, watching sunlight make patterns on the walls while she took copious notes. Then, I borrowed her books.

Spiritual Midwifery traced a band of brave hippies in buses from California to a farm commune in Tennessee. Along the way, they learned how to deliver their own babies.

As a Christian, I was supposed to want to be like Helen. As a woman, I knew I longed to be more like Tina. Allan said, "I think you go to too many visits."

Gently, Tina talked to me about facing my fears about birth. What would come out of me if I was in so much pain that I became uninhibited? What might I say in the madness of pain?

The *Spiritual Midwifery* mamas got into their births without negativity or pain—it was all about surges and love and welcoming new life. Labor had a high—a series of waves that opens a woman's body and floods her with feel-good chemicals. Tina's books said birth could empower, and a strong birth could even heal past sexual trauma.

I hadn't said anything about tree hollows and Troy. Or about my wedding night either. But Tina, like Michael, saw through, and I understood now why Allan didn't like her.

I rested in the shade of Tina's sequoia, confident that I was capable of a safe, normal delivery full of love. My body was young and strong. I'd gained good weight. I had women guides to support and hold me.

I think I trusted my body for the first time.

I remembered too well that virginity didn't teach me how to be a wife. What if birthing didn't teach me to be a mother?

There was a new course at church recommended by Dr. John F. MacArthur, president of the Southern Baptist Convention and friend to Dr. Vines. Gary and Anne Marie Ezzo attended MacArthur's church and wrote *Preparation for Parenting* and *Growing Kids God's Way*. Signing up to attend the course seemed as natural and innocuous as registering at Toys "R" Us for a crib.

Anne Marie was a NICU nurse and her experience informed the medical advice. She wore a puritanical black dress with an oversized lace-trimmed collar. She giggled and deferred to Gary, and I struggled to imagine how she handled herself in a neonatal nursery. I recognized her *Fascinating Womanhood* hallmarks with mixed feelings. How could I take a woman who coos seriously?

The Ezzos started with sin. Infants are born with a sinful nature, one of the base elements of the depravity of man. While newborns don't make cognitive decisions about moral rights and wrongs, they're biologically affected by sin at birth. Left to their own with weak mothers, they'll break the marriage and ruin the family.

I read the chapters carefully. As a nanny, I wasn't worried about newborn care. But I feared sleepless nights. A tired Allan was an unhappy Allan. I needed to fix that before it happened.

The Ezzos said our happiness came down to how I fed the baby. The secular world encouraged feeding a baby "on demand" with attachment parenting.

"Mothers are told to endlessly carry their babies, sleep with them, breastfeed them day and night without any regard to routine. They exalt the child as the center of the family universe." The Ezzos said husbands had to watch out for this evil.

Parent-directed feeding was his solution. Feed the baby when they wake up, interact a little, and then lay it down for a nap. This predictable pattern was neither a schedule nor chaos, and it stabilized the hunger/sleep cycles for proper infant management—essential for keeping the peace.

I studied and highlighted the pages. If I got it wrong this time, I wouldn't be the only one who paid for it now.

My baby was born on a blustery day in March, full of wind and white sunshine. I was twenty years old.

Labor surged over my consciousness and took me to a hidden place, a world of eternal mothers. Azure swirls and golden stars flowed into an ocean of love that surrounded and held my body. Pain that pushed away pain that wiped my soul clean.

"Tia, open your eyes and watch your baby being born," Jo said. My hands helped lift a slippery red baby to my chest.

A beautiful boy came from *me*. I gasped and sobbed, overcome with love for him. His wrinkled body arched back, and he looked at me with dark, watery eyes of recognition.

Hi, baby.

We were in our own world, a shield cast by light, love, and longing. My ears registered sounds of laughing and cleaning up, but my vision didn't extend beyond the baby.

A key in my chest unlocked some sacred part of my heart that had saved itself for this particular little boy, and I opened it to him. *I'll be here, baby. I'll be here. I'll show you everything I can, and I will never, ever leave.*

Even though Gary and Anne Marie warned me not to, I fell in love with the baby. I spent hours letting him sleep on my lap, propped up on my knees so I could stare at the incredible beauty of him, his peaches-and-cream skin, his long fingers that grasped mine tightly as he slept. He was a serious little man with a wise old soul and eyes that said he'd been here before. I inhaled his scent until my lungs ached and my head dazed. Baby-high, *hi baby*.

Our days settled into a rock-a-bye rhythm and breastfeeding came easy. A diaper service delivered a bundle of soft white diapers each week. We walked beneath massive oaks and sycamores. I played Brahms's lullaby and Bach's *Jesu* and Rachmaninoff's sonatas. I forgot everyone but the baby.

And then, like a cramp, reality returned. Allan, overjoyed I'd borne a son "to continue the family line," said I belonged in a red tent, referring to the Old Testament practice of isolating bleeding women until they stopped leaking everywhere. My blood and milk flowed constantly, abundantly. "Your body is disgusting," he said.

Reluctantly, I looked up from William. Helping Allan learn to be a father was part of my job.

I chose an evening when he'd had time to relax after work, read his Bible, and eat part of the casserole I'd made. William needed a new diaper.

"I'll be more involved with him when he's older," Allan said. "Babies are women's work."

"If you wait, he won't know you later," I said. "Taking care of him now is how you spend time with your son."

It surprised me, but he listened.

Allan became adept at changing cloth diapers with pins and held William high on his shoulder when he shrieked with gas. He created a litany of sweet nicknames and laughed when the baby laughed. He became an engaging daddy.

I learned that when Allan's shoulders twitched forward and then back, it meant he was afraid—but open. He didn't want to admit weakness, but if I responded with gentle instruction, he eagerly pitched in. I remembered his childhood. Of the two of us, I was the one with the better father. What if Allan learned how to be a nurturing father . . . from me?

Helen was right. The difference was being attuned to my husband's needs. Motherpower showed me how to pay attention. By being a good mother, I'd be a good wife. My vigilance would make us happy.

Mentor

ATTENTIVE MOTHERING CAME EASILY. MY FOCUS WAS ALREADY centered on the baby, without distraction. I didn't blink when Allan said I needed to quit the orchestra and stay home more. Or when he sold his car to use Gladys and be a one-car family so that I'd have no choice. I pushed William in the stroller often, mastered the Ezzo feeding rhythm, and daydreamed about our happy future. Vigilance was the way to maintain peace and I felt stupid for not realizing it before.

But I needed to teach my baby not to cry. Crying unraveled everything and reminded me how easily my control could slip. William only cried at 2 A.M., which I didn't think was too bad for six weeks. He was a "good" baby, everyone told me. But crying at night woke Allan, even if I jumped up quickly and raced to the cradle.

"Some children have a greater propensity to cry, which is not necessarily a signal that their basic needs aren't being met," Gary wrote in *Preparation for Parenting.*

Allan reminded me that Gary had warned us not to react. Instead, we should stop and consider why the baby is crying. Then, discern what to do to keep our emotions from controlling our actions. Gary warned not to indulge a crybaby lest we grow a self-centered baby headed for hell. I thought this was a lot to consider at 2 A.M. I was exhausted. And I didn't think William was a "crybaby."

Sometimes I reached a hand over in bed.

Allan said, "Don't you dare. I have work tomorrow."

Gary, Anne Marie, and Helen knew exactly what would happen if I didn't figure out how to keep William quiet. "A prominent characteristic of abusive parents is thoughtless emotional responses directed toward innocent children. Too often sleepless nights and children trained to be demanding fuel those responses," Gary warned. Helen had a chapter on how trying to "change your man" created marriage problems. She said that even though a wife had a moral and sacred obligation to protect her children, which might mean taking them out of his presence, she also had to "accept even cruelty as a human weakness and not judge the man."

So, unable to change Allan's "masculine fault," but understanding how he reacted when he was tired, I knew Allan's backhand could land on William, the way it landed on me. I needed to get this under control, and I had no idea how I'd do it.

I wondered if I could reach out to Tina. The support she'd given during pregnancy and labor had helped me become a better mother. I'd healed so fast after delivery. And the hippie women in *Spiritual Midwifery* were older, busy homesteading, and lived peaceful lives. I called her.

"Hello, my love. How are you feeling with that sweet precious baby?"

"He's so good," I said. "My dream come true. But I'm having a problem at night and wondered if I could get your advice."

"Certainly! I'm hosting a group of new mothers at my house to talk about breastfeeding and newborn care. Why don't you come see me then?"

I wasn't sure how I'd get to St. Augustine without a car but maybe I could take Allan to work that day. I thanked her and then prayed it would all work out.

The whole world smiles at you when you're holding a baby. Our first Sunday back to church was no exception, and I felt everyone's eyes conspicuously on William first, then me. Needing a private place to breastfeed with modesty, I scoped out the nursing room in the Preschool Building.

This was my arrival into the mother club. I fumbled with the buttons on my dress and the tuck of a blanket over my shoulder, so I'd be covered while feeding. I wondered why we had to be so modest, if we all had boobs and babies and there were no men around, but all the other mothers covered and learned to sweat serenely. The problem must be mine.

The *American Gothic* woman was there too, nursing her tenth baby with her oldest daughter seated on the floor. The girl was thin and pale, with waist-length dishwater hair. I guessed her to be around fourteen, although maybe younger. Twelve? She was so sweet and childlike it was hard to pin her age. She seemed to be waiting to take over.

"I'm so happy to see you've had another baby! I used to watch your family from the orchestra. My name is Tia. This is William."

My face spiked red-hot. Too loud, too fast, too much.

"Blessings on your miracle," she said. "I'm Judith Small."

Eager like a puppy, I kept going, dropping all the intel and observations I had of this stranger. "I had William at home as well. Isn't Tina wonderful?"

Judith nodded, unsurprised I knew about her without knowing her. "It's good we have her, although it will be even more wonderful when we have a Christian midwife. Jo graduates in a few years. Some of Tina's practices suggest witchcraft. We've had concerns about paganism."

I'd heard about pagans at camp. Pagans chanted blood spells for Satanic worship. I couldn't imagine sweet and soft Tina casting spells over Christian babies as they were born, secretly consecrating them to Satan. Although . . . she did love nature and herbs. And she told me she went to the ocean to swim nude after William's birth to give thanks for my baby.

"I'm Anna," said the girl at Judith's feet. "Our baby's name is Justice."

Anna spread a blanket on the carpet, and Judith handed the baby down to her. She put Justice, the *American Gothic* baby, on the blanket. He was old enough to crawl, and when he rolled over to try, she flipped him to his back and centered him on the blanket. "No, Justice. No." He reached his arms up to her and his lower lip curled like he might cry, but he didn't let it go.

"Oh, poor little fella," I said.

She turned to me and said, "Too much holding spoils them. Blanket training teaches obedience. We have a book we can bring you if you're interested, right, Mama?"

Judith smiled with approval. She straightened her blouse to return to church.

But I'd had a sudden urge to ask her about babies and sleep. Nervous words tumbled out.

"Can you teach me how to help my baby sleep through the night?"

Judith seemed sincerely glad I asked. She and her husband hosted in-person classes for the Ezzo method and mentored young pups like me.

"If you've tended to his needs before bed, he's manipulating you into holding him or nursing more. He might even be trying to get into bed with you. Your baby won't learn to trust you'll come back if you never leave him."

I turned red. Bringing William to bed with me was something I wanted, because it would be easier to feed him quickly before Allan woke and got upset.

Gary and Anne Marie said co-sleeping was third world and deadly. And indulging a mother's need for convenience produced an insecure child. But the third risk was an angry father. I wrapped my arms more tightly around William, napping in my arms.

"But if I let him cry and don't come to him, aren't I teaching him I won't come when he needs me? He's so little," I said.

Judith tucked her chin like I'd suggested the circus. "Of course not. You've met his needs. Let him cry it out for a few nights, and pretty soon, he'll stop. Trust me: everyone will be happier for it."

I believed her. I'd known it since Hannah. Special Christians had the answers. They had confidence, a calmness that their alternative choices were right. Special Christians were like a church within a church. And I wanted into that club, so bad.

"We're attending Tina's mother-and-baby class this week," she said. "Would you like us to give you a ride?"

I marveled at how God answered prayer.

Judith and Anna, along with four other mothers and their babies, picked me up on Thursday. She had a fifteen-passenger van that had been donated by someone who "loved big families," and Anna smiled and said "to God be the glory," when she told me.

William cried the whole way. Rather, he screamed like a terrified banshee shrieking about the dead. Tongue curled, tears streaming, bulging purple face. I'd never seen him like this before.

I checked his car seat buckles, diaper, clothing for pinches or strings, popped diaper pins, wicked moisture, access to suck his thumb. I would've unbuckled my seat belt and whipped my boob out to nurse him if I'd had an ounce more confidence. But I just dug around looking inept and dumb.

The other mothers chatted and laughed as if nothing odd was going on. I tried to feel reassured by their lack of concern. I felt Judith watching in her rearview mirror.

Tina's house was full of so-happy-to-see-you moms. I nursed William outside as soon as we arrived. Exhausted and sweaty, he gulped with relief. I was sorry I'd come, sorry I'd done this to him. Both of us wanted our ordinary bubble on the couch.

As soon as I tried to take him inside, he broke out in wails again.

Tina came to me outside and held him on her shoulder. He hiccupped, curling his mouth into a sad pout. Tina sang, "Shhhhh, little man. Maybe Mama ate something that's not agreeing with your tum? Is that it?" William warbled into her neck.

I tried to remember if I'd eaten cabbage or pepper or garlic. Was I feeding him anxiety-spiked breast milk, transferring my worries to his tiny tummy? Inside, the mothers laughed at someone's anecdote. Tina said, "I have a remedy you can get at the natural food store. I'll write it down for you, love."

I felt Judith's stern eyes and remembered what she'd said about witches.

William screamed the whole way home. When Judith dropped me off, I carried William inside, spilling tears of humiliation that I was this bad as his mom.

As long as our day had been, we had an even longer night that night. William's shrieks and wails rang in my head, heartbroken accusations of my failure to help him. He couldn't understand that I took Judith's and the Ezzos' advice so I could protect him. He screamed to be picked up and fed.

I cried into my pillow as he cried into his cradle, and I begged God to help my baby please stop crying. Allan said, "You have to be the parent; he has to learn so we don't have to go through this every night."

I knew it confused and scared William that I was breaking our magical bubble of love and trust. And as loudly as he screamed from across the room, a voice inside of me screamed to get up and retrieve him. The mother

I wanted to be—responsive, attentive, and kind—didn't let her baby cry for hours in the night.

I got up to pace and cry, walking back and forth, praying and wondering if I was doing the right thing.

So

Many

Hours

Later,

His exhausted screams lessened into mewling, quiet pleas. I lay in bed hating myself, my bed soaked with tears and breast milk.

Finally, in three nights' time, he slept through twelve hours. When my milk supply settled out, I slept all night too.

Judith congratulated me on facing the first challenge of motherhood. Allan and I earned a certificate from the Ezzos' course.

"Don't wake a sleeping baby making the next one," joked Judith's husband, John. Allan laughed; I did not. I didn't feel ready for another baby, but Allan didn't really touch me anyway. He waited until he needed "relief."

Each morning Allan tiptoed to the bathroom. He studied the Bible on the toilet instead of walking down the hall so he wouldn't wake William. Complementarian gender roles led to more responsibilities for him. He explained them one night while I was chopping carrots for soup.

"Interpreting Scripture is part of the biblical mandate for headship," he said. "It's my job to teach you what we believe. It's part of my biblical role as your husband."

I scraped the carrots into the pot and turned on the gas. "What's headship?"

Sproul Jr., MacArthur, Piper, Ezzo, and John Small teaching Bill Gothard all recommended the same structure: An Umbrella of Authority. Christ over the husband over the wife over the children. Men were the head of their household, accountable to God and the authority over their wives. John gave Allan a thick red textbook from Gothard's Institute in Basic Life Principles—pages and pages of special rules to follow so we'd be loved, happy, and headed for heaven.

I got more responsibility too. When William was a year old, my magic kingdom increased to a tiny new-to-us little house down the road from my parents: twelve hundred square feet, three bedrooms, one bath. A realm to rule as queen of my home.

Dad sunk pressure-treated posts in the ground between two tall pine trees and I strung lines for drying clothes—Allan's, mine, William's, and a new set of onesies for the baby on the way.

Twenty-eight hours of stalled labor. A drive across town to the hospital where Tina's backup OB delivered. "Tia, do not push," spoken while crossing the bridge. The duh-dunk of pavement lines and contractions. The high white light of the moon. "She's having the baby!" while we were still outside, in the hospital's driveway.

Wheelchair.

Elevator.

Bed.

Breathe.

Breathe.

Push.

Breathe.

"You have a girl!"

A daughter. Hear her mew like a new kitten across the room. *Give her to me. Why is she so far away?* "Tia, we're just going to take her for a little while. Your baby needs help breathing."

This time the azure river in the hidden world of mothers came with shields and swords. That ancient love surrounded and filled me again, but it also came with a hot-flame rush of primal, fierce protection, a wind that blew through and around me and my baby. I tried to get up off the bed and go to her. *Give her to me.* They felt like words I roared.

"Tia, stay put," Jo said. "You still have to deliver the placenta."

Judith had warned me that hospitals would vaccinate without my consent. And my baby wasn't crying.

"We have to take her to the nursery," they said.

"Go with them, Allan," I said. "Don't take your eyes off her for a second." And he did. As he had before, Allan listened to my motherhood.

I pushed, and the veined bag of cord and blood came from me as though torn. But of course, it feels that way, like blood will not clot, that your bleeding will never stop. Breathe. Cry. Flames settle to embers that burn in a mother-heart forever.

When they finally brought me my pink little rosebud baby, she looked at me with skeptical, curious eyes. I wanted to hand her the world, the key to the entire planet. *Be who you want to be, baby girl.* I promised to be her sword and her shield and to teach her how to use them too.

Katie liked early mornings, happy and bright. She slept soundly at night, almost right from the start. My keen daughter watched us like a bird and figured out how to fit in fast, born hypervigilant and sweet. Before Katie, I wondered how I'd love a second child the way I loved William. And then she got here, and my swollen heart outgrew my chest. Now I wondered how I'd ever felt alive without her.

Judith worried I relied too much on instinct and intuition. "The Bible says, 'lean not on your own understanding.'"

I was at her house to learn more about the IBLP, while John counseled Allan through the red textbook. Katie slept at the breast and William sat next to me with a book. Justice sat on a blanket watching, and he looked like he wanted to crawl over and play. But he didn't leave the boundary of the blanket.

Judith said Proverbs 31 was our blueprint for life, the model woman.

But the Proverbs 31 woman made me tired. It bugged me the Bible never gave her a name. She gets up before sunrise. Selects wool and flax, weaves fiber, makes clothes. Makes food from scratch for her family and all their servants. Looks at a field she likes. Buys it. Then plants a vineyard. She makes snow clothes, bedding, linens, and sells sashes on the side. She speaks wisdom. Is never idle. She stays up late at night, working, cleaning, praying. She snacks and naps, instead of feasting and sleeping. Her children call her blessed. Her husband sings her praises. But she doesn't have a name. She's no one outside of what she does.

"Women of God don't care about having a name for themselves," Judith said. "She's a utensil, useful to her husband and blessed by God. What could be better? If you're feeling personal ambition, Tia, you need to repent and ask Jesus to help you die to yourself. Just read."

She quoted Paul. "If you keep yourself pure, you will be a special utensil for honorable use. Your life will be clean, and you will be ready for the Master to use you for every good work."

Even though I knew some translations use *vessel* for *utensil,* I got her point. The point of Christianity is propagation toward the end goal of taking dominion. Men do it with propulsion. Women do it through servitude.

"Train them up in the way they should go, and when they are old, they will not part from it," she said. "You probably struggle so much because you weren't trained this way from childhood."

I thought about the woods and the farm, the creativity of it and freedom to roam and explore. The feel of my paintbrush pressing into pigment. Our giant church. Hannah's mother dying. Rapture plans. Marci and Troy. Summer camp and screaming preachers. Gonga-rhea. Quick engagements and failed compatibility tests. No, I wasn't raised with the special rules from childhood—but I'd grown up knowing there was more to happiness and heaven than I'd been told. I knew I needed more than Jesus and his blood to save a wretch like me.

There were many more days like this one at Judith's, sometimes with other mothers from church. I studied the rules, studied their example, and tried to keep my questions to myself.

But dying to myself didn't have the glorious and holy impact Paul said it would. The woman in Proverbs was someone, until she became a nameless example. And like the slip of a hand beneath the ocean's waves, nobody saw me vanish as they focused on what I did instead of who I was.

Formula

I KNEW I WAS HEADSTRONG AND STUBBORN. PEOPLE HAD TOLD ME that my whole life. And now I had the domino of a new mentor to help me solve my personal ambition, before I headed for hell and took my babies with me. I knew I needed more help—books and Bible verses weren't enough to prevent dents beneath the wallpaper when Allan slammed my head.

I'd asked Judith if I could sit at her feet and learn, like it said about older women teaching the younger in Titus. I got to join the mother club of Gothard women spreading through First Baptist. We sat together and nursed our babies, discussing Scripture, child training, recipes, and household rules.

"We follow biblical principles, not instincts," she said.

To the red textbooks she added supplemental books to help me discover where I'd been deceived, and how to develop godly character. "I recommend you start with humility."

As I studied, I could see: it was plain that *I* was the problem in my family.

Allan had an idea to quit his job.

"I want to go to Columbia Bible College in South Carolina," he said. "Study the Bible full-time."

My stomach twisted. *What's Bible college going to get you? Bible knowledge won't pay your bills.* I could still smell Dad's sawdust and sweat. But I bit my argument. He was so excited to have a new plan that he flipped me over for relief that night.

I'd just started feeling settled in our new house and with two babies. I'd started a garden and we'd gotten a puppy—a floppy black Lab named Emma.

I even thought about taking my paints out again, just for fun. My parents were a stroller walk away and Monica was home from college. I didn't want to move.

I turned to the mother club for help. Judith said, "Disunion invites hardship."

"Remember your umbrella," Kay said. Kay had eight children but wasn't poor, because her husband did something with shipping. She hired tutors to help homeschool and all of the kids took violin. "It doesn't really matter what you think. You go where he goes, and you do it with a cheerful smile."

I thought of South Carolina's seasons and hills, trees and woods. This could get us out of Florida. Not all the way to Michigan but at least a little bit north. That made me want it too. I told Allan, "Let's do it. Let's plan. I'm with you all the way."

I didn't want to have a baby a year, especially if Allan didn't have a job.

Even married, birth control was a sore subject. Judith and the mother club and the IBLP all said: quiverful families didn't try to open and close the womb. That was God's job.

"What's a quiverful?" I wondered at the next mothers' gathering at Judith's. She nursed baby number eleven and Anna waited to take over.

Anna rolled her eyes. "Mrs. Brown. Sometimes I think you don't know anything! A quiver holds arrows. The Bible says children are like arrows unto God and happy is the man who has his quiverful of them. If you were headed into battle, wouldn't you want as many arrows as possible?"

"Well, yeah, but we're not headed into battle."

The women laughed. "Y2K is coming! And America is becoming more liberal and godless every day. *Of course* we're headed into battle . . . especially at the polls," Kay said.

"I'm so thankful for a husband who votes God's way," Judith said.

"Speaking of Y2K, I need to order more wheat berries, Judith," said Kay. "Do you have the Breadbeckers' phone number?"

I switched Katie to the other breast and wondered if Allan and I would have a quiverful someday. How many kids was that? How many were enough? I asked.

"Who would ever tell God they'd been sent enough blessings?" said Kay, shaking her head. "Trust me, you want as many as God will give you."

I'd been on the pill when we conceived William. And I'd asked Tina to fit me with a diaphragm after that. I could keep that in every night, so if sex happened, I was already ready. But we still had Katie that way.

Maybe pregnancy was more about longing and God than it was sex. Because I had always wanted lots of babies, like *Anne of Ingleside*. And I wanted them so badly that even though months passed between Allan's five-minute bursts of no-touch, no-talking, get-on-all-fours relief, birth control couldn't stop God or override longing. These children were meant to be.

"You don't want God to have to send a trial to get your attention," Judith said.

No, I didn't want that. I was still learning to be married, to be a mother. And there was always a rule or principle I'd overlooked or didn't know. I didn't want God to have to teach me a lesson.

It turned out Judith had other worries about my level of surrender.

A few weeks later we sat at her table sipping herbal iced tea and eating dry popcorn. Soft gospel Muzak played in the background, a James Dobson recommendation.

"I'm concerned about the way you dress, Tia," she said.

I looked down at my jeans and striped sweater. Both were loose and covered me from neck to ankle. "What do you mean?"

"Your jeans. Do you understand that your son will form his first views of sexuality based on your appearance? Your jeans can turn him on, even at two years old. Your jeans are visible to the other boys and men in our fellowship, and they're a distraction," she said.

A flush reddened my neck. I was tempting the older sons of the mother club because I wore *jeans*? "What should I wear?" I asked.

She nodded and opened the thick red textbook. "I'm so glad you asked. This will help you learn discernment. Wisdom booklets can help. In fact, let's come back to dresses in a little bit. I think you might need work on your attitudes about birth control."

Wisdom booklets addressed the topics mothers worry about—education, family, marriage, faith, and finances. These were matched with the corresponding commands of Christ: Repent. Follow Me. Render unto Caesar. Pearls before

Swine. Receive God's Power. There were forty-nine topics and commands. A concerned mother could find a wisdom booklet to match any burning concern she had for her family.

Judith said the character quality I needed to hone was security versus anxiety. I was sinning by feeling anxious instead of trusting God, and I needed to strengthen feeling secure in His provision.

She gave me a stack of booklets and sent me home.

"What Should We Do When We Face Tests and Trials," I read later, rocking Katie to sleep like a rebel. Sometimes I held the babies while they slept to stop and savor time because both of them were growing so fast.

The booklet started with the verse, *All things work together for good to them that love God.* Bad things are really good things that God gives us to discipline us into maturity.

Family size was an opportunity to yield to my sinful nature and trust God. Bill Gothard urged women to give thanks, rejoice, cry out to God, and overcome evil with good.

I didn't understand, at least directly, what this had to do with birth control. I wasn't saying babies were bad. I just wanted to space them out a little.

I carefully laid Katie in her crib and walked to William's room to peek at him. Still asleep.

I called Judith. She said, "Pray that the Lord opens your eyes to His wisdom. The Lord opens and closes the womb, Tia. It's your spirit that needs to change."

I flipped through the materials Judith gave me and looked at a photo of Bill Gothard. He looked short and hawkish, and smiled like he wanted you to buy his car. His careful hair and glistening skin defied age, and I couldn't pin him to an era. Was he as old as my dad? As old as Dr. Lindsay? I couldn't be sure. Never married and not a father, he seemed to know a lot about how mothers should behave.

Nap time was almost over. I pulled out a booklet from Tina's house on Natural Family Planning.

Timing ovulation was a chemical- and barrier-free way to control pregnancy. So, I'd know which days were impossible to get pregnant. This was knowledge, not a barrier. And since sex was rare, the chances of conception were low. Another baby would take a miracle and probably one we couldn't afford.

What I knew for sure was that all of that Proverbs 31 work wasn't enough to pay the bills. My worries lined up like tiny socks on my clothesline. Our financial ends didn't meet. We were broke, and sometimes I had to choose between milk for the kids or gas for Allan's car. Bible college would probably only make it worse. The last thing we needed was a baby right now, when Katie wasn't even a year old.

But when I asked the mothers about stretching money, they got excited.

"Try *The Tightwad Gazette*!"

"This is why we use cloth diapers and hand-me-downs! Free kids!"

Judith said being poor was good because it helped me surrender more and trust God. But couples frequently fight about money and Allan and I weren't any different in that regard.

But why couldn't I work? Maybe I could do something from home? It seemed to me my family needed a second income, and for me to make more of a contribution. Maybe that would even bring Allan relief. And the Proverbs 31 woman had made clothes for money.

Judith said a good wife is a thrifty wife. "Put more effort into pinching pennies," she said. "Don't take on more work and deceive yourself that the time away from your family will help. It won't."

It turned out I was good at thrift. Clotheslines, cloth diapers, gardening, fresh bread. I even figured out that cloth toilet wipes with a squirt bottle of water worked like a homemade bidet. That was ten dollars I could save on toilet paper to help buy food.

Everything I needed to know I learned from *Little House on the Prairie*. I took my homekeeping vocation as seriously as a pilgrim crossing the sea. Making a single income work depended on the thrift, creativity, and perseverance of a hardened pioneer.

But connecting with Depression-era thrift only worked as long as I didn't wonder about the world. About the new TV show called *Survivor*, or movie trailers, or the cute, new lower-rise jeans at Target. It worked when I didn't think about Monica having a career or Michael acting in New York. I wasn't an Old Testament Proverbs 31 woman. I was twenty-two going on forty. And, if I stopped moving too long, sadness crept up my legs like ivy.

Judith upped the ante of my training. Allan got it too, from John. Our babies played and made noise, squirmed, and ran around. Judith said, "I have a book you need to read."

She handed me *To Train Up a Child* by Michael and Debi Pearl. "I buy these in bulk to hand out," she said. "It will teach you how to correct your children."

This was the book that taught blanket training—what I'd seen Anna doing with baby Justice the day I'd met the Smalls. While I often put my babies on a blanket with some toys in the nursing room or at mother club, they often crawled off to explore.

"You have to do more than put them on the blanket, Mrs. Brown. They need a consequence if they move," Anna said, more than once.

The Pearls wrote that parents of terrible children looked like Holocaust victims who'd just escaped a boxcar. They warned we'd have to nag our children 666 times to get them to obey. The solution was their recipe for how to train children to please you. They recommended training to commands, military-style, with quiet, controlled voices. As soon as a child learns to crawl, the parent establishes training sessions with the switch.

On page nine, the Pearls described switching their four-month-old's legs to keep her from crawling up the stairs. William was two, Katie eight months. I'd never switched either of them, which is why I got an F for blanket training.

I put the book on the shelf and made myself too busy to read it. Judith noticed my lack of results.

"Many children are harmed by their mother's weaknesses, Tia," she said. "When you train infants for obedience, there's no need to punish when they're older. Look. Don't use a switch from your tree as your spanker. Those dry out. Use a glue stick from the craft aisle or a small line of PVC pipe." She took a long white tube from her diaper bag and demonstrated against her palm. The spanker whistled and slapped against her skin.

I flinched.

"It should sting," she said. "You want repentance. You want your child to avoid what precipitated the switch."

I didn't want this next thing. My blood churned like a swirling undercurrent against the tide.

Allan and I left the babies with my parents for a weekend and visited Columbia Bible College. He sped up and down the humid hills and talked about getting the house ready to sell.

"But what are you going to do with the degree, once you have it?" I asked. I was hoping he wouldn't say "be a pastor" because I didn't want the pressure of being a pastor's wife.

"Probably get another one after that," he said. "I'll need a master's and then a doctorate. I want to teach. I love studying the word of God."

I stared out at the trees wondering how we'd feed a family on degrees.

Since I still wore jeans sometimes, Judith came back to dresses. "A good wife is a modest wife," she said. "You must learn how to avoid eye-traps." We were at her table again with iced herbal tea and dry popcorn, while her children watched William and Katie.

Eye-traps sounded like some kind of mask or hood. But they're distractions designers place in clothing on purpose to trigger lust.

V-necks. Tapered waists. Diagonal lines. Roomy armholes. Designs that accentuate shape. I thought of Helen and her dislike of plaid and mannish colors. Gothard took *Fascinating Womanhood* even further, down to the ankles.

I couldn't afford new clothes, but Judith had an answer for that problem too.

"Denim jumpers," she said. "They're economical, practical, modest, and plain."

"You'll avoid unwanted male attention if you dress properly, Mrs. Brown," Anna added, refilling my tea.

"It's through the eyes that we transmit sexual information to the brain for mating," Judith said.

When Anna left the room, Judith whispered, "And your husband may prefer it if he knows there's nothing on underneath that jumper."

I almost laughed out loud. I couldn't even turn my own husband on. No underwear was supposed to help? And if all the women in jumpers wore no panties, didn't that turn on other women's husbands too?

But I got the gist. Jumpers were boxy and easy, removing the temptation to look cute.

Like my bedroom before my wedding, I boxed up all my jeans. I threw away anything with a V-neck and realized with horror that most of my clothes were too immodest even to give away.

Allan liked the new jumpers. "Add a head covering," he said. "I like it."

I laughed to keep the mood light, swallowing a shadow down my throat. I felt ugly and matronly, old before my years. But it turned him on, and that night he flipped me over. When he finished, I lay on my stomach and watched the moonbeams shift across the floor, counting the days since my last period.

That autumn, I resisted stenosis by taking photos of every happy small detail I could find.

I loved taking photos because photography stopped time. It caught moments in my fingers and offered proof. I could say, "Look, we were happy." But also, a photo could remind me of what I forgot. Because increasingly, I forgot whole days.

I'd be standing at the clothesline, arms raised to pin a tiny sock, and wonder how I'd gotten there and where were my children. Turn, frantically to find the babies right there at my feet. Or I'd fall asleep sitting up and reading. Wake up not knowing when I'd opened the book. I didn't know what these spells were, but they made the day pass faster. Zoning out got me closer to sleep. It was like daydreaming or time travel—I didn't know the word "dissociation."

Days hung on me like humidity, my thoughts trickling down my back like sweat.

I felt like I was disappearing. Photos proved I was still here, even if I was never in them. Someone, even a nameless someone, had to have taken them.

The religious news insisted we'd all be gone soon anyway. Y2K was coming, the end of the world. Even the scientists couldn't be sure of what would happen.

Judith schooled me on toxic vaccines and dangerous doctors. On how to stockpile homeopathic medicine, wheat berries, and canned goods. The Baptists said we'd be raptured first, but as Reformed Calvinists now, Allan said we might be here for half of the tribulation. We needed wheat berries and batteries to prolong getting marked with 666. My head echoed with the icky thump of some girl's head. Would it be mine? My daughter's?

Tears at the clothesline and cicadas in the trees, their fragile shells stuck to the pines. Sobs choked their way out of me as if I didn't want to let them go, as if my body felt it had to fight me.

When was the last time I laughed?

Spoken to a friend my age?

Loneliness ate me from the inside out so that I wondered if I didn't have a third baby inside me but a spirit of loss and sorrow. A good wife is a fertile wife, and a woman is saved through childbirth, but I felt more lost than any field I once wandered.

I reached up to pin a sock to the clothesline and then bent down for another one to do it again.

The Smalls noticed my children weren't making progress staying on the blanket. Judith asked if I had any questions on implementation.

I mustered up every shred of intuition I still had left. "I'm not sure that book's for me," I said. I knew I couldn't be the mother I wanted to be if I used this book. Not even close.

Judith nodded. "That's fine. But setting up your child to be rebellious puts them in danger of hell. Is that what you want?"

Hot acid rose in my throat, triggering an old and familiar stomachache. What if my children were left behind? What if they burned in hell, and it was my fault? What if Y2K came and the clocks never rolled over and everything exploded, and we died? Was I being the kind of mother who could bring her children to salvation?

Maybe I should try one more time.

Later that week, I spread a blanket on the lawn and centered my roly-poly sunshine girl in the middle. When she crawled to the edge, she reached for a leaf with her dimpled hand. I helped her explore rather than eat it.

"No amount of training is going to override the certainty of sin developing. But the training we give can make it easier for repentance to follow sinful indulgence," the Pearls wrote. Children weren't naturally sorry, he said. Instead, they needed pain to teach them to repent their sins.

I scooped up my girl and kissed her face. I didn't think a baby could register repentance. There was no way I was blanket training.

To my relief, Allan wasn't in favor of switching them this young either. And he said he'd tell John Small that himself. But after he got home from the men's group, he said, "John says this works for marriage too."

Chilled, I hid our copies behind some others on the shelf.

Putting my foot down, albeit gently, about blanket training made me feel like an adult and whatever Allan and John's conversation had been, he didn't push me on it. I was taking what worked for our family from the Gothard formula and leaving what didn't. After a while, the rules seemed simple.

Home birth, homeschool, pay cash, plan ahead, court your daughters, court your sons, study Scripture over academics, eyes ahead, eyes on God. Wives stay home. No birth control. Live simply. Raise a new army for God.

All I had to do was obey Allan and teach my children to do the same. Then we wouldn't have to worry about boys like Troy or scary lessons at camp or even rapture drills. Gothard lives held fewer dominoes.

We could be Christians in the year 206, 1506, 1896, or now. The timelessness of our lifestyle made me trust it had to be right, because it had lasted for so long. I had the balance figured out until Dr. Lindsay picked on the babies.

Dr. Lindsay was pro-nursery. He didn't like having his sermons interrupted by a loud squawker with an expensive nursery right across the street. And when one of the Gothard children cried in service, he said, "You know, we have an excellent nursery," in front of thousands of people.

The mothers were embarrassed. The fathers were up in arms. The quiverful declared First Baptist no longer family-friendly.

"It's a husband's job to teach his family, not a pastor's," Allan said. Calvinists put the father in charge of everything. Allan said we needed to change churches. First Baptist commercialism grated against quiverful priorities of simplicity and living set apart. And God told him we needed to worship as a family together more.

"It's called Family Integrated Church," he said.

My parents took it hard.

"But you grew up here," Mom protested. I smoothed it over by saying we'd still have Sunday dinner together every week. I talked up Allan's devotion so she wouldn't hold it against him.

"He wants to be Reformed," I said. "He follows John Calvin." The Calvinists focused on sovereign grace and the authority of Scripture. Calvinism didn't sound that different from being Baptist to me. The change came down to family worship and headship, as far as I could tell. And the exodus of Gothard families was because the pastors picked a fight. Men don't like it when another man tells them how to live.

When the thunder and contractions began in January, ten weeks too soon, I stood in the darkness and prayed. I pleaded again, as I had so many times in the previous months, "Dear God, if I should have diagnostic testing, please let me know." Judith was against OBs and ultrasounds but something inside me felt off. Intuition, instinct . . . something was screaming.

I knew what I always knew, deep down inside: I was headed into hell because as a sinner and a woman, I had hell inside me as well as coming for me. And being a good Christian or following all the rules wasn't going to change the darkness ahead.

Heart

MEADOW-GREEN LINOLEUM WITH FLUORESCENT LIGHT REFLECTED
in the wax squares. The hem of my denim jumper, the toes of my brown loafers.
A soup-can voice paged a doctor as Allan and I walked toward the exit. We'd
already heard the words our doctor murmured. Allan pushed the click-clank
bar of the metal door that led outside to the sky to the sun to the car.

I needed to breathe.

Two chambers two chambers two chambers echoing with every step. Words
in a sinus rhythm underwater on the ultrasound, still ringing in my ears. I
knew what two chambers meant because this had happened to friends. I'd
prayed for the miracles. I'd attended the funerals.

To have the ultrasound at all was a failure. Judith warned me sound waves
harmed unborn babies. She encouraged me to have a "completely noninva-
sive pregnancy." I'd tried, I had. I'd told Jo no to the backup OB and no to
his recommended peek-see "just in case," weeks ago. I'd been Judith's faithful disciple and Allan's obedient wife.

And then, thunder in January. I woke up with contractions, ten weeks
too soon.

Allan took me to the hospital.

Someone else watched my children.

Dr. Gaudier, with his lilting Latino accent, said, "Oh yes, I definitely see
two chambers here."

I needed to breathe.

What we'd done was walk into an unplanned land blanketed with fog and confusion. We had God solved with routines and rules. So there wasn't a plan for when the bough breaks. Unplanned land is full of held breath and waiting.

Dr. Gaudier ordered bed rest. Friends from Country Road Baptist, our new church, helped with William and Katie. My parents too. At home, I sat in bed, shopping catalogs for car seats some days, talking to grieving mothers about caskets on others. On Mondays, I visited a procession of new doctors.

Everywhere we went, they sketched drawings of the heart.

One-two-three-four. Here are the four chambers.

Left and right. Two very important sides. Each does a different job.

Two lines to indicate a channel. The ductus brings oxygenated blood to the left side of the heart.

Arrows in a flow. Here's how it works in a healthy rhythm.

Blue blood. Red blood. Atriums and arteries. Ventricles and valves. Rooms and rhythms. These were rules and routines that were never meant to be broken.

"Your daughter's heart has two chambers."

Two chambers meant her heart could not receive blood from her lungs. A missing ductus and chambers broke the flow. Of course, this wasn't supposed to happen, but for now, it didn't matter. This is because in utero, for all babies, the lungs aren't working yet. When routines and rules are followed, sometime after our first breath, the ductus opens.

But my baby was two chambers too short, and she didn't have a ductus, so sometime after her first breath, she'd die. It wouldn't matter that she was fat and full-term. The routine and rules were broken.

"Sometimes it looks like SIDS," the cardiologist said. He resembled Jerry Falwell. "Babies go home from the hospital just fine—and then sometime in the next three days that ductus never opens. Parents check the cradle and find the baby has passed."

Has passed. Like a car in traffic. Like a phase. I looked at him and blinked. My mind toyed with other things that pass. Gas. Feelings. Kidney stones.

The doctors' fascination seemed endless. They couldn't quite see the full extent of her defect, but infant heart repair was a rapidly growing field. The cardiologists weren't *sure* she would die—it depended on the severity of what they saw after she was born. The chances here made them eager and optimistic.

"So, she might not be stillborn?" I asked the surgeon.

"She might not," he said. "Let's look again." I kept hoping they'd see something new in the galaxy of the ultrasound screen. They'd see they'd made a mistake.

An amnio—that long thin needle puncturing my womb while I prayed she'd hold still and not stab or scratch herself with it—happened. How far I'd come from Judith's admonishment to avoid medical intervention during pregnancy. It made me dizzy to realize the nagging worry in my blood had been right and that Judith and the rules had been wrong.

I needed to breathe.

The amnio confirmed the baby didn't have a chromosomal defect. Down's or something else like it would affect our options at delivery, Dr. Gaudier said.

The word "options" sent me spinning. Options mean there's a fucking possibility the doctors are wrong. Options mean swapped ingredients that don't ruin the recipe. Options mean doorways, means of escape, rapture plans, and coping. Options mean miracle births. The word "options" helped me exhale.

I compiled pages and pages of questions that no one could answer until she was born.

Would she be able to breastfeed?

Would we be able to bond with her in the NICU?

Would we save her cord blood to help in a situation where she might need a blood transfusion?

To their credit, the doctors were kind and patient with me. But not one of them could tell me if I could expect skin-to-skin contact with a baby so close to the margin between life and death.

Allan and I named her so we could pray specifically. I didn't want God to get mixed up. I wanted to pray for my daughter, not an idea.

Clara.

I forced myself to imagine the letters in cursive on a birth announcement and never a grave.

On the ninth Monday, I was strapped to monitors so they could track her heart rate. It decelerated. They moved me across the street to the surgical floor.

Mom was with me. Jo arrived, and then Allan. Labor proceeded more quickly than the doctor predicted.

After four hours, her head crowned. The nurse panicked because I wasn't supposed to deliver in a regular room. She threw up the side rails of my bed and rushed me to the OR.

We careened down the hall, sometimes slamming into the walls and doorways. I felt Clara's head as it emerged from my body. I put my hand down to touch her as the bed slid into the green-tiled room full of shining steel and bright lights. Someone pushed my hand away.

"One push, please," said a masked face.

All I could see were faces above me, masked faces with eyeballs and gowns and lights. I heard myself crying and calling Clara, and I reached down again to help her be born. Hands held my arms back. I felt her shoulders leave me and the wet warmth of her body slip out of me. And just as fast, half of the faces turned and went with her. They whisked her away to another part of the room or the next room where I couldn't see.

No azure river. No swirling stars. No hidden world of mothers. I lay blinking at the white orbs above me, wondering what had just happened.

Someone wheeled me back to a room of faces I didn't register and voices I couldn't hear.

Three hours later a nurse came in with two Polaroids.

"I got you a photo of your baby," she said, trying to cheer me up. I held the squares with my trembling fingers.

In one, a nurse with long brown hair propped Clara up on a table bed. My baby was fat, with arm rolls and a head full of spiky red hair. Her perfect and wide-open mouth in full cry. I saw an IV in her navel, a band on her wrist, and tiny heart monitor stickers on her chest. She was pink and beautiful. In the other photo, she lay on her back, with one pop-eye open, peeking out at this world she now lived in.

Lived in, my heartbeat reverberated.

"She's seven pounds, seven ounces," the nurse said.

I burst into tears and breathed.

That night a new routine emerged.

The nurses on the recovery floor didn't know what to do with me. I didn't have a baby with me, and I didn't want their medicine. I'd brought my own Extra-Strength Tylenol. Leaning on the handrail, I walked down the hall to the elevator, past the rooms of mothers with their new babies. Destination: NICU.

I put myself on an every-two-hours Ezzo milk schedule within my first day postpartum. It began with scrubbing to the elbows in hot water and astringent medicinal soap. Clock a full three minutes. A clean gown over my clothes. Through the waving doors to the ward. Clara, arms and legs open like a sweet pink frog on a warming bed. Stroke her skin, smell her head until milk lets down. Head to the pumping room and pump. In an hour and a half, start the process over again.

Unplanned land had weird rules. Sometimes, no rules. Days here stretched so that time warped. The warp created a space I could sit inside with my baby. The real world felt far, far away.

Allan came when others could care for William and Katie. I steeled myself to trust they were okay, a difficult maternal skill I'd call upon for years to come. A mother of more than one child will eventually find herself unable to be two or more places at one time. But this was the first time I'd ever been separated from them and the stretch felt like torture designed to snap my ligaments like dry rubber bands.

One nurse said to another, "That mama doesn't need us. She's strong." I understood then strength was to keep moving. Walking forward and pumping every two hours kept me moving. Finding ways to keep moving became salvation.

On the third day I learned what the small counseling rooms with tissues on the tables are for.

The cardiologist and pediatrician sat across from us at the table, drawing hearts again. Blue blood. Red blood. Atriums. Arteries. Ventricles. Valves. Rules and routines are broken.

Her defect had a name now: hypoplastic left heart syndrome. The doctor made a list of three bullet points, like a Dr. Vines three-point sermon.

"You basically have three options here," he said.

I sighed with relief. Options leave room for the miracle.

"Option number one is a transplant. We can put her on the list and wait for a new heart. She'd need to go to Gainesville because we don't do transplants here yet."

Clara would be number three on the list, and infant hearts are a long wait. The medication to keep her heart working, for now, would only last a week or two.

"Your second option is surgery," said the doctor. "It's called the Norwood procedure. It re-plumbs the heart, so half of the heart can do the job of the whole heart."

I sat straighter. I'd heard of this before. "How often do you do it?"

"A couple of times a year," he said.

My parents had an Amway friend whose baby had this surgery in Atlanta. And a friend of a friend of a friend at First Baptist went to Boston. So I asked if transferring was possible.

"Yes, both have extensive cardiac units. They do this procedure many more times a year than we do, probably fifty in a year. Obviously, that makes their current success rate much better. Your insurance will cover that. We can arrange medical transport."

"What's option number three?" Allan asked.

The two doctors pursed their lips and looked down. "It's called compassionate care. We make her comfortable. You let her go."

Let-her-go. A one-two-three punch to my sternum. Who lets a seven-pound, seven-ounce pink and beautiful baby die when there are *options*? Head spinning and dizzy, I watched the doctor's mouth move.

"With her other defects present, I need to say it's a viable option. You may not want to put her through the rigors of surgery and recovery with those other question marks present."

I tipped my head to the side, curious. What did he mean, *other defects*?

A horseshoe-shaped kidney they weren't sure would be an issue. Extra creases on both thumbs. Cleft soft palate, inside her mouth, but who cared? Clefts were repairable. Her head circumference, slightly smaller than the rule and ratio, with almost no fontanel.

"We're not sure what else this points to," he said. "But defects like these usually mean something."

I wondered what kind of a monster lets their baby die because there are too many creases on her thumbs.

Then, out of the corner of my eye, I saw Allan lower his head.

I took a quick breath. Squared my shoulders. Tipped my chin and spoke for us all, a first, and with all the motherpower I could muster.

"I only see one option here," I said as steady as I could. "Please help us get to Atlanta. I want to try the surgery."

A children's hospital is another universe within our universe. No one in there gave a damn about traffic or paychecks or TV shows or politics or any other kind of worry I once called life. Allan wasn't in charge. Neither was Judith. As near as I could tell, neither was God. I didn't once think about Bill Gothard or Piper or MacArthur. Helen who? *Check out my fascinating pajamas. Aren't they masculine and feminine and clean? Do you think I care if you find me attractive?*

They flew us to Atlanta on a Learjet—Clara, in a glass incubator with portals. It was my first flight. Below us churned a storm. Above us, only stars.

Surgery was scheduled for the day after we arrived, April 4, 1999. Clara and what she needed were all I could see.

The nurses made dropping my baby off for surgery the same as leaving her in the church nursery. "Say goodbye to Mom," sang the nurse, Theresa. We stood in the hallway outside of the surgical wing at the crack of dawn.

I bent my head low to kiss Clara, warm for maybe the last time. "Come back to me," I whispered. Babies don't always make it out of heart surgery. Clara's procedure was eight hours long.

The nurses prepared us for what she'd look like by taking us to visit another baby patient.

In surgery, the heart swells considerably, and the body retains fluid. So, a week-old infant will look four months old when they come back, shiny and bloated, rolled like the Michelin Man. Their chest will be open for a week until the swelling goes down. There will be more tubes and wires than there will be baby on the bed. The nurses run an oscillating fan on the baby to keep the fever down.

"It's a horrible shock if you're not expecting it," the nurse said.

It was a horrible shock anyway.

It took Clara a week to look like a fourteen-day-old infant again. A week of dreams and waiting.

Her chest was open for all that time. They kept her asleep and immobile. Drainage tubes pierced her side. We waited for her heart to go from an apple back down to a walnut able to fit within her ribs. And then finally, they stapled her chest and put on new bandages.

Her eyes woke from the paralysis first—astonished orbs before the rest of her body began to respond and reanimate. She looked wise, an old owl of a girl.

I needed to breathe. I sat next to her bed and tried to force in air.

But fear rattled through me. Had we been wrong to be invasive? Who were we to decide a baby should go through this? Who was this selfish? Her *mother*?

My fears came in Judith's voice, and my head swam with bright lights and accusations.

"Tia, do you feel okay?" The voice sounded like it came from underwater.

I blinked—the new nurse. "You look like you might have a fever," she said. She checked it, and I did—over 102. She told Allan to take me across the street to the adult emergency room at Emory.

I laid my head on a paper pillow and cried because now I couldn't even sit by her side. *Failure*.

"We need a clear urine test. One without blood," the nurse said. "Have you been taking care of yourself?"

"My baby has HLHS." Letters filled in for big, life-altering words. "I'm two-week postpartum. Still bleeding."

An intern came in and did a pelvic exam and a Pap smear, stretching and hitting every skid mark from Clara's quick delivery as he did so. "We need a clean catch. If you can't give us one, we'll have to cath you."

I tried to focus on the sneering, spinning face. He snapped the glove streaked with my blood and threw it in the trash.

Another student doctor came in and repeated the exam. "We're concerned you have an infection in your womb," he said.

Why was Allan just sitting there?

"Then give me antibiotics," I croaked. "If it's a uterine or a bladder infection, please just give me whatever you prescribe for that. My baby is waking up after a week in a coma. I need to get back to her." My milk had come in.

Large wet circles from leaking stained the front of my gown, and my heavy breasts ached.

Another student came in for an exam, this one in my rectum. "I'm worried that we should admit you."

I thrust myself up and closed my legs. "You will not admit me! I need antibiotics! I need to go back across the street! I need to get back to my baby! I need to pump my breasts! You need to let me go!"

"Ma'am, we're concerned about infection and postpartum psychosis."

"I need an ADVOCATE!" I yelled. Amy, a new friend whose heart-baby was also in the CICU, had told me that "advocate" was a magic word in the hospital. *Once you say the word "advocate," they know you aren't stupid, and could sue them for ridiculousness.*

An hour later, the summoned advocate called the social worker in the CICU, who explained all I'd been through. They wrote me a prescription for a UTI and finally let me go.

The magic word had worked. And by wielding it, I'd advocated for myself. It felt . . . different.

Six Mondays in, Clara remained on a respirator but now had cycles of being awake. I could sing to her, put tiny socks on her tiny feet, and dangle a mobile from her warming light. Allan went home to work.

My parents juggled childcare with their jobs. Allan's parents traveled to help, but our homesteading routines stressed them out. My mother-in-law skipped the clothesline and dried my tiny socks in the dryer. She bought convenience dinners from the freezer section and stocked my pantry with luxuries like plastic wrap and paper towels and lots of toilet paper. When I spoke to her on the phone, she cracked, "Golly, girl, you don't have to make this life so hard!"

The families in my church strained to cover the gaps, and none of us knew when or how it would end—but still they asked when they called for prayer updates.

"Tell us what it's like there."

"Today's a good day," I said, keeping it simple and hoping no code alarms sounded while I was on the phone.

That week eight babies died.

Not every baby is strong enough to withstand heart repair. Sometimes their bodies have adjusted to being broken. Sometimes even the most talented surgeons can't change fate or the hand of God.

The God-rules didn't work in here.

Despite her slow progress, the nurses started to ask if I had a plan for when we went home.

"Three babies under three is hard enough, but your third one is medically sensitive. Are you set up for that at home?" asked Lauri, the social worker. I both relied on and mistrusted her. Her job was to support the families in the CICU. But she also screened them for needs and problems. So it was important not to let my cracks show and part of me was glad Allan had gone home.

But he came back for Mother's Day. He hadn't brought my babies, which is what I wanted most in the world. My arms ached for an ordinary day: laundry, sippy cups, carrying them on my hip. He met me at the Ronald McDonald House—RMH—where I was staying.

"I need a break, Tia," he said. "It's not easy-street for the rest of us while you're up here."

What makes you think a heart ward is a vacation sat on the tip of my tongue. But he said, "I want to visit the Reformed church here this weekend."

"Clara's saturation is strong enough for me to hold her today," I said. "I don't want to go to church."

"Excuse me?" He looked at me like I had three heads.

"And even if we did go, it should be one of the churches supporting us. Not a new one."

But Allan said, "No. I've already looked this place up on the internet. Go get dressed." He took a picture of me in front of the RMH standing in the ivy. "Happy Mother's Day," he said.

Halfway through the service, my milk came in. "I need to go pump, Allan. We need to leave," I whispered.

He shrugged me off, leaning forward to pay closer attention to the pastor. Warm milk seeped from my nursing pad onto my dress, making an unmistakable dark blue mark on my breast. Finally, I got up and left the sanctuary.

I could hand-pump the milk into the bathroom sink if I could find it. Searching for the restrooms, I wandered through the hallway.

Allan came behind me and grabbed me by the arm and steered me out to the car. Fury radiated off his body, and his eyes burned bright.

"What is your problem?" he seethed. "I was enjoying that."

I got in the car. He started the engine and gunned it, driving fast and taking turns hard.

"You're a shit mother, Tia. And a shit Christian. And I'm sick of you being up here instead of home where you belong. It was a bad idea coming up here. It's too hard on everyone. You're a special kind of idiot to think I'm not going to take the kids and leave you. I could do it too. I can make sure you come home to an empty house and never see any of us ever again."

I panted and held on to the side of the car door. Atlanta traffic forced him to slow down, and he had to hit the brakes a lot to avoid rear-ending other cars. I didn't know what I'd done wrong. "I just needed to go pump, Allan. It's just that time."

"It's just that time," he whined back, mocking me. "Your fucking excuses. Your weakness. You're a slob, is what. A sick, slob wife who needs to get the hell out of this car."

He'd stopped on the top of an overpass and then reached over to push the car door open. "Get the fuck out," he said. He pushed me out onto the concrete as the line began to move.

As Allan drove off, I crouched and hugged the concrete barrier.

The driver in the car behind me looked like he couldn't believe what he was seeing.

"Are you okay? Miss? Are you okay?" The man wore khakis and a nice shirt, probably on his way to see his mother for Mother's Day.

I stood up and brushed myself off. Lauri couldn't find out about this. "Oh, sure. I'm fine. I needed to get out. I was feeling carsick."

"You're barefoot." I'd kicked my shoes off in the car.

"I'm fine," I insisted. The man slowly drove behind me until I was off the bridge. I spotted Allan and the car in the parking lot of a barbecue restaurant. Like that night on the beach, the passenger door was already open, and I got back in.

As we drove back through the heart of Atlanta, I stared at the houses and their watching window eyes seeing my shame. Real life could find me in Atlanta. Real life was what Clara and I would go home to. Christian wives kept their husband's secrets and they protected their family's appearance.

On our eighth week, my parents came to Atlanta with a cooler. They took home over fifty quarts of my frozen milk. Allan brought William and Katie up with him, and we walked through a green park across from Emory. For a little while, we looked like any other family with small children rolling down the green hills.

At night I spooned their bodies and prayed they'd forget my absence. I prayed their bodies wouldn't remember their mother had left. I felt like I'd abandoned them, even if it was to save their sister, and I couldn't stretch the word "mother" enough to cover two places. Years later, when I learned about attachment wounds in early childhood, I'd grieve the impact of their mother leaving at three and eighteen months. I'd grieve the failing of my capacity.

Finally, the doctors removed a chest tube and drainage bag from Clara's lungs because she could breathe on her own. We moved to the step-down unit, out of the CICU.

Nurse Audrey loved Clara and listened to my worries, but she cautioned against carrying the burdens of the other parents. "Don't get to know these folks too much," she said. My heart didn't know how to break any further. That some dark angel crossing over Atlanta had spared the life of my baby didn't make sense; every parent begged the same God for salvation. But I knew Clara couldn't die. Healing was only a matter of time. *You have to believe the miracle can happen.*

I started to wonder what would happen if I told my parents about Allan's episodes. Or if I told the pastor Allan hurt me. Allan had been the one to threaten leaving . . . but was it possible for me to leave him?

Would a judge let me keep William and Katie with a medically sensitive baby and no job? Nine weeks postpartum, three years married, three babies. The women here thought I was crazy. They were nurses and social workers, doctors and therapists. They used daycare. They'd been in college at twenty-two, not caring for their third kid.

But I didn't get a chance to wonder long. That morning Audrey came in and announced we'd be going home soon.

The nurses taught me how to insert an NG tube, take her blood pressure, and clean her chest scar with a swab and bubbling peroxide. I learned how to watch for sweat because it could signal her heart was working too hard. And I had to know if her lips and fingernails were turning blue from low oxygenation. "These are signs you need to get to a hospital," they said.

I called my dad to come get me. Clara would transport in an ambulance. Allan and the kids waited at home. This long night was almost over. On May 26, I fell asleep happy, hopeful I'd weathered the lesson God sent well enough to go home and try my best again.

The hallways rang CODE BLUE ROOM 202. CODE BLUE ROOM 202.

I sat up in the recliner by the crib. Bleary forms flooded in. Blinding lights thrown on. *Our* room was 202. I tried to put CODE BLUE and 202 and OUR ROOM together. I reached for my glasses.

Peter, tall, dark, and tender, whispered low in my ear, "Tia, I need you to get up and come with me." Peter often stood over us and prayed "For Clara and her mother to have miraculous healing." I followed him without asking where we were going.

The room was full of so many doctors and nurses that we could hardly snake our way through to the door, and the hallway was crowded with medical staff. Everyone comes for a Code Blue until they're sure they have who they need. Peter led me to a treatment room down the hall, just bigger than a closet, and handed me off to Nurse Angie.

Babies in the step-down backslide to the CICU all the time. They get infections in their blood and air in their intestines. Their pressures destabilize. I sat on the rolling stool and prepared myself not to go home this week but back to the floor. Back to RMH. Back to twenty-four-seven nursing care. Tonight was a setback, but just part of the experience. Our friends Amy and Amanda went back seven times. Seven follow-up surgeries, in just a single month. This was just that.

I called Allan at home and told him. "They're working on her," I said. "I'll call you when we're back on the floor."

Angie made small talk. She had a farm in a nearby town being swallowed by development and Atlanta. She worked three days a week and raised chickens and goats for the rest of the week. Allan and I had talked about a farm. We'd talked about moving to the mountains. I imagined my three little sweet ones chasing a flock of chickens on a green hill.

An hour passed. A nurse came in for a handful of supplies—a crash kit of some kind. The nurses exchanged looks. I shrugged my shoulders and settled in to the long night. I'd call RMH as soon as we got on the floor. Book a new room. Get some rest.

The doctor came in. Strange. He was looking down at the floor. He wouldn't look me in the eye. My eyes registered his white lab coat and the navy embroidered script of his name on the left pocket. His first name was Angel. I noticed his long straight brown lashes and the heavy tear that clung there.

"I'm so sorry," he said softly. "I'm so very sorry."

Sorry. What was he sorry for? I waited for him to say she was in the CICU, and I could see her now.

Blue cursive. *Angel.* I'm so sorry.

And then I knew.

My bloodcurdling howl flung my consciousness into the air above. I left myself and floated over the room, hovering near the ceiling tiles. Below me, my devastated body writhed and sobbed on the floor. I watched two nurses try to hold me. I heard one of them say, "Oh, this is bad. This is really bad."

The room, and the nurses, held me down as I strained to climb the wall. I couldn't escape. I couldn't get out. "I need my baby," I wailed. "I need to see her. I need to hold her. GIVE ME BACK MY BABY!"

Marrow to blood, breath gone, I felt myself dying, and I waited to go with her. I remembered hearing other people say, "I could never survive the loss of my child." So, I spread my arms wide and clung to the cold linoleum floor and I waited to die too.

But that isn't what happened. We sat there, all of us on the floor together crying, until the nurse breathed with me, breath by breath, and somehow, I calmed down.

I came down back inside myself. We sat there together until the hour of death had come and gone.

A knock sounded on the treatment room door. "She's ready for you now."

I nodded. Angie helped me stand.

Amy had told me once that if my baby ever died, to hold her as long as it took for me to feel ready to let her go. When she said that, I wondered when any mother would be prepared for that. But as it happened, an order established itself, and my spirit knew the hour.

Her body was still soft when they brought her to me—pliable and somewhat warm. They'd opened her chest on the table. Angel and his team had tried to resuscitate her three times during that hour, and at some point, they'd reopened her chest to massage her heart. They'd stitched and taped her closed again. As I held her, Clara's mottled body stiffened beneath the pink blanket. I begged God to let this be a mistake.

I kissed her cold cheeks. They were hard beneath my lips.

I stroked every curve, every red hair on her head. I sang her lullabies and rocked her by the window, the city lights casting a white glow in our darkened blue room. Ashes to ashes, we all fall down.

The nurses came and asked if I was ready, but I wasn't. Letting go meant forever. So they closed the door and left me, rocking, crying, talking to my girl.

I wanted a witness. Someone who knew this and knew me from the inside.

Dad was asleep with his cell phone turned off. Allan was at the airport waiting for a flight. I called Jo. Midwives always answer their phones in the quiet, dark hours of the night.

My heart knew her voice in the thinnest places: deep within the surreal wave of a contraction, deep in the drowning waters of grief. I trusted her when she said, "I know you need to be alone with your dead."

My dead.

My baby was my dead.

These words were the truest grounding I could have had. My baby was not sleeping. She would not wake up. My little baby was dead.

I had to hold her until my dad came. Until Allan came too. I had to show them.

I heard breakfast carts rolling outside in the hall and smelled coffee as the sun broke through the skyline. And still, I rocked Clara's body.

I told her about how I'd dreamed of being her mother and about her sister and brother. How there's so much more enclosed in a dream. We dream the high points and forget the layers and nuance of the shadows. Life becomes more than we can imagine.

"We're changed now, you and me. You've changed me forever, Clara, and I can't ever go back to what I was," I said, kissing her head. I didn't even know what I meant by that. Only that I'd never be the same again.

Dad was there then. He cried with me. He held his granddaughter and took photos of her fingers, cheeks, and toes for the first time. I counted this as one of her miracles.

You were loved, sweet baby. You were loved.

When Allan cracked the door to our room, Clara's body was heavy—time measured in the weight of cold blood. When I looked into his bright blue eyes rimmed in red from his tears, his gaze laser locked onto mine, lucid and true.

"Oh, it's real." His voice cracked like spring ice on a frozen lake. "It's real. All this time, part of me didn't believe it was real."

I watched the one other person who knew what it felt like to be Clara's parent fall to pieces. It parted a veil that hung between us.

We sat together on the bed with our dead and sobbed, finally unified, in grief.

I saw how my motherhood included him, depended on him. There was no way to have them without him. I knew I could make our lives better without tearing them apart.

Lauri came then and sat down beside me.

When she offered to hold my baby, I passed Clara the way any new mother sets her baby down for a minute. Just a minute. But that minute broke the spell I was under.

Lauri cried as she left the room with my dead.

The funeral held such strange moments and memories. Dappled sunshine and shadow. Time spells and tiny horrors, little details I wrote into my heart.

Like how she's buried in the blue dress I bought for church testimonies of her miracle. And how when we had the private viewing, I scooped up her body, following maternal instinct to pick up my baby. But you don't hold the body at a viewing, because embalming water flows.

And how infant caskets look just like igloo coolers. She's got two left shoes on her feet. The peach roses were delivered bright orange.

Two geese, a duck, and several squirrels attended behind the pastor. They listened to the eulogy better than I did.

Light broke through the boughs of the trees.

A lumbering Navy plane flew overhead.

I don't know why these are the details that stood out so loudly. Only that the brain does what it must to cope. And who knows where God was . . . only that rules and routines don't solve Him. The savior doesn't always save.

Clara's gravestone bears a butterfly and the words EVERY DAY WAS A GIFT.

I don't remember going home.

Part Three

———

IN THE WAY

Trapdoor

FOR

a

long

time

there

were

no

words.

I sat in silence, a half-glass of yesterday's tepid water.

Echoes of life called from beyond me—distant and canned, the way a crow calls from an acre away. By the time a fragment of sound reached me, and my mind registered what it was, the maker had moved on. For a week, no one left me alone with the children.

Blink.

Somehow the Very Concerned let me drive the car. The car always took me down Lone Star Road. The car turned right into the memorial gardens. The car parked. My feet walked.

Clara lay nestled between the roots of a massive oak tree in the Garden of Love. Cemeteries are fields of grief and shadow, echoes of what was.

I sat on the Thackerson's bench holding her bloodstained blanket because my arms hurt so bad. Empty Arms Syndrome, Amy called it.

But after the funeral I sank eight feet too. Feelings, tears, time, and language all hovered above me, out of reach.

Blink.

I was changed—the way a malformed heart is reworked—but my body couldn't process the surgery. My body bloated and leaked and drained with pain. The acuteness of my grief made holding an appearance impossible. Losing Clara cracked me open.

Katie reached to be picked up. I looked at the strawberry-blond solidness of her, at how much she'd grown in two months. Curls at her neck. Dimples in her elbows. She started crawling up my lap, the poor big sister who'd never know her sibling.

But children bring grace. They unlock the living among the dead. Katie's petal-soft skin on my skin, the animation in her bones, quickened the parched marrow in mine. My arms wrapped around her and squeezed. I cradled her head in my hands and inhaled the sweet aliveness of her.

"Mama home," she said.

I thought I'd cried all I could the night Clara died. I was wrong.

The shock of all I'd been through started to sparkle with vivid, sharp edges. I couldn't stop crying.

My tears dropped into the dishwater. They splashed on William's blond head. They formed wet stains on my shirt. Tears backlogged in my face until it swelled. Involuntary salt water seeped from me until I felt like I was melting.

People wanted to help.

Nothing helped.

I dehydrated.

A card from among the hundreds of sympathy cards offered the advice of an old mother who'd Been There. *Go to the ocean,* she wrote. *The ocean is a vessel of tears.*

I cried at the cemetery because no one asked why. But I sent racking sobs into the sea. The waves drowned my sounds and sorrows. The ocean received pain and offered relief, undulating calm and violence, at once a dangerous and tender thing. I threw myself open to the sea.

I found the hollow inside of myself there, as if I were a conch shell, the siphonal canal that wound into a spire, housing my soul. By screaming rage into the vessel of tears, I entered the chamber I'd held locked for so long.

I wasn't only grieving Clara. My daughter only handed me a key and led me inside.

The room echoed like a cavern, anger reverberating in the walls like wind. WEDDING NIGHT and MOUNTAIN DOCTOR. He was YOUR BEST FRIEND and RAPTURE and LEFT BEHIND. Inside of me, inside of sobs, inside of the ocean I crept through the room, listening. SUMMER CAMP and MICHIGAN and TROY-TROY-TROY.

NO ONE LOVES YOU UNLESS YOU FOLLOW THEIR RULES.

I pressed my hands to the sides of my face and unleashed the furor of unfairness, of violation, of interference and denial into the waves of the sea. I screamed until any voice I had was a salt-hoarse whisper. I went home drained and sunburned.

Blink.

In time, I could handle the grocery store.

The cashier recognized me from when I was pregnant. "Where's your new baby?"

"She's dead."

"Oh, I'm so sorry, honey . . . I guess sometimes God needs a new rose for his garden."

Fuck God and his garden of dead babies. My hands fumbled to count out the right amount of cash. My brain tried to remember numbers. My eyes and breasts leaked. *Fuck the rapture.* Outliving your children is hell. What kind of mother can't hold her children? A shit mother burning in hell, that's who.

Worse than the cashier was the procession of sad Christians who didn't know what to say with their cream-of-crap casseroles.

"If only we'd prayed harder for a miracle," they said.

I sat and looked at my dumb empty hands in my dumb empty lap. What did they think God was? A fucking vending machine? If miracles depend on the intensity of prayer, then who's God in that equation? And who prays harder than a mother?

"Mama, help me tie my shoe," William said. My babies pulled me into reality with their visceral, physical need. It was the only language my spirit understood. Because of them, I was still a mother and my lap didn't have to be empty.

But there came a morning when I couldn't get up. I lay in the bed hearing Katie call, "Mama! The sun's up!" and my legs wouldn't move.

Allan was at work.

William stood at the door. "Mama awake?"

So began the zombie days. The reanimation of my corpse stiffened my limbs and left me in a trance. Nothing wanted to move. I slogged my way to the kitchen to make juice. I skipped laundry. Skipped the dishes. The kids went barefoot all summer and didn't need tiny socks to be washed and hung at the clothesline. There was no need to pray.

While they watched *Blue's Clues* on the TV someone gave us, I lay on the floor next to them watching shadows on the wall.

Allan came home and did baths and bedtime. We sat on the couch in silence watching *Survivor* and *Big Brother*.

He left in the morning for work. I ignored Judith's calls—and anyone else from the mother club too.

Blink.

Dad built a treehouse with a bridge at their house and Monica helped me watch the kids play. At their house, no one yelled at me to PAY ATTENTION and WHY AREN'T YOU WATCHING THE KIDS the way Allan did at home.

Like after dinner, when I stood at the sink staring at the mutable clouds, my hands in suds, and Katie turned her plate over, refusing to finish her beans.

I looked at Allan as if he were a strange octopus behind the glass. "What are you talking about?" I said. "I'm right here."

Maybe he needed to scream. Allan didn't go to the ocean or the cemetery. His eyes didn't weep until his body dried out. He didn't eat cashiers and church ladies. Allan went to work. The man I felt connected to in grief vanished the same way the twinkling chess player once had—but now I knew for sure he was in there. If only I held out long enough, I knew I'd find that man again and receive the blessing of having waited for God's best. But Allan folded Clara into himself, so that whatever his experience of her was, I couldn't find it.

"Leave him to his book," Dad said. "Bring the kids over here." And so, Dad built the kids a treehouse with a bridge to offer some laughter. He'd recently bought a computer with a dial-up connection to the internet. So, while the kids played with Monica, I sat down before the large square monitor and turned it on. Some static and beep sounds later, I was online.

I wanted to find homeschooling curricula. William was three—old enough for preschool. I'd attended Jacksonville's homeschooling fair the previous year and heard about Sonlight. It used real books instead of textbooks and was compatible with a method of hands-on learning and nature study I liked called the Charlotte Mason method. The library lover in me wanted my children to know literature and Sonlight had an online forum where moms could ask questions.

The forum was divided into categories like rooms. There were spaces to discuss home management, curriculum organization, book choices and reviews, and homekeeping issues like meal planning and stain removal. Sonlight embraced a Christian worldview, so I knew these women were safe, even if Judith and the Gothard mothers might not think so.

The first several times I went to the boards, I stayed in the general discussion room. Then I saw a board called "Edu-Anon."

The Educators-Anonymous board centered on the idea that our public education had failed us as women, and we were in recovery from it. By educating ourselves, we could improve our minds as we homeschooled our children. It was run by a woman named Julie B in Cinci—that was her handle.

My skin prickled with electricity. No one in my real life knew I was in these forums, reading about ideas other than Gothard and the IBLP. This was a secret, but it was *my* secret—and I knew I had to keep it anonymous. "Edu-Anon" promised conversation beyond OxiClean and meal prep. With a little cleverness, I could educate myself.

I was hooked.

Exploring my own education—even just saying those words—gave me an idea of how to process the impact Clara had left on me. What if by getting better, I could make our lives better? What if, instead of fighting Allan and resisting all the time, I poured myself into being the best Christian wife and mother ever?

I still woke up panicked my baby was out in the rain when it stormed. I still counted heads in my rearview mirror and realized one was missing. Anxiety nipped at me to walk faster, that I'd forgotten something. I'd left someone behind. I'd miscounted.

Was it even possible to get better?

I broke one of Judith's rules and went to the library. I told Allan the kids liked story time and didn't mention I used that hour to roam the aisles to keep up with what I was learning online.

I ran my fingers over the spines of hardcover books, tracing the artifacts of language, leaning against the shelves and finding comfort in the familiar scent of old pages. Here was a home, here was a safe space.

I read about fetal microchimerism. When a woman is pregnant, her baby sends cells into her body, which attach to her heart and organs and bones. The cells migrate to the wounded, broken parts of the mother that most need repair. In autopsies, the researchers found fetal DNA within a mother's heart. It happens early in pregnancy, so even an early miscarriage can cellularly alter a woman for the rest of her life. She literally carries her baby in her heart.

I already knew she was in my heart. I could feel Clara's cells inside of me. They'd already nestled into my ventricles valves atriums chambers. She'd already unlocked long-hidden pain and occupied my hollows. And now that a fourth baby grew inside of me, I could feel a fertile will to survive the dark days that climbed like a vine up my spine.

I wrote about Clara and grief on the forum and the other mothers didn't flinch. Our conversations branched out—art, music, travel, ideas. Sometimes, because we'd all come from different backgrounds, this included R-rated movies, solo travel, secular music, and feminist ideas.

When the owner of Sonlight thought our conversations were too radical for a Christian environment, we left their forum. Julie B switched her handle to Jazz and announced a new website: the Trapdoor Society.

Jazz knew theater. She wanted a women's society that offered a way of escape. Her guidelines:

"The Trapdoor opens a door to discovery—discovery of beauty in the arts, music, literature, nature, film, philosophy, theology, and relationships. We've talked about Jane Austen's books, home décor, movies like *The Princess Bride* and *Hamlet, Enchanted April* and *O Brother, Where Art Thou?*, meiosis and mycosis, nature journaling, U2 and Beethoven, Andrea Bocelli and Sting, Shakespeare performances and Broadway shows, Impressionist art and Sister Wendy, how to teach kids and how we learn, too."

Seeing in color again began with blue.

I typed in www.trapdoorsociety.com and a deep sapphire page loaded. I clicked on a photo of a blurred angel and a scrolling lamppost against a periwinkle sky and landed in Trapdoor's lobby.

I found myself surrounded by the heroines once more. *Jane Eyre* and *Wuthering Heights* and *O Pioneers!* Then *Cold Sassy Tree, Jewel,* and *Pride and Prejudice.* My Trapdoor friends and I explored stories—themes, characters, impact.

BethSC posted about personality tests. Colleen discovered an Austen-style wedding around the same time Jazz's daughter studied Edwardian dance. One of the Rachels shared a contrast of the Hepburn/Bogart *Sabrina* with the newer Harrison Ford version. Carolfoasia started reading the Great Books. Susan posted writing prompts. Carrie shared her equestrian dreams. Notebooklady asked what art we had on our walls. Dalissa taught us about Fluevogs. Stephanie explored sad movies as therapy.

Old corners inside of me filled with light. Words—essays, novels, posts, ideas, films, classics—cracked the layers of suffering, hardship, and ugly secrets. I wanted character arc and growth. I craved what it meant to be "well read" and educated, to watch *10 Things I Hate About You* and identify the Shakespearean roots. To find the poetry in Eminem and Coldplay lyrics. I learned "liberal arts" were also called "humanities" and I suddenly thirsted to understand a culture I'd lived outside of for so long.

When Jazz posted about bhags—Big Hairy Audacious Goals—I wondered if I had any. What did it mean to have an idea and explore it, without first considering if God or your husband or your family wanted you to?

At the library, I found the aisle of cookbooks and another on wine. I was hung up on Jesus's first miracle. Maybe it was because my daughter's miracle life had cracked me open and the people at church thought her death was failure. Or maybe it was rage at the idea that we could believe hard enough to make God change His mind. But it pissed me off when the pastor said the wine at Cana wasn't real, that it wasn't more than juice.

Wouldn't the wine of Cana be the best wine in the whole wide world? And what did that even mean, *the best wine*?

I posted the question on Trapdoor and Beth suggested I make it a project. I wondered if it could be my bhag.

Allan started coming home to changes.

"Oh, you cleaned the house today," he said.

"Thanks for making dinner," he said.

"You cut your hair?"

"You're wearing jeans!"

A small praise band formed at church and I announced I was going. Allan stared at me and swallowed. I could see him doing the math of it—should he pounce on my brash rebellion or be glad I was finally out of bed? That night I drove to the church with my flute on the seat beside me and stopped at the cemetery on the way. When I wrote about it on Trapdoor, I called him my "dh," short for "dear husband," and sang his praises for agreeing to watch the kids.

Liam was born after a flawless pregnancy. The obstetrician, cardiologist, and geneticist granted me a clean bill of fetal-maternal health. "Your daughter's defect was a fluke," the doctor said, clearing me for home birth.

Jo and her assistant sat beside the pool Allan filled in the living room. I loved the nest of it, moving alone in the warm water, no bright lights or tiled ORs or lemony astringent soap near me. Louis Armstrong sang "What a Wonderful World" from the stereo.

I put my hand down as my baby crowned and helped him be born. My baby boy opened his wide blue eyes while still under the water and gazed at me with wonder at his calm journey earth side. My heart held cells from William Katie Clara Liam. When the azure river and swirling stars came this time, I saw I was surrounded by their love.

There came a time when the dominoes had names—human, indelible benchmarks. While I emerged from grief into self-discovery and a new baby, Allan had been busy connecting with other patriarchs.

Doug Phillips entered our home as a name in a men's forum and a shiny catalog that came in the mail one day. Allan frequented his blog. Doug heralded the Christian Golden Age, a time when Christian values will rule America. Evangelical homeschoolers led the charge and raised the army. Genesis 1:28 ordered us to: "Be fruitful . . . take dominion."

Doug's Vision Forum offered curricula and toys for classical, traditional, Christian homes. Full-page bleeds and beautiful resources appealed to wannabe men of valor and women of virtue. Phillips showed us the patriarchy could be poetic, dramatic, and aesthetic. This was no Gothard ugly red textbook.

Doug's toys for boys included spy glasses for detectives. Wooden shields, swords, and guns. Rock hammers and utility belts for creation-themed adventures to Raise the Allosaurus. Pocket knives! Costumes to dress up like a puritan or patriot. Teepees. Davy Crockett caps. Covered wagons, zip lines, bush knives, and telescopes.

Doug Phillips played dress-up a lot. His wife, Bealle, bore eight scrubbed-clean children the way a teapot pours out tea: with a delicate smile on her lace-framed face. The appearance she maintained of their family was enviable and lovely.

Vision Forum sold toys for girls too. Six historically dressed dolls. Pewter pincushions. Calligraphy sets. Books on homekeeping. Jacks and dominoes. Tea sets.

Doug led men on issues that mattered to patriarchal leaders. Male dominance, Christian dominion, female submission, child discipline, political influence, and *Titanic*-level valor. The ideal Vision Forum father cared about what happened in Washington, taught his boy to be a rough-and-tumble man, taught his daughter to shave his face and serve him, and kept his wife fruitfully multiplying.

I didn't talk about Vision Forum on Trapdoor. Like art school and youth group when I was a teenager, I wanted to keep my two Tias separate.

On Trapdoor, I wrote a piece on the color blue while listening to Enya's "Caribbean Blue," calling attention to the zit-zit-zit of the neighbor's sprinklers and the slap of my flip-flops against the bottoms of my feet. Noticing details helped me feel alive again. Inspired, I picked up a book from the library: Annie Dillard's *The Writing Life*. I wondered if it was too late. Could writing be a bhag?

"How we spend our days is how we spend our lives," she wrote. I counted days in loads of laundry and tiny socks. The Psalmist prayed, "Teach us to number our days." There was something to time and presence, the temporal and eternal.

Words satisfied like food and poured off the excess pain so I could better hold it. I wanted more. The forum wasn't just about connection and conversation. Something alchemized inside of me when I posted, and words full of thoughts that were my own became a freedom I craved.

In 2000, the conversation centered on politics. Some of the women weren't voting for George W. Bush—not everyone on Trapdoor was Republican or even Christian. I didn't want to tell them I wasn't allowed to vote. I suddenly felt embarrassed about our lifestyle, the way I couldn't let Lauri see my cracks in the hospital.

Allan learned about Head of Household voting from Doug's blog. He said our household was voting for a Reform Party candidate—Donald Trump or Pat Buchanan.

Allan liked Pat best because he was a Nazi sympathizer. Allan called mixing the races "mongrelization," and liked David Duke—Pat appealed to him. When Pat visited Bob Jones University and gave a speech about taking America back, he said he wanted to rebuild Gideon's Army and prepare for Armageddon. I thought he sounded like an angry idiot.

Of course, it didn't matter what I thought. Head of Household voting means the men vote and represent the household. A year or so ago, I hadn't cared much when Allan said Doug Phillips encouraged men to make this a rule. But now that I read about politics and watched other women debate issues online, I wanted to cast my ballot too.

"Well, this could be a close election," Allan said. "As long as you vote the way I vote, the women might help. I'll think about it. By the way, we're going to be changing churches soon too."

I started cleaning clean things and rehearsing what I'd tell my family about another church change.

Issues of *National Review, World* magazine, and *Tabletalk* by R. C. Sproul Jr. stuffed our mailbox. Biblical commentaries replaced *Survivor, Big Brother,* and TV time altogether. *Sinners in the Hands of an Angry God* was Allan's favorite evening, Johnathan Edwards's frightening reminder that annihilation depended only on God's whim. He listened to Sproul Jr.'s Basement Tapes, Piper's *Desiring God,* and AM-dial preachers in the car.

We bought a bigger house and Dad came to help me with a clothesline.

"Why is he moving your church again?" Dad asked.

"He says Baptists are weak," I said. Allan's actual word was "pussified," but there was no way I was using that word with my father. "He wants a truer following of Calvinism and for the kids to be baptized."

Dad huffed and exhaled, trying not to interfere.

The more Allan learned about TULIP and John Calvin, the more it bothered him Clara wasn't baptized.

"She could be in hell, you know," he said. "Let me teach you about TULIP."

I held my breath in the horrible image of my baby in the flames I'd once seen in Sunday School. Allan continued talking. He went on about TULIP for days, until I could paraphrase it in my sleep.

Total Depravity.
Unconditional Election.
Limited Atonement.
Irresistible Grace.
Preservation of the Saints.

TULIP meant humans were depraved from the start, but some of them were elected to be saved. Jesus died for only those selected souls, and if you were chosen, His grace was irresistible—you couldn't say no. If you were one of those lucky-duck saints, you'd be preserved no matter what came your way, saved whether you liked it or not.

Suddenly, sweaty nightmares of broken baby body parts burning in hell returned, and I woke up in a screaming panic to count the kids. What if Clara wasn't elect? What if she burned in hell while I was out here reading Harry Potter and learning about wine?

"Read this statement of faith," Allan said. "The Presbyterians support headship and the church we go to needs to be in alignment with our values." He pushed his desk chair back so I could read his computer screen.

A wife is to submit herself graciously to the servant leadership of her husband even as the church willingly submits to the headship of Christ.

"What about Judith and John and the group?" I asked. Changing churches meant leaving our mentors.

"Pussy Baptists," he said. "Milquetoasts. I want a stronger faith. And by the way," he said, "we're voting for Pat. If you can't do that, you can't go."

In Florida and the country, the count came down to the popular vote, dangling chads on ballots, and the Supreme Court. George W. Bush was the new president. I stayed home because he'd catch me lying if I voted for someone else, but I wondered how it would've gone if women like me had voted. I'd liked what Gore had to say about the planet. His convictions struck me as more compatible with protecting creation—the very first mandate God ever gave humans.

R. C. Sproul Jr. was a jolly-faced red-bearded Calvinist preacher. Allan started reading his column in *Tabletalk* magazine, a publication of Ligonier Ministries, run by Junior's dad. Junior lived in Bristol, Tennessee, and pastored Saint Peter Presbyterian Church.

Allan told me about it over glasses of jammy red wine under the magnolia tree because we did that now—drank wine. New Calvinists loved wine and I'd done enough homework now to conduct a tasting. I knew I liked Pinot Grigio and that Pinot Noir made me want chocolate. Riesling was too sweet and Cabernet reminded me of swaying hips and Nina Simone.

"The church members homestead," he said. "They grow their own food, bake their own bread, brew their own beer. They make merry." He laughed and raised his glass to the dusky sky.

I laughed too—and our shared humor felt like friendship.

Bristol sounded like Vision Forum cosplay for grown-ups, so I checked out *The Self-Sufficient Life* and *The Encyclopedia of Country Living* at the library. I liked the idea of moving to the mountains when the kids were older. It would be cool to go to church with a bunch of families who were happy and wholesome, and not as mean and stern as the Gothardites.

I didn't know what was said on Junior's Basement Tapes or in the men's forums Allan frequented. Only that they were talking about what mattered to Christian men. I didn't worry about it. Life felt great. Allan was happy to have so much research, he got promoted at work, and I threw myself into happy-homemaking and homeschool.

I had the flow down of what it meant to be a vibrant Christian wife and mother. I was a Manager of My Home—our day divided into fifteen-minute capsules as recommended by Teri Maxwell's MOTH book for homeschooling mothers.

I read out loud to the kids and taught them math with blocks. We used workbooks to practice their handwriting. Play-Doh and cookies, splatter paint on canvases laid out on the grass. Our favorite was "school outside."

"Edeh-fant," Liam said, pointing at a cloud.

"Elephant," corrected little-mama Katie.

My babies and I spent hours at the parks, libraries, and museums. William climbed trees. One grandmother paid for William's violin lessons and another ballet and tap for Katie. Patent leather gleamed as her metal taps clacked on the parquet floor.

At nap time, I stepped through the Trapdoor.

I had a little pile of secrets now, either about real life from the Trapdoor girls or about Trapdoor from Allan, secrets I mulled while scrubbing the cracks in the baseboard and using OxiClean to whiten sinks.

Like egalitarianism—where marriage partners are equal. BethSC posted about it. She was thinking about not being Protestant anymore. Maybe Catholic, maybe nothing. Maybe she wouldn't spank her kids anymore. She mentioned "non-coercive parenting."

I'd never heard a Christian woman say that out loud. We'd skipped the Pearls' infant spanking, but we used a wooden spoon now that they were older. I hated it. But discipline is how parents maintained order in their homes and kept their families from hell. So, what did it mean if spanking was a choice?

I couldn't talk about Beth's idea in front of Allan or he'd take the internet from me, the same as he'd taken Michael. But I wondered . . . what if I just tried these things? What if I tried to teach the kids without a spanking? Could I teach them God's rules without pain?

As if she knew what I was hiding, Judith sent an email, admonishing me not to forget my first love: The Psalmist grieved too, Tia. But you must beware of little foxes that ruin the vineyards. Allow your heart to remain true to your living family.

"Little foxes" in the IBLP referred to secret, hidden sins that spoiled the fruits of the spirit. But what I was learning on Trapdoor felt like eating the fruit of the spirit. I felt more love, peace, patience, and kindness when I learned, not less. Christians talked all the time about joy, but nothing we did brought me that feeling. In contrast, motherhood, learning, and making choices that rang true in my body felt good.

Was I being tempted again to use my free will or was writing my "hidden art," as Edith Schaeffer and Mary Pride suggested was possible in their books *The Hidden Art of Homemaking* and *The Way Home*? If writing was my calling, according to Mary Pride, then it would become my ministry, and I wouldn't have to hide it anymore.

But if writing was a little fox who'd ruin my vineyard, I needed to kill it the way Christians killed their wills.

I tried to dump those thoughts like cold mop water, but the questions wouldn't go away. Maybe I needed Trapdoor because I was trapped.

Katie called me to "Look, Mama!" from the magnolia tree. She swung from the branch to the swing set pole to the chain and down, like a little monkey. I was glad she played in shorts and not a cumbersome dress. Some of the Gothard daughters even swam in dresses, which made them look like they were drowning.

Beautiful Girlhood from Vision Forum lay beside me on the lawn chair.

Girls should look at things from their parents' side and smile often. The girl who would come to perfect womanhood must learn to be obedient.

Katie ran across the yard and crashed into arms that weren't empty anymore. William piled on and then little Liam. I'd found beauty for ashes, the oil of joy instead of mourning, like it said in Isaiah. A monarch fluttered by. On "Edu-Anon" my handle was Clarasmommy. On Trapdoor I was Tia. At home I was Mama.

Allan and I hadn't had a fight in ages. I felt loved, even as I navigated the rules.

There was a Springsteen song that came out in those baby years on the *Jerry Maguire* soundtrack. I heard it late but I knew the secret garden Bruce described. I knew how to be here and how to stay a million miles away. If I was trapped, I also had a brief escape, a trapdoor to fall through and step offstage. The rules were salvation because they showed you where the lines were drawn. And once you knew that, it was easy to find where the colors fit inside.

Maze

A SENSE OF BOTH FREEDOM AND VICTORY FOLLOWED. NOW THAT I knew how to color inside the lines, I could show up in each space the way I wanted. Unlike school, I wasn't going to graduate from Trapdoor and lose it. As long as I kept my life at church, and with Allan steady, I was free to explore art, writing, and ideas with my friends online. And I was glad for that escape, because the Calvinists were relentless.

At least with Judith and the Gothard moms the rules were immediate and practical. Wear this. Don't say that. Go here. Never go there. But the Calvinists attributed everything to eternal security, election, depravity, and giant end goals—like world dominion. They debated theology endlessly, thirsting for the right answer to solve the mystery of God.

Our new pastor explained. Humans are depraved worms in need of a savior but we're such filthy sinners—insects, really—that we don't deserve to be saved. Thankfully, a limited few are elected for heaven. Christ and His grace are irresistible to the chosen—we're unable to say no to God. Even if we try, it's only a matter of time and suffering until we're broken and returned to Him. This is why Christianity hurts. Suffering aligns us with Christ, and it's a good thing when love hurts—that's how you know it's real.

I thought about my hurts. I tried to reconcile how they were gifts from God. The Calvinist God was angry and wrathful. As if he'd been waiting for the chance, Allan read me a quote from *Sinners in the Hands of an Angry God*.

"The bow of God's wrath is bent, and the arrow made ready on the string, and justice bends the arrow at your heart, and strains the bow, and it is nothing

but the mere pleasure of God, and that of an angry God, without any promise or obligation at all, that keeps the arrow one moment from being made drunk with your blood."

Life felt that way—that at any moment, the cup could spill. The glass could break. The ice could crack. The arrow could fly. The only way to soothe an angry God is to make sure you tiptoe quietly. To make sure you're pious enough to never break any rule. I needed to mind my spiritual manners because I'd been mistaken to forget the tempestuous anger of God. Annihilation was just one holy mood swing away.

Determined to stay on track, I ordered *I Kissed Dating Goodbye* by Joshua Harris from Vision Forum. Doug Phillips wrote about courtship on his blog and recommended daughters stay home to serve their fathers before marriage. I sat down on the lawn chair to read while the kids played under the magnolia tree. Harris was young and handsome, a gentleman with a fedora on the cover.

My courtship curiosity overrode any logic about young children, years away from getting married. I wanted to know if courtship could spare my kids my pain. What if I could spot dangerous flags for them before they got hurt? Now, I knew how to avoid a Troy. I knew how to avoid an Allan too. Maybe courtship would help them land in a marriage more like my parents'.

And there it was on the page—another reminder that we're only loved if we follow the rules.

The Bible teaches that if we truly trust in Jesus Christ, we die to our old way of living. And we can no longer live for ourselves—we now live for God and for the good of others.

I looked up. Is that what I wanted for my daughter? To stay home and serve Allan while he did (or did not) find her a match? To lose herself in making other people happy first? I thought back to the moment of her birth, to the sword and shield I'd felt rising inside of me. What I actually wanted for my daughter was to have a life absolutely nothing like mine.

William and Katie continued progress on their fort. Liam toddled around, trying to "help." Their faces, stained orange from Popsicles, all turned and looked at me. "Come see, Mama!"

I set the book down. I didn't want her to live only for the good of others, burdened with invisible and silent pain for their convenience or preference. I didn't want it for me either.

The neighbor kids tumbled out their back door. I let the kids talk through the fence. Judith Small had taught me casual associations and playmates were dangerous. It's why so many families bought land out in the country—to avoid neighbors and have greater control over their environment without curious eyes on them.

"Hey, Tia!" Denice was puppy-cheerful, like life was one giant open door.

"Can't talk, sorry. I have chores. I'm working on a new chart to manage my home better." I was always tweaking the MOTH chart.

"What's 'manage your home' mean? You mean housework?" She laughed. "Y'all are the weirdest people I've ever met."

I went inside, thankful she didn't know the half of it.

That week at the pediatrician's office, I picked up a copy of *Parents* magazine. A woman named Michelle Duggar was featured—she had fourteen children following in a line. Nine boys, five girls, two sets of twins. The girls all wore boxy red jumpers.

Michelle's husband was in politics. She managed her household with charts I recognized from MOTH. Her laundry and shopping routines were the same as Judith's. They drove a bus that seated twenty-four, used a fifteen-passenger van for errands, and had a mobile home they used for vacations to "conferences." When the article said she homeschooled using a character-based curriculum, I knew in an instant she was a Gothard mom.

How interesting this article was in *Parents*. Why would a secular readership want to know the life of a big fundamentalist family? If Gothard-life was going to be featured in the mainstream, what about the secrets we kept? The way the Pearls recommended spanking babies and the way women couldn't vote. What would happen when the readers of *Parents* found out women had to obey and that we didn't vaccinate our kids?

On Trapdoor, Devmom asked, "Has anyone tried Netflix?" It was a new service where we could order films straight to our house on DVD, no Blockbuster trip needed. You created something called a queue of interests and favorites and then, three discs at a time, they came in the mail. I missed movies. I missed Michael.

Nikki described her queue of self-education and exploration. Carolfoasia shared a review of *Divine Secrets of the Ya-Ya Sisterhood*. Notebook Lady's post said, "It's a woman's prerogative to change her mind."

But how? Movies gave me ideas, but what power did I really have to implement any of them? If I admitted I wanted to change my mind about anything, the dominoes would immediately start to fall. I was loved only when I followed the rules. Could I risk the anger that followed stepping out of line?

I clicked on the Book Lover's room but quickly closed it out. Allan had assigned new books for me to read and they weren't the kind I could write about on Trapdoor.

"They're your priority," he said. "I'm studying Federalist marriage and covenant theology. You're going to study submission." We'd had fights again— sit-on-my-head fights. Allan said there was a solution to our ongoing conflict.

Doug Wilson was a gravel-voiced patriarch and pastor in Idaho who wrote a series of paperback books on how we should practice covenantal theology in our homes. He looked the part of a wrathful God. The stack of thin books reminded me of the angry Pearls' books, packed with opinions, sold by slick Doug Phillips. One idea always led to another but clearly these men were connected.

Reforming Marriage. Federal Husband. Wilson's point was that Christians had to study discipline, theology, and war so we'd be ready to usher in the Christian Golden Age.

In Hebrew, the italicized word translated mankind *as* Adam. *In other words, God created Adam and his wife, male and female. He blessed them, called them Adam. She was, from the beginning, a covenantal partaker in the name of her husband. God does not call her Adam on her own; He calls her Adam with him.*

The book said a man needs help, and the woman needs to help. That's her job, her created purpose. She's his "helpmeet." On his own, man's unsuccessful. He can only function to his full capacity with a capable, amiable woman helping him along the way. And she'll only be happy if she surrenders and serves him.

This was why Allan said I needed to start asking for his permission. And why the money I was starting to make taking photos needed to go to him first.

He needed to take over balancing the checkbook and review my library selections. He needed to approve my grocery purchases and meal plans.

"But why?" I asked. "I'm capable of doing all of that. How is more management helping you?"

"Because the husband is responsible to God for all that goes on under his roof," Allan said. "Responsibility gives authority meaning."

This worried me. Allan already struggled under pressure. The benefit of me working hard to improve our lives was that Allan came home with less on his shoulders. It seemed to me he'd be happier if I relieved him of extra work—not if I added to it.

But Wilson and Sproul Jr.'s agrarian covenant theology was what Allan wanted for our family. He was convinced this accountability and control were the key to our happiness. How he handled it wasn't my business. That was between him and God.

Allan took all that he learned and issued new rules with tighter, more defined lines. Under the surface, anger brewed.

He wanted me to call him "my lord."

Wear only dresses.

Cover my head with a scarf to show submission and modesty.

And he wanted me to stop showing anyone what I'd written or made, such as a forum post or a scrapbook, unless I'd shown it to him first.

I took a break from Trapdoor to skip his show-and-tell. It was safer to tell my friends I needed to take a hiatus than show Allan what I'd been learning. But in my efforts to be different after Clara and to be the best wife and mother possible, this escalation didn't feel fair.

I tried being too busy and thrifty to go back to dresses. "Honey, I'll get to it. I just bought all those jeans last year."

I tried humor, giggling when I called him "lord."

I completely blew off the order for him to approve what I made before showing it to others. I just wrote and created less.

Allan turned to the men's forums where husbands could get advice on how to make their wives cooperate.

"You're not getting it," he said. "A wife shouldn't nullify her husband's voice. You're always raising your head higher than mine. You demean me."

"How so?"

"You don't ask permission and I can tell you're hiding something. I'm going to conduct a Tia-audit," he said, smiling. "I need a full accounting of everything under my roof. And that Bible study at church, *The Excellent Wife*. I want you to go. You spend too much time on that damn computer."

Tread carefully, I heard in my head. I'd created a delicate balance between my thoughts and behavior, my inside and outside, my real world and the virtual world. That line was tightrope thin now. The worst thing I could do was set Allan off.

"Alright," I said.

"Say it correctly," he said.

I took a breath and looked at the wall. "Yes, my lord," I answered.

Shockingly, Allan's audit included sex.

His need for relief ruled our frequency. I knew better than to ask. He hated my taste and smell, even after a shower. He hated fluids, touching, kissing, and breath. So our current pattern was that we didn't have sex until he had to have a release. Then he'd reach for my right breast and squeeze it. That was my signal to roll over. Always from behind, always a few thrusts, then I could lie back down.

How was an audit going to include sex? I didn't *have* sex. Sex happened to me.

"Are you saying you'd like to do it more often?" I asked, hoping he wanted me.

"I have a mandate from God to meet your needs," he said.

"Oh."

I wasn't sure what to say or do. I didn't want more instances of what we already did. What I longed for was to be kissed and held. I wanted love that felt good.

Or did I? As soon as I had this thought, I realized I'd wanted that as a new bride. Now I just wanted him to stay off me. I wanted to say no.

"What I think would work is for you to have an orgasm more often. I will wait for mine until you have yours. Can you do it on my command?"

I stared at him and then bit back a laugh, knowing he'd backhand me if I let it out. Orgasm on command? *That's so romantic.* I could probably fake it.

I nodded as he dictated our sex schedule, including the time of night and how long he'd wait before telling me to finish. He looked pleased and optimistic, the way he was when he bought new school supplies.

You're a utensil. Maybe if I could see where he was going, I could better prepare for the changes. I read more of Wilson's books, searching for clues.

It is lawful for a godly husband to admire, kiss, taste, and caress his wife wherever he pleases. The woman *is* a garden and she *has* a garden. Wilson quoted Song of Solomon and said women should not taste their lover with pursed lips and neither should men. Christian lovers should be "deep and lasting."

Federalist men were virile and loved sex—Wilson's book was clear on that. Covenantal men were not finished in three touchless minutes—they took dominion. Allan was trying to take Wilson's advice and the Pearls' too. A book called *Holy Sex!* came in the mailbox.

As the audit continued, I read less, worked harder, and lost weight. When I couldn't control anything else in my life, controlling my food felt good. The pain of hunger was reality I trusted.

I developed a compulsion to have the house clean. I watched the kids playing instead of playing with them, scrubbing harder when it hurt. Hands. Knees. Bleach. Corners. *This isn't the mother you want to be.* I sorted bins of baby clothes and broken toys. Picked out crumbling, yellowed caulk from the cracks around my sink. Laid beads of shiny new caulk. Moved furniture around, sometimes twice weekly.

My body got smaller. People noticed.

"Why are you losing weight?" asked Tammie at church. "You were already thin."

"Just busy," I answered. I asked Allan for permission to buy some new clothes.

Allan said, "Denim jumpers. That's why Judith recommended them. You don't need new clothes every time you go on a diet."

One size fits all. The woolly curtain of sadness overshadowed everything.

I didn't want my kids to have a sad mom. I could clean, plan, and come on command, but I couldn't make myself feel happy. I remembered my mom, during those blizzards, snowed in and isolated, in over her head. I understood her tears and shadow. It's the drape of There's No Getting Out of Here.

Allan was changing too. As I suspected, the pressure was getting to him. His eyes were darkening, enthusiasm waning. He came home from work tired and didn't want to keep auditing my days. He kept saying I wasn't submissive enough, as if my presence signaled a chore he resented.

The Excellent Wife was more of the same when it came to authority and headship roles. But it homed in hard on attitude. Chapters on how I needed to work on my bitterness, accept my fault, and understand love was a choice were interspersed with tips like, "Eighteen Ways to Glorify Your Husband."

Reading, sleep, food, hobbies, and exercise were examples of false saviors bad wives turned to instead of Jesus. Biblical submission could be my joy and fulfillment if I'd let it.

In 2021, Grace Community Church in San Antonio, Texas, would share a video of Martha Peace responding to the torrent of bad reviews online about *The Excellent Wife*. In the video, she stands at a podium refuting that she thought it was okay for the husband to beat the wife. She laughs and says, "No, I said 'call the police and have him arrested.'"

But I held her garnet-colored book in 2003. The internet barely existed, and YouTube not at all. Martha's book said women came to her saying they were hurt by their husbands. They were hurt so much they had "bitter thoughts" listed in her chart. Thoughts like:

"I can't believe what he's done to me!"

"I will never forgive him."

"This is more than I can bear. There is no hope."

"I hate him."

"He's repulsive."

"I wish he were dead."

That sounded like more than bitterness to me. But Martha wrote: *If you are bitter and will not forgive then you are being wicked.* She wrote, *The wife who is disrespectful may experience severe consequences,* and that *your husband may rebuke you.*

I understood the word "rebuke" meant a stern, sharp reprimand. Synonym: correction. We used words like "rebuke," "correction," "discipline," and "training" interchangeably. When did rebuking become abuse? Even when we talk about disciplining or rebuking children, we didn't use words like "beat" or "strike." We called it correction.

Books, memories, and thoughts tumbled together like a quilt in the dryer. Martha's chapter on respect reminded me of *Fascinating Womanhood*'s instruction against trying to change masculine faults and how to speak with a soft tone. She called to reverence the same way Dr. Wheat had in *Intended for Pleasure,* and said to call our husbands "lord" the way Doug Wilson had in *Reforming Marriage.*

I felt like Martha spoke alongside the secrets I kept of our private kingdom. Women like me read books like this to help our painful marriages. We read because we struggled to stay in marriages that hurt, and even if she never said, "It's okay for the husband to beat the wife," she did say:

Wives sometimes face very frightening circumstances because of immorality, physical or verbal abuse, irresponsibility, threats of leaving, or use of alcohol/drugs by their husbands. Anyone might be frightened if their husband was behaving in any of these ways. What can a wife do to overcome her fear? The key to overcoming fear is finding some biblical ways to show love to God and love to her husband, since "perfect love casts out fear."

To reinforce this, Martha offered a chart contrasting fear thoughts and love thoughts. Anger, drinking, and irresponsibility were answerable by praying, "God will give me the grace to get through it." She quoted Romans 13:1 about governing authorities if a serious criminal offense had been committed. But most of the women I knew who read *The Excellent Wife,* myself included, minimized the extent of the harm we experienced, and didn't call the cops.

Martha's encouragement was to overcome my fear by finding ways to show love. The problem wasn't Allan's behavior then, but my fear of him. Fear was a sinful response to sorrow.

There was a chart in the back for dealing with a heart of sorrow.

If this was more than I could stand . . . 1 Corinthians 10:13. God would help me through it.

If I couldn't take it anymore . . . 1 Corinthians 10:36. I could do it as long as God deemed it necessary.

If I didn't want him to hurt me anymore . . . 1 Corinthians 10:31. I was to let him and glorify God.

If I wished for a gun to kill him . . . Vengeance belongs to the Lord.

If I wanted to kill myself . . . I was to continue fulfilling my duties whether I felt like it or not.

I stared at the chart. So many women wanted to kill or die that a whole bestselling book was needed to rebuke them? That's a lot of angry women.

The book said to practice smiling.

I went to our bathroom and stood in front of the sink. The tense woman peering back with plain-Jane hair and glasses looked forty-eight, not twenty-eight.

I forced my lips into a smile. It looked fake. I shook my head.

My eye caught a photo of the kids on the windowsill. Immediately and involuntarily, I smiled. But then I turned to the mirror. Sincerity dropped my guard and showed where I was vulnerable.

The whole point of this was how to appear happy while feeling miserable. Pleasant while suicidal, even. I sighed. The old woman looking back at me slumped her shoulders.

Hag.

I tried clearing my mind. Have no thoughts. I attempted invisibility, with dull and vacant eyes. Now, smile.

Success.

A serene and simple woman gazed at me. She looked like Judith and the pastors' wives and the women in the Vision Forum catalog. She seemed unstressed and unbothered, able to fade into the background. Her light dimmed into shadow until even I couldn't find her at all.

A few days later, I pulled into the driveway, home from Target. Unloading the car, I looped grocery bags up my arms. Doing it in one trip made it look like I'd bought less.

He sat at the computer, his back to the door, and startled when I stepped inside.

A flash of movement caught my eye out the family room window. I counted heads. One, two, three—

"The kids are outside," he said.

I stood as though wearing concrete shoes, eyes now locked on his computer screen.

A woman hung trussed like poultry, mouth gagged, eyes blindfolded, vulva bare and open for easy fucking.

"It's not what you think," he said.

I set the bags down. My body felt as hollow and fragile as a cicada shell clinging to a pine tree. I heard the tick of a metal snap in the dryer, the low rumble of a Navy cargo plane overhead. *He doesn't watch porn,* I thought. What was going on?

He pushed back the desk chair and got up. "It's art. Research. Don't worry about it. I have something to discuss. But, first, let me help you with the groceries."

Art. I paused, trying to do that math. I looked at the dark background behind her, the spotlight on her labia.

He hefted a bunch of bags. "Looks like someone spent a bunch of my money," he said.

"What if the kids came in right now and saw that, Allan?" I let my voice hiss and rise, feeling hot anger burn my throat. "That's not just nudity. That's cruel."

I'd never seen anything like it. I wondered if the woman was even alive. Could she breathe like that? Could she move?

"Oh c'mon," he said. "Correcting women for bad behavior is hardly a new concept."

"You're calling that correction? Close the screen. I don't want the kids to see," I said. I heard him click the mouse, scoot the desk chair.

I stood in the kitchen now, looking out the window at the three of them build a fort. Liam tried to keep up, and William struggled to be patient with his baby brother. I kept to the side so they wouldn't see I was home.

I tore off a sheet of Saran Wrap to seal the rest of the morning's bread, forcing my hands to be busy. I thought correction meant reminders. Conversations. Maybe a visit to the pastor, at worst. The Federal marriage books talked about meeting the church elders when there was a problem.

Allan leaned against the kitchen doorway. "A man can't haul his wife to the elders every time she's in rebellion," he said. "It's impractical. The solution is Christian discipline. I'm on a forum for Heads of Households. There's one for women too."

I wiped the clean, bleach-scented counter again. Then reached for the broom and swept the squares of golden sunlight on the wood floors. The bottoms of my feet searched for the cold stability of our foundation. My eyes darted for the door.

Over the next several weeks, I obeyed his command to learn more about being Taken in Hand. He directed me to membership forums and even a handbook.

"They have threads on what constitutes spankable offenses. How to conduct a spanking, how to use time-outs and the corner, and what happens afterward."

"You want to put me in *time-out*?"

"It's often used in conjunction with physical discipline." He hurried to his next point. "Christian Domestic Discipline repairs problems in the marriage. And it's done in love. Every spanking resolves with intercourse."

"So, it's sexual." My stomach clenched. Wife-spanking was kink in church clothes.

"No. Godly discipline is done in love, and sexual unification is God-designed to bring a husband and wife closer, like in the Song of Songs."

"But, you don't even like sex." My words hung in the crisp tension between us.

"Actually, that's not the case," he said coolly. "I realize now that your rebellion is a cockblock. It makes me not want you. You disgust me with your opinions and individualism. This will solve all that. I'll be able to make rules for you to follow, and when you break them, I'll address them without anger. Read the definition," he said.

Domestic discipline is the practice between two consenting life partners in which the head of the household (HoH) takes the necessary measures to achieve a healthy relationship dynamic.

Christian Domestic Discipline elevated BDSM kink by bringing in God. It promised an end to random fights and violence.

"Like Wilson's book says, Tia," he said. "Discipline must be painful. So, instead of punishing all of us, CDD allows me to punish just the one responsible."

My shoulders collapsed, unable to absorb that this was real. Allan left the family room. I read the words over and over again, dizzily walking in walled circles. Fragments of old questions drifted in like a breeze rustling the curtains of a forgotten window. *Can I leave? Can I do this on my own? What else will I lose if I lose my marriage?*

To be spanked like a child. It hadn't happened to me since I'd been a child myself. My dad had the duty—Friday night consequences for a week's transgressions while he was working out of town and Mom struggled with Monica and me by herself out in the middle of nowhere. These were unpleasant events, but never anything I'd felt I needed protection from, and we usually screamed and cried more at the outrage of getting spanked on Friday for something we'd done on Monday than anything else.

I leaned against the bookcase and sat down on the floor, with Jane Austen and Willa Cather and Tracy Chevalier at my back. It was just so *embarrassing*. What adult woman says to any other adult that she goes along with this? And if she can't talk about it to anyone, if it's that much of a secret, what recourse does she have if it goes too far? I suddenly felt so small, so alone, and so in want of a rescue. Who loved me, even if I sinned against heaven, even if I couldn't do this thing demanded of me?

The closest chance was my mom. I was careful to cry out for help without divulging details I'd never be able to take back. "I can't do it anymore," I said. "Our fights are too much."

She released a London-fog sigh, the kind that precluded Great Patience. "Tia, you can't get a divorce," she said. "You haven't even tried counseling yet."

"I can't afford counseling," I said. "Allan would never let me pay for that."

"I'll pay," she said. "Call First Baptist's counseling department. I'll pay for your sessions. But, for the sake of the kids, you have to give this a try."

Looking back, I can see how I stepped out on the edge of dangerously thin ice but wasn't committed or confident or even scared shitless enough to cross. I wanted permission to fail without compromising our appearance. Like a good wife, I protected our image more than my safety. I tested my primary attachment bond to see if she'd hold me, even if I committed the terrible, awful sin of divorce. Even if I went against everything I'd been taught. But I didn't grant her the knowledge that would ignite her own fire shield of protection. If she knew he was hurting her daughter, she'd rise up. My parents would get involved. There'd be war. So, I let her think we just fought a lot. That we fought so much I was on the edge of desperation and wanted out. My confession rang more of exhaustion than danger and she toed the Christian-lady line: fights and disagreements can be fixed.

I decided I had to be honest with the counselor, where confidentiality was required.

The letter I wrote to John-the-counselor was six pages long and I told him everything—my wedding night, the way sex happened, the way he sat on my head, Mother's Day in Atlanta, CDD—everything that hurt. John would save me, I knew it. Pastors and counselors were shepherds who protected vulnerable sheep. He'd defend and rescue me because it wasn't possible a husband from a respectable Baptist church could spank his wife. It just wasn't possible.

I drove downtown and parked in the same garage I'd once used before orchestra rehearsal. It was weird to be back at FBC. I knew my way around here from memory, every snaking hallway and age-level floor. My relationship with Allan began here. What if it ended here too?

"Hello, Mrs. Brown. How can I best serve you today?"

The counselor led me to a room full of books and sat behind a glistening wood desk in a tufted leather chair. Allan would love a study like this. I glanced at the certificates on the wall and noted close, smiling eyes behind his glasses. I felt grateful to be in a safe place, finally able to release my secrets.

With a tremor, I gave him my letter. "Oh good. It's helpful to have notes," he said.

I watched as he scanned the violence. His face paled when he got to the part about the spanking. But I relaxed as I started to feel sure of his advocacy and protection. Somehow, the kids and I would be safe.

"Mrs. Brown, I see this all the time," he said, folding my letter and handing it back to me.

"You do?" I felt dizzy. How could he see *this* all the time? Was it mainstream? Did everyone do it?

"Yes. I'm constantly handing out the same advice to wives like yourself."

I sat forward in my chair, anxious to hear the words that would help me get a divorce.

"What you need, Mrs. Brown"—he paused—"is to honor your husband more. Do what he asks. Less of what he doesn't. *Honor. Your. Husband. More.* You need to ask yourself what you are doing that's driven your husband to this point, and you need to submit to him."

My veins ran cold. My body numbed like anesthesia. I mumbled a goodbye and walked like a zombie to the van. Submission. Respect. The problem wasn't what was done to me but how I reacted.

I turned for home disoriented and dissociated. Over the St. Johns River, I wondered how I'd gotten there. Why was I driving on the bridge?

I recounted the list: First Baptist. Allan. Honor him, Home. My brain strained to rationalize.

What if there was wisdom in appointments over outbursts? What if knowing when the pain would come helped me hide it?

Like a teabag steeped in hot water, the elements came together, only I'd never held a cup so hot. I walked through our home on my tiptoes. What ultimately tipped my scale was a faint pink line on the stick.

I was pregnant with number five. What if random violence and fighting were what caused Clara's defect? What if I could prevent that from happening again by helping Allan stay in control?

"How's that contract coming?" he asked a few days later, referring to the contract agreeing to channeled violence.

The floors gleamed with lemon Pledge. The yeasty scent of fresh bread hung in the air. Steve from *Blue's Clues* entertained the kids. *Mail time, mail time.* As he said this, I listened, never slowing the stroke of my mop. But it felt like the screws on me tightened.

"There's a script on the forum," he said.

"Can't you print it?" I said. Sometimes he gave up on ideas when they required extra work.

"Stop stalling. It needs to be in your handwriting. Get it done."

Later, I wrote the promise on ivory stationery with sticky black ink that smelled plastic. *I will not accuse my husband of domestic violence due to Christian discipline.* My stomach clenched with hopelessness, imagining a lawyer holding it in my face, saying, "But you wrote this yourself!"

No one told me there's no level of submission that's "enough." In a cage, a tiger can circle. In a maze, a rat can run. She can determine the bounds of her freedom and move her will within them. But submission is not a cage. It's a vacuum. As you give, the container squeezes harder, removing all air.

He warned me we'd do it soon, "over something small, to get used to it."

A week later, I stood in the kitchen, sliding a metal spatula beneath fresh, hot sugar cookies to frost with the kids.

"You showed those photos to Cindy without showing me first," he said. He was referring to a photo session of my friend's dog. I'd delivered the proofs at a fellowship.

"She was eager to see the proofs," I said, shrugging.

"That's against the rules. Go to our room," he said.

I froze.

"Don't make me repeat it."

Numb, I passed the kids' bedrooms in the hall. "They're outside," he said, and I realized he hid this too. I felt on par with them, unadult and small.

He motioned for me to get on the bed on all fours.

He started to pray, then took off his belt.

I buried my face in the pillow, and as he struck me, I silently screamed into the feathered down. But, like women in a vacuum, I made no sound.

Keep

ALLAN RALLIED AS IF HE'D STEPPED INTO HIS CALLING. AS HU-miliated and ashamed as I felt, he was as high and confident. Hitting me was no longer taboo—it was holy. And having a sanctioned outlet when he churned out of control helped him regain equilibrium. I could see how women ratio-nalized discipline as a method to keep the peace.

He was reading Wilson's book *Federal Husband*. *"Federal comes from the Latin,* foedus, *which means 'covenant,'"* he said. *"Wherever there is genuine fed-eral headship, the head as representative assumes responsibility for the spiritual condition of the covenant body,"* he read.

Federal Husbands imitate Christ by assuming responsibility for the sins of their households. Wives submit to their covenantal husbands the way Christians submit to Christ. Allan said years of Bible study finally felt like a culmination.

"I want us to start practicing family worship," he said. "I'm going to start teaching the kids Latin, Greek, and the Westminster catechism."

I spent most days wandering, scrubbing, shopping, mothering in a haze. I felt yanked back in time, to the years before Clara, before Trapdoor. I stopped eating more than a chicken tenderloin for breakfast and a small portion of whatever I made for dinner, even though I was pregnant. Except for a protruding belly, my body shrunk, and my spirit did too. I remembered what Reverend Brewer had said all those years before. "There's no way two lights can shine in this union."

At my first midwife appointment, Jo said, "Tia, your blood pressure's really low."

I muttered something about being so busy. She encouraged me to add in some snacks. "We've got to keep you healthy," she said.

Deep inside, a quiet voice whispered, *Why?*

Allan continued to thrive.

He hummed hymns while he stirred cheesy eggs for the kids. He had "wrastle time" with them, rolling on the floor and laughing. He brought home a shaggy brown dog he named Xenos, the Greek word for "stranger." He played chess with William and Katie and volunteered to mow the grass.

He ran catechism drills.

"What is the chief end of man?" he asked.

The kids would answer in their high and tender voices. "The chief end of man is to glorify God and enjoy Him forever."

"Good!" Allan cheered. "And what do the Scriptures principally teach? William, you go."

"The Scriptures principally teach what man is to believe concerning God, and what duty God requires of man," William said.

I listened from the kitchen, my hands kneading dough, recalling being taught what to believe to keep out of hell. Did I even know Jesus? Or God, for that matter?

"Katie, what is God?" Allan asked.

"God is a spirit, infinite, eternal, and unchangeable in His being, wisdom, power, holiness, justice, goodness, and truth." Her voice rang clear, even with the r's in "pow-ah" and "twooth" because she'd lost her two front teeth.

I sighed and rolled the dough into loaves. What did it matter to wonder about God, if His mysteries could be explained within a few lines?

New books arrived: crudely published papers and cassette tapes made in someone's basement for Allan. *Created to Be His Help Meet* by Debi Pearl for me.

I resisted another Pearl book. But the women at church buzzed about how much wisdom this particular book offered for wives struggling with difficult husbands. I remembered a sermon by Dr. Vines. "It's not important what's done to you. It's how you react that matters."

Debi agreed. Her book didn't dispute men were awful sometimes. She often called them stupid jerks. But a man's stupidity didn't relieve his wife's responsibility to respond in a submissive, cheerful, radiant way. Doing it right could even change that "selfish old man." If wives did a better job, planning ahead and joyfully smiling, their husbands wouldn't be jerks. They wouldn't cheat, look at porn, or otherwise behave badly.

Debi had several assignments to help wives do it right. Use the Crock-Pot for dinner. Offer the children only one breakfast. Serve the same lunch every day, without variety, unless Dad is home. A simplified lifestyle helped her focus on serving her man.

But also, it was important to understand that rough sex, with a "token" struggle, satisfied men who needed to conquer. Anxiety and depression signaled wives had forgotten their enthusiastic duty. A woman was a Jezebel if she thought she should teach her husband anything. Fat women were pigs. A woman without sexual desire needed to focus on ministering to her husband. Women near forty were teetering on the edge of mental instability. Menopause or pain were lame excuses. Reactions defined us and God told us what to think.

Alternatively, I could be what Debi called a "dumb-cluck."

The day you stop smiling is the day you stop trying to make your marriage heavenly, and it's the first day leading to your divorce proceedings. Wives who failed to respond well to their husband's insensitivities would find themselves struggling to pay rent in a "dumpy-duplex" while their children struggled in daycare. This wife could comfort herself that she'd stood on principle rather than allowing him to humiliate her, but she'd sleep alone for the rest of her life.

Accepting my man for who he was would avoid the sin of divorce and rejection from God for following Eve, Jezebel, and Satan.

I hid within rules and routine as though they were a veil, granting Allan the right of way.

Inspired to be a Federal Husband, Allan took me on date nights again, out to dinner and the bookstore or a walk on the beach. He held my hand and called me his Good Thing and Cookie Jar. He said I was the Tia he remembered meeting.

"Submission is sexy," he said, obviously turned on. I fell back on my practice and smiled, and as the contract required, I thanked him for his attention.

From time to time, I wondered how binding it would be in court.

What if I burned it?

What if I lost it?

But Allan no longer had the crazed look in his eye. Maybe this was God working in mysterious ways. Maybe this was why, for centuries, the traditional wedding vows included the words "to love, honor, and obey." There was a release in letting go and giving in.

Despite the happy high Allan usually rode, I still committed mistakes. Like wasting money at the grocery store. Or neglecting to say, "Yes, my lord," when told what to do. I'd canceled three midwife appointments to hide the stripes on my thighs after his loving correction.

Jo lived in Orlando now and the distance terrified me. In my dreams, I cried I'd give birth alone. Then I'd wake up, make breakfast, set out the books for homeschool and art time and field trips. I'd grab the camera and shoot the evidence of a happy childhood. Falling back on rules and routine got me through day after day. I tried pushing away reminders of Annie Dillard that how we spend our days is how we spend our lives. I didn't want this misery to be how I spent my life. But I knew there was no escaping Allan. There'd be no escaping his angry God either.

Ever so slightly, the way humidity rises in milliliters per cubic centimeter, Allan's moods began to shift. He said he wanted to move out of state.

He tried to buy property in Mississippi and Arkansas and the Canadian Rockies, sight unseen. He promised he'd find a job until our self-sustaining farm was up and running. We'd live off money we'd made on this house.

Cheap land was probably cheap for a reason, I suggested, but he said we'd be creative. We'd figure it out and the more secluded and off-grid it could be, the better.

How would I protect my children in the wilderness?

My dreams twisted with the sound of rattlesnakes. Distant thunder rumbled in the low-pressure system surrounding us. Florida's oppressive humidity reminded us of its feral nature, its submission to being stripped by wind and punished by rain. Storms were the only way its wildness was ever tamed.

That year the hurricanes blew unabated, one right on top of the other. Charley, Frances, Ivan, Jeanne. The clouds pursued without pause and the submissive trees bent to the gusts, their roots digging in to remain standing, and only some of them succeeding.

At our homeschool PE group, the kids played soccer while the mothers sat in chairs and talked. Sue and Martha went to church, but they didn't seem as strict or covenantal as Allan and me. They went to Disney as a family and talked about movies. Homeschooling had all kinds and this was the livelier side of the same group that held the Smalls.

"Did you hear about Karen Lucas at First Baptist?" Martha said. Gossip from the big church still got around. I remembered the Lucases were Sunday School teachers. Role models.

"She went crazy," Martha said. "Went Rollerblading through her neighborhood naked as a jaybird. Titties swinging in the wind."

"During the hurricane?" I said.

"Yep," Sue said. "Jeanne. She couldn't take it anymore."

"Storms drive us all crazy," said Martha. "But what makes a good Christian woman do something like that?"

I knew what would trigger a smiling Christian woman into streaking through a storm on roller skates. Debi called it *giving in to the 40,000 thoughts*. Allowing our anxieties and hormones to rule instead of our husbands.

But maybe she was wrong. Maybe 40,000 anxious thoughts meant something was off about that man. I bit the thought away, unwilling to face the consequences of arguing about the Pearls.

I drove to my final Orlando midwife appointment after Frances swept through. The orange groves of Central Florida were gone, the fields scarred and stripped bare. I drove past acres and acres of pine trees snapped in half, their broken splintered fingers grasping toward the sky for salvation.

Jo made a lunch of creamy chicken enchiladas. We rocked on her porch and hung out as old friends for hours after my appointment needs were met. I'd gained no weight, but my blood pressure was good, and I was four centimeters dilated. I still had a few weeks to go. Her assistant, Mary Ann, would come over and do my home visit next week to make sure everything was in place.

"The insurance company says it will only pay two thousand dollars. Allan asked if you could adjust your rate to that so that it won't cost us out of pocket."

"But my fee is twenty-five hundred," she said.

"I know. I feel horrible about this. He really doesn't want to pay the remainder."

"Tia, I have to pay Mary Ann from that remainder. The insurance payment is already a discount. That's supposed to cover all of your prenatal care, and trust me: it doesn't come close."

I swallowed hot dread. I knew Allan was impassible. And if I pushed, he'd make me have this baby in the emergency room, at the mercy of whatever doctor was on staff at that hour. This wasn't fair to Jo. She deserved to be paid. My eyes throbbed, and my vision was swathed in colored stars.

"Look," she said. "Lie down. I can tell this is stressing you out."

"I'll get you paid. I'll figure it out."

"I believe you. Let's focus on your health for now. I wonder if this fear you have of delivering alone is actually a reminder of your own strength." Jo was pushing back at my panic, refusing to pet it. "Women do sometimes catch their own babies. They have since the beginning of time. Deep down, you must know that you can do it if you have to. The point is, Tia, you're strong. You've done this before. Your body knows what to do. You can trust that. You can trust yourself."

When I got home, Allan wouldn't make eye contact as I recounted my visit with Jo and her encouraging words about how even if I was alone, the birth would be okay. The tension increased all evening long, through dinner and family worship time. He grew agitated by something he didn't want to talk about. As we got ready for bed he spit reminders at me.

"Don't even think about leaving me, Tia. I'll take those kids. I'll make it so you'll never see them again. Do you understand me?"

I swallowed and stared at the wall, keeping my back to him. "Yes, my lord."

Discipline was the line I'd crossed that I couldn't come back from without losing them. The kids had no idea of my life behind closed doors, and it had to stay that way. We had to stay. I had to thrust my roots in deeper and find a way to remain standing through the storm.

This required not letting Jo see bruises. Not allowing myself to labor unattended around the kids. Coming up with five hundred dollars on my own to keep everyone happy. I had to keep going, so damn sad about it or not, because it was my body covering our cracks.

The baby came in a slow rush. I wanted Allan to go away. I didn't want him to touch me as I rocked and swayed this child through my back, through my hips. He was bigger than the others, I could tell. He was not sliding into the birth canal as much as he was incrementally plugging it like a solid cork stops wine inside the bottle.

The only way to keep Allan off me was to tell the women I wanted to be alone, which meant they stayed off me as well. The two of them sat under the magnolia tree, allowing me to labor on my own in the house.

But I craved their hands and their steady voices and longed to be outside with them, hugging that tree and squatting through the contractions. Instead, I lost myself inside Mindy Smith's lilting album of love and strain near the breaking point. I danced to the edge and then felt pulled back in, holding on for just one moment more, and then another, and another.

Six hours later, I was fully dilated. And then, I pushed for four hours, gasping at the solidity of his body, at the effort it took to writhe in tandem with him inside me.

I crawled on all fours in the water, groaning ancient sounds embedded with more than mere pain. Jo and Allan refilled the pool with pots warmed on the stove. On breaks to walk around, I pressed against the wall, pleading for the station count to advance, for his head to come closer to crowning, or the ring of fire to come.

The fire always comes. My giant baby finally emerged into the water. Amniotic fluid rushed out from behind him, uncorked. There was blood, and the purple-white cord, and then his protesting wail. His head was round and redheaded.

Jo guessed him to be ten pounds, and Mary Ann laughed in agreement, no betting before weighing this time.

I'd delivered my fifth baby. I lived in a five-child house. I felt complete, and at the end of something, and a current of deep knowledge surged through me. Whatever came next, this would be the last baby. I would not have to do what I'd just done ever again. I was done.

We named him Gavin and the midwives went home.

Allan said he needed to sleep, so I was on my own for nighttime feeding. Gavin nursed for twelve hours and my head jerked to stay awake.

The next day, Mom dropped off William, Katie, and Liam. Mary Ann called to check on my postpartum progress, my bleeding, how nursing was going. "And I do need you to pay us that money, Tia. We attended your birth in good faith that you were going to be making that up when you could."

I started to panic, feeling like I was being pushed out of bed. I couldn't fight with Allan or take discipline while recovering from birth. I couldn't bear defrauding my midwives.

"I don't have that money," I cried. "Allan won't let me pay you."

Mary Ann sighed. "Please don't cry," she said, her voice cold and calm. "We don't need you getting sick right after having a baby." Her words stuck in my mind. Sick from crying? Could I get physically ill from emotional distress? But at the moment, I ignored her and cried harder.

"I'm so sorry! I can't even work for it right now. You have no idea what will happen to me if I take it out of our accounts! You have no idea," I sobbed.

"Shh. Calm down. We can talk about it later, maybe at your two-week appointment. Just concentrate on the baby, on healing, on making good milk. It will be alright."

But it wasn't alright. Allan didn't let me pay, and he didn't let me go to my follow-up appointment either. "You don't need those witches," he said. Mary Ann let it drop, and Jo never spoke to me again.

I registered losing Jo as a casualty of war. A blinking loss into the horizon of bereft acceptance but also confirmation that I was done having babies. I could not imagine having a baby without her and now she was gone—so I could not have another baby.

Allan knew Jo had become dangerous, so he created a situation that would break our bond, and it reinforced the lesson I'd learned with Michael: women having friendships that supported them first as people, with any role they filled relegated to a secondary interest, was a threat. Jo saw through the bullshit too and I'd probably offered her a lot of it, always protecting my family's image over being honest with her, while clearly writhing in enough dysfunction to cause a friend worry.

If I'd told Jo, "He'll spank me if I pay you," she would've helped me escape. Just like if I'd told Mom, "I can't do it anymore because he hits me." Until or unless I was willing to truly cross the ice to safety, the casualties would pile up.

Mentors were allowed. Judith Small was to me what Jo or Hannah or even Marci never would be: a fundamentalist who touted the purity of an idea over the human need of a friend. As Clarasmommy, I'd ranted on Trapdoor about putting ideas before people—it was a safe place to explore concepts I'd never utter aloud in my life as Tia. Trapdoor and the topics we studied there taught me women supporting women led to ideas. To underground networks and whispers that led to freedom and change. Women supporting women looked like phone-chains and tunnels and "you can stay with me" and "you're stronger than you realize."

I'd noticed the patriarchs sabotaged that support—or forbade or denied it—sometimes through the voices of other women, because the wives needed to remain small, isolated, and alone. Without the service of submissive women, the whole patriarchy would fall. Children would go astray. Western civilization would go to ruin. Young Christian wives trusted the voices of older-women mentors, even when the advice they gave led to more abuse and pain. I knew because I was one.

The books on my shelf taught that wives were homemakers and should beware of friendships or anything that took their attention away from their husband and hearth. Wives must stay busy serving.

I threw myself into our days. Moving was strength. Moving was healing. And there was plenty to do home alone with four children.

Katie, deeply enamored with her living baby doll of a brother, learned how to change his pinned cloth diaper and keep him for an hour in the morning while I got a little more sleep. But as much as I needed her help, it bothered me to ask it of her.

She was seven. I understood now why mothers trained their daughters to be keepers of the home. They needed their help because they needed help. A daughter would have to do. But I didn't like how it felt to lean on her this way. It took from her childhood to para-mother her brother. She was still little—and needed to be able to put down the baby doll and go play with something else.

Anna Small had done that from the time she was Katie's age. She'd been the voice in the nursing room as a teenager, while her mother returned to service. She'd been unavailable as a babysitter for hire because her mother needed her at home. And now she was Anna Tinker with nearly as many children as I had in half the years. Every ten months she got pregnant. If she had ever dreamed about becoming something other than a wife and mother, it would have evaporated long before dawn.

Years later I'd learn there was a word for this practice—"parentification." It means giving a child adult responsibility that isn't age appropriate. And while they're charged with more than their small hearts, minds, and bodies can handle, their own needs are neglected. But at the time, even without knowing what to call it, resistance wedged into me like a seed. The mother I wanted to be—responsive, attentive, kind—and the protector I promised to be was at odds with relying on my seven-year-old for childcare while I slept.

The honest truth was I couldn't do this all on my own. If I left Allan, the kids would be ruined, and I'd go to hell. But if I stayed, they'd become like me. And if I stayed, I allowed huge gaps I was beginning to recognize widen and thrive. I pleaded with the silent sky for a way to get out of this mess. There was no use talking this out with Allan. He had his eye on deeper theology.

"We are no longer going to be Christmas-keepers," he said one day. "Enjoy that tree while you can because this is your last one. Tell your family. We are no longer holding one sabbath day higher than the rest of the week."

This was part of his new covenantal theology. While I was busy with the baby and lost in my own world with the kids, he'd been studying the Protestant Reformation and the Puritans.

"Christmas is our favorite holiday," I begged. "It's a huge deal in my family. I can't just tell them we aren't doing it anymore."

"Find a way to say it, Tia, because we are abstaining as of next year. Keeping Christmas is over."

His other new beef was the war. As the conflict with Iraq intensified, he brewed fears he'd be reactivated as a reservist. At work, his boss wondered what kind of idiot could be so unpatriotic and un-American that he would say anything against the war on terrorism.

The Christians we knew were angry about the burkas we saw on the news. It was un-Christian, they said, to force women to be invisible and uniform. But I silently laughed at that. American Christians had burkas too. I wore one. The denim jumper *was* the American burka.

Dinner became story time about terse exchanges with his coworkers. It was always something. Allan wanted a promotion to sales, and he pressed to be considered for a territory that was opening soon in northern Mississippi.

"I could put you and the kids out in the country, out in the woods, and I could drive my sales territory. We'll make much better money with fewer threats to our freedom."

But his boss refused to promote Allan. He said he was too black-and-white for sales.

He got fired on a Monday.

He'd punched his boss in the office, in the foyer where they received guests. He should've been arrested, but I knew his boss was trying to be kind to the kids and me, out of pity. You can't find a good job if you've punched your boss and lost his nine-year reference. We had one paycheck coming, with no severance.

On Tuesday, Allan told me to get the house ready to sell and make arrangements with friends of ours to live in Tennessee while he looked for a job.

"Why Tennessee?" I asked. The world felt like it was spinning.

"You'll like it there. Four seasons."

But his specificity shone like neon. I asked again.

"The church I want us to join is there. It's covenantal and Reformed. The entire congregation homeschools their kids. They offer paedocommunion and paedobaptism. The men are Heads of their Households. The women submit. You're going to like it there."

The map of his unplottable motives revealed the path ahead.

On Friday, we listed the house. She said there was a housing bubble in Florida, and we'd make a considerable profit. We listed it for fifty thousand more than we'd paid just three years before.

On Saturday, he left for Tennessee.

On Tuesday, we got the winning offer.

Three weeks later, we'd signed, deposited the check, and loaded Dad's trailers for our move north. There wasn't any time to think about why a thing was the way it was—only the time it took to do it. I was Allan's helpmeet, not his conscience, and it was my job to cheer him on.

Covenant

HE'S DONE A LOUSY JOB OF PICKING THINGS OUT ON HIS OWN, THE voice inside me said. We pulled into Knoxville on I'll Kill Ya Highway. It's actually Alcoa Highway, but it was called that because so many people died on the snakelike downhill. The apartment Allan chose was on the hill.

Our two-bedroom apartment was a thousand square feet, on the third floor, at the top of a steep hill my mother immediately knew would ice over solid in the winter.

"Where in the heck did he find this place," she said, not really asking.

We stood in white rooms with mushroom-brown carpet and absorbed the new reality. The kitchen window offered a view of azure ripples, the ample flanks of the Blue Ridge Mountains calling from the horizon.

"I guess we'd better get to work," Mom said, and together we unpacked a four-bedroom house into a two-bedroom box.

They treated us to barbecue before leaving. I sensed Dad had the same hesitation he'd shown at the wedding. His eyes said, "Are you sure you want to do this?" But I was too far in now; you can't be a runaway bride nine years and five children in. When they drove away and left me there, I could tell there was more than *we'll miss you* on their minds.

We had a Saturday to ourselves, and then it was time to see the church that drew him here. I'd unpacked the Sunday clothes, the hairbrushes, Katie's Mary Jane shoes. On the drive over the long Tennessee River bridge, I wondered what the other women were like, and what kinds of groups and ministries they had, like a book club or Bible study.

Allan described Pastor La Touche as classical and intelligent, with a taste for tailored, vintage suits and antique trains. His wife, Veronica, was an artist from South Africa. They were part of the Covenant Reformed Evangelical Church, which had split from the Presbyterian Church in America (PCA) along with Doug Wilson and R. C. Sproul Jr., who pastored Saint Peter Presbyterian in Bristol.

The congregation met in the chapel on the campus of a Seventh Day Adventist mental health sanitarium, in the hills of West Knoxville, on the wealthy side of town. Allan pulled the van into a parking lot full of vans just like it, with families just like ours filing into church. Girls in long dresses, boys in short-sleeved dress shirts and khakis. We looked different and uniform all at once.

Our family stepped into the dimly lit sanctuary. High wooden beams and stained glass windows felt very different than the large theatrical auditorium with TV lights I'd entered at William's age. I wondered what he was thinking, and if this move out of state felt to him the way Michigan had felt like fallen dominoes to me.

The congregation sang familiar Presbyterian hymns from the hymnal—all the verses for "Be Thou My Vision," and "Come, Thou Long Expected Jesus," and then from the printout in the bulletin, "As the Deer Panteth."

As the deer pants for the water,
So my soul longs after you.
You alone are my heart's desire
And I long to worship you.
You alone are my strength, my shield,
To you alone, may my spirit yield. . . .

Jesus was always a metaphor: a lover, food, water we thirsted for. No wonder we wouldn't know Him on the street.

A boy of about fourteen played the cello on the stage next to a girl on the violin. Their mother played the piano. Families sat together in each row, with the men on the aisle, their wives beside them, and their children down the row as far as each family's fertility had provided.

Dudley La Touche covered his tailored suit with a white robe. The wool of his trousers stuck out at the bottom, and the blousy sleeves cuffed pale hands at the wrists. He stood to lead us in prayer. He seemed keen on his diction, volume, and oration skills.

At his "amen," I rose with the baby and the diaper bag to go to the nursing room in the back. I could still hear the sermon because they piped it through a speaker into the darkened room.

The pastor opened with a story about Jehovah's Witnesses who come around the neighborhood and how they try to convince you that Jesus is not God.

"A JW told me, 'We spend five nights of the week studying the Bible, studying that Jesus is not God.' The JWs say that! They don't believe in the incarnation. They don't believe that God could be anything other than monistic, the modern invention of the Arian heresy. They are delusional!"

La Touche's voice was emphatic and crisp, with sarcasm, wit, and a Southern drawl sneaking in where it could. I got the feeling he was sharing with us an inside joke, and if we laughed when he laughed, we were in. But on Trapdoor, we shared about listening to people tell us for themselves what their beliefs were, and laughing at people behind their backs at church felt as nauseating as it did back when the pastors at First Baptist poked at segregation.

There was one other mother with me. She introduced herself as Rafaela. Young and model-pretty, with gentle manners and a smiling voice, she said, "Welcome." I felt old enough to be her mother, even though there were probably only eight or so years between us. She did not want to talk.

"My husband encourages me to follow the sermon," she said.

So we nursed with silence between us, as La Touche's voice over the speaker cackled about poor sinners who didn't know how right we were. Perhaps they were predestined to hell, perhaps they craved the Lord's table. If they did, they'd find us and not the other way around. We fulfilled the Great Commission by bearing a quiverful. We let our families be the light unto the world.

After the sermon, the families approached the front of the church as households. There was no final invitation or altar call, like in Baptist churches, because we were God's elect. Nobody here was lost. Fathers led their families to the front, aisle by aisle, while the piano played.

A white-clothed table held chunks of fresh bread and goblets of wine. This was no Southern Baptist Communion with dry cracker crumbs and plastic cups of Welch's. Babes in arms gulped and laughed.

"The gifts of God!" Pastor La Touche said.

Allan beamed. Here was the table where he wanted to feast. Here was the culmination of his faith.

The pastor walked to the back of the church where he passed out candy to all the children who'd been quiet throughout the service. Dappled sunshine broke through the leaves of the changing trees. Husbands and wives approached us to welcome us. "It's good to finally meet Allan's wife," they said.

William ran around with some boys his age, and at some point removed his shoes to climb to the top of the flagpole with his hands and feet, like a monkey. Everyone laughed.

"I'm glad to see you haven't raised a weak, frightful boy, Allan." Pastor La Touche clapped Allan on the back. Veronica smiled with sparkling doe-eyes, kindly. Our boy was a "real boy" and "all boy" and had just proven that to the whole congregation.

But I exhaled, relieved a church of covenanters didn't seem so bad. Theology solved, I relaxed knowing I could relate to these women over homekeeping and homeschooling. We'd have plenty to talk about.

Allan's new job selling air tubing required traveling across state from machine shop to shop, trying to nudge out competing brands and existing relationships with established salesmen. The job was entirely commissioned with no salary, and he wouldn't get a check until he made up the loss created by the previous employee. So, we were going to live on our savings in the meantime.

His schedule also meant I'd have a lot of time on my own. And since Allan had a company truck, I now had the minivan and could take the kids out.

My first stop was the Great Smoky Mountains visitor center, followed by the redbrick Blount County Library, complete with a clock tower and glass rotunda. We strolled through the meandering Greenbelt Park shaded by ginkgo and sycamore and took our first field trip to the Sam Houston Schoolhouse. I found u-pick farms for juicy blueberries fat and warm in the Tennessee sun and a week later, an orchard for speckled red apples. We came home to the small apartment tired and quiet, with baskets full of books and fruit.

On Monday, we joined the homeschooling co-op, a loosely defined group of Christian mothers from all kinds of churches who got together to teach literature, history, geography, and science. On Tuesday, we joined Cub Scouts and American Heritage Girls. Wednesday, we went hiking in Cades Cove, Gavin strapped to me in the Maya wrap and the other three running ahead over rocks and trees. We saw kestrels, phoebes, and crows, meadows, mountains, and streams.

In the woods, spires of goldenrod reminded me of roaming the pastures in Michigan. The canopy of trees punctuated with white sunlight rustled something in my heart, the way a breeze disturbs an old pile of leaves. *Something is right here,* I thought.

The domino of a church friend.

Leah and her husband, Mike, had moved to Tennessee for a Covenant church as well, kindred thrifters from someplace else. Leah shared she also wanted a woman's Bible study or book group, but she'd been cautioned to stop asking.

"The elders feel that women getting together is dangerous, because of our propensity to stray from spiritual topics into gossip when unattended by a head of household."

I remembered what Judith said in a Character Study once. Tale-bearing was one of the little foxes that ruined the vine. Women lacked discernment and hid sin on their lips; we needed men to keep us in line.

So, Leah and I got together on our own and skipped the idea of a group. We schlepped our kids from pumpkin patch to picnic playground, canning jellies at each other's homes, and sharing recipes for homeopathic remedies. On Sundays, we played it down, both of us aware not to flaunt any close bond.

Because Allan demonstrated an understanding of covenant theology and Headship of his home, Pastor La Touche and the elders, Watson and Hyde, were ready to extend their offer within a few weeks' time.

"I'll caution you, Tia," Pastor La Touche said, licking his pink lips. "Covenantal membership is something we take very seriously. It's easy to come to the Lord's table and join with us. It's not so easy to leave."

I wondered why he addressed me. Allan wanted a covenant bond. He said it was accountability and submission to God. My opinion didn't matter.

We joined and signed our names into the registry of the church with a contract that specified the terms of our membership: how we promised to conduct ourselves as a household and under what specific terms we'd be allowed to leave.

"That day will never come," Allan said, shining with enthusiasm.

"Your family is under our authority now," said one of the men. "With patriarchy comes hierarchy."

"Thank God!" Allan exclaimed. The men all clapped each other on the back and said to give all glory to the Lord.

I was glad when Sundays were over. We'd worshiped, fellowshipped, and napped. On Mondays Allan left for work and I could get back to what I was doing.

On Trapdoor, we argued about homosexual union. I was glad we didn't call them sodomites, the way the Pearls did in their book. It seemed to me that if someone like Michael wanted to get married to someone who loved him, that would be a good thing. It was at least his own business. But our worldviews clashed and some of the women were as vitriolic as any Calvinist I knew. Conversations unraveled and topics stalled. I needed somewhere to go online when Trapdoor was having a bad day.

I had an idea. Our families wanted updates. My grandma missed her grands. Emailing them all separately was getting long. But there was a new thing called a weblog that anyone could do, even if you didn't have your own website like Doug's blog on Vision Forum. I entered Blogspot.com and opened an account.

I titled it Living Deliberately, from our favorite Thoreau quote, and because that's what I'd decided I was doing here. I'd determined to make Tennessee an adventure for the kids, a mountainous discovery of stories and starlight in the wonder of an ordinary day. Within minutes I had posts up about our orchard visits and field trips. Then I emailed anyone who got my Christmas cards the link.

We measured time in Sundays. Morning service, potluck dinner on the grounds, late afternoon Psalm sings. Sometimes we spent the whole Lord's Day together as a church family. The other women didn't spend their weeks at co-op, Scouts, and field trips, and I didn't talk about Trapdoor or time when we conversed briefly after church.

Reformation Day approached and plans needed to be made for costumes and field games. Golden late-autumn sunshine shone through trees covered in yellow leaves. Blackbirds cawed from the heights. Rafaela had a question about teething because her baby was waking to nurse more often at night and she had another one on the way.

She wrapped the blanket around her baby against the bright cold, as did I mine. She looked ashen, too worn out to be pregnant and nursing successfully, and I suggested weaning her son so that the calories could be spared for the baby. Our husbands joined us then, talking about guns and the shooting range.

Ryan, her husband, put his arm around her shoulders. "Well, it's time we should be getting home. Mommy's getting a spanking."

His words slammed into me like a punch and my jaw dropped slack before I caught my reaction and swallowed it down. Had he just said that out loud?

Ryan winked at Allan, who laughed and put an arm around my shoulders as well. "H-o-H duties call."

Allan turned my stiffened body toward the car. *Of course.* He'd wanted a covenant Phillips-Wilson-Sproul-Pearl kind of church for a reason. How could I have been so blind?

Even as I asked it, I knew that out of sight was out of mind. This was the reason why mainstream Christians didn't think the Duggars' lifestyle was anything but charming. Maybe a little weird, but to each their own. And why mainstream evangelicals wouldn't guess zealous Presbyterians were raising future politicians with dominionist theology. Even I, who knew the underbelly of what popular theologians taught but rarely spelled out in print, had convinced myself that this covenant fellowship was just agrarian, wholesome devotion. And I trembled from the reminder of how the patriarchs held control. It was hiding right in front of me all along.

As it happened, Allan was gone too much and the apartment too small for him to follow up with his HoH responsibilities, that afternoon or in the weeks and months that followed. Logistics offered reprieve and I spent more time without him than with him home. I used the extra time to expand my writing.

Language poured out of me the way water comes from a spring. Pastor La Touche talked about that sometimes, about how giftedness came naturally, because it was put there for the Lord's pleasure. His favorite movie was *Chariots of Fire,* and he mentioned the foot race often in sermons. "And when I run, I feel His pleasure," Eric Liddell says in the film. Pastor La Touche didn't talk about this concerning a woman's giftedness, only a man's, because a woman's role was in supporting her husband in the pursuit of his dreams, not chasing her own.

So, I kept my blog family-centered. I bought a key chain digital camera and uploaded photos of the kids. I wrote about poetry and prayer, recipes and reflections on art, local food, and favorite songs. I told my new friends at co-op about it and several of them started their own as well. This created a blogroll in the sidebar and we checked in with each other's blogs every day to see if there was something new. The need for new content gave me an idea: What if I started posting book reviews?

I started with the easy ones—titles we discussed on Trapdoor like *Girl with a Pearl Earring* and *Pride and Prejudice.* Then one day I turned on Oprah. The topic was how to stay in shape throughout motherhood. There was a woman in the audience—tall, blond, fit—who said she had ten children. Oprah, amazed at how great this woman seemed to juggle everything, called her "unforgettable." Her name was Kathryn Sansone and her book, *Woman First, Family Always,* was a bestseller. I decided to buy it for a review.

Her book activated a fire within me, setting off a cacophony of judgment tangled with envy, a nerve I couldn't silence. She wrote about prioritizing *her* needs, using baby formula and scheduling workouts, while grabbing quick naps in the car. I'd never heard a mother talk about motherhood while considering anyone but the baby, the father, and the family. Her refusal to be selfless landed like blasphemy—but it wasn't that I envied a life so exhausted that I napped while waiting at the bank. It was the idea that JOY (Jesus, Others, You) wasn't the only way to live.

"Your swing post-baby isn't SUPPOSED to look like your swing pre-baby," I wrote, fingers furiously stabbing the keyboard. "I'm still operating under the (mis)conception that motherhood often means 'others first.' Isn't that one of the great mysteries of motherhood? You put the child's need before your own OFTEN. That doesn't mean you neglect yourself, but 'self' isn't the core of the decision process."

In part two of the review, after I'd finished reading it, my post leveraged the superiority of sadness. "Yes, I admit to strong envy of her mudroom, where each child has a cubby with their photo, seasonal sports equipment, and daily needs all neatly hung in a row! But that doesn't make this book a 'word of wisdom I can use in my down times.'"

I cried where Sansone wrote she'd never rocked a baby to sleep. I couldn't imagine doing motherhood without the rituals that kept me going—and I didn't know how to appreciate what I couldn't imagine. So, I judged her instead.

Monica's developer husband, Jake, called one night and taught me to monitor my site analytics. Traffic surged ten thousand, then twenty thousand and more, until my Living Deliberately blog of recipes, book reviews, and reflections was averaging eighty thousand hits per day. "You've discovered the magic of keywords, Tia," Jake said. Words like "Oprah" and book titles helped readers find me in the search engine. "You seem to have a knack for it," he said.

As comments increased, so did my posting frequency, and I had a new list of online friends and fellow bloggers I checked in with every day. I was stunned to see the seed of my words germinate this way.

The elders wanted a word.

It was because, in my enthusiasm over a little success, I'd blurred the careful line I knew from experience to hold: when there's more to life than church, keep it to yourself. Christians don't understand outside-world priorities. I was splitting into two lives again and I'd failed to keep my two Tias separate.

What happened was that I'd spoken with Mrs. Watson at the latest Psalm sing, the two of us setting out trays of sandwiches for the children, and I'd told her about my blog. I liked Mrs. Watson and her gentle cheer. I wanted to be her friend. But her husband gave me the chills.

Elder Watson seemed to sweat rage. On his antiperspirant surface, he presented as a rugged Scout leader and successful business executive. He wore cuff links and carefully oiled his hair so that nothing was ever out of place.

His militarized children were as scrubbed and orderly as if they'd stepped straight out of a Vision Forum catalog. But I sensed a thin veneer over teeming emotion, fire-hot and clammy. And what tipped his mood most was the sound of a woman's voice speaking before she was spoken to.

I could tell right away that Watson didn't like me. He eyed me the way a cowboy circles a wild mare whose independence threatens his dominion. I felt like he knew things about me he shouldn't have known, intimate and private. And while Watson seldom spoke to me directly, I could tell the side of his face paid attention when I spoke to his wife.

"How did you even know how to do that?" She pulled stacks of plates from her sideboard for our refreshments.

"It's easy. Blogspot walks you through the steps. Then you just write when you want to."

"Oh, interesting!" She seemed as fascinated and awed as if I'd just told her I'd figured out how to land on the moon. "And how do you come up with things to write? And the time for it?"

"I write during nap time. And for the content, I'm mostly just reporting to family out of state what we're up to, so they can feel more involved."

"Oh, I see. So, it's a family thing." She smiled. "That makes sense."

Mike told Leah he'd overheard a conversation between Elders Watson and Hyde. Watson was indignant that my blog was "absolutely not just a family thing." He said I had a voice that overrode the authority of my husband by representing us in my own words. Elder Hyde, older and kindlier, suggested Watson give me some time to settle in. "She's away from her family and they've been through a major life change. Perhaps we mention it to Allan in passing."

"Maybe you should take a break," Leah told me.

But I ignored them all. *Go ahead and disapprove,* I thought, digging in. I wasn't willing to give up writing again. And if I had two Tias within me, I knew I'd also chosen a favorite. I liked writer-Tia way more than church-Tia.

Reformation Day came and went—"Lutheresque" beverages and bobbing for apples, archery and field races in Puritan costumes. Allan took a second job working at UPS to help pay bills. The house money was running out. We moved into a small rental house in the center of town with a big sloping back-yard where the kids could play. Allan left at 3 A.M. and I didn't see him again until seven at night. I filled the hours without him embracing our life in the mountains, charting the moon and the seasons, filling bags with library books, and spending lots of time with co-op friends.

One Sunday in January, the elders called Allan for a meeting over dinner. When he got home, he sat on the edge of the bed and summarized while I put away stacks of clean clothes.

"The elders and deacons read your blog," Allan said.

"Good," I said. "Maybe they'll be reassured that it's not worth getting up-set about."

"No, Watson feels strongly about two things: you are out of the house too much and your writing should be in my name."

"But you aren't the writer!"

"I'm your authority and the head of my household. Your blog is speak-ing for our house. You are out of line representing us without my approval."

"Tell me one thing I've written you have a problem with, Allan." It was unlike me to push back, but I kept going, my voice suddenly strong. I wanted the right to my words. This was my solo creation, from my hands and from my mind. I stood straighter, my spine like a rod, my toes digging into the ground.

Allan looked down and away with a sigh. "I can't. I don't read it."

"Exactly. I'm writing about our homeschooling trips—my observations—and housewives read it. What's Watson so curious about, anyway, that he'd read my little-old-lady blog every single day?"

"He's watching over the flock, Tia. It's his calling."

"Whatever. The blog is mine, and I'm not breaking any rules." I kept my body moving, anxiety flowing through me like electricity on a wire.

"You are if I forbid you to write it any longer." He sizzle-whispered the dare.

But instead of heart-stopping fear, my body released a surge and I spit the facts as they sparkled before me. "Then you'd better have an answer ready for Grandma. Because there's going to be a family uprising if the blog just dis-appears."

He was silent at that. He had appearances to maintain with my family. There was a lot of our truth he wanted to keep from them. And, I suddenly realized: visibility meant safety. *Stay where I can see you,* Mom used to say.

I stared at Allan, daring him to try taking this away from me. He looked old, heavier and thicker than he had when we were young, like cold chowder. Working two jobs was taking a toll on him, and his skin was gray and pale from a lack of sleep and sunshine. He was overdue for a haircut, but I gave bad ones, and he refused to go to a barber because of the cost. He was thirty-two going on fifty-two.

"What if you just run your posts by me," he said, defeated. "So I can tell the elders your writing is under my supervision."

I chewed my lip. "You're rarely home and I post every day. What if there's no time for that?"

He sighed. "Just do the best you can, Tia." He got up to shower.

Winning didn't feel like having won. At the end of his religious quest for covenantal belonging, Allan appeared more whipped and exhausted than triumphant patriarch, without spark or fight, without spirit or zeal. His shoulders bent with burden and regret, like an ox caught belly-deep in mud.

Did that mean I was now at the plow? If it did, this wasn't the direction I wanted for us. Maybe it wasn't even the field. Wives were supposed to support their husbands' vision, but if Allan was breaking and I had the power to change things, I didn't want to be a patriarch's wife. I wanted what I'd always wanted: to be an artist mother writer hiker friend.

I wondered if there was a way out for us, a way back to recalibrate, a way to make this hard road work for us. I vowed to work harder to keep my two worlds separate. I didn't want to have to choose this time.

Part Four

———

SHE SHOULD GO

Pastoral

AN UNATTENDED WIFE IS A PROBLEM. BY REFUSING TO FOLLOW
the God-rules, I'd undoubtedly sin more and run my family into trouble. My
haughty spirit and rebellious words would re-crucify Jesus. Everyone around me
would suffer until I succeeded in pulling us toward hell. So went the sermons
without mentioning anyone by name. The pastor urged the patriarchs to keep
their wives in line. I sat in church knowing exactly who he was talking about.

The covenanters upped their game.

Suddenly, the wives reached out, inviting the kids and me over for playdates.
And while I was skeptical and socially unsure, my children weren't. William
traipsed through the fields with the elders' sons and Katie played house with
their daughters. They loved their new friends and feeling accepted, even though
I knew there was a directive and agenda behind the precipitous attention. I
forgot to tell them not to talk about Harry Potter with their church friends
and not to mention the library. I didn't warn them about how to live two lives.

I tried asking the mothers what they were reading and what ideas they
were thinking about but the only answers I got back involved menu options
for the next Psalm sing, courtship, or homeschooling curricula. That I was
their project and assigned task hung in air that never left the room. The at-
mosphere clouded with an awkward fog of inequality and superiority, like a
perfume I couldn't name. And when their efforts failed to decrease my posting frequency, Watson shifted tactics.

"What you need, Allan, is better employment. One job."

Having Allan home more often would offer better oversight. He wouldn't be too exhausted to monitor my behavior. He'd have the energy to properly run his household and hold accountable those out of line.

"Why does Watson care so much?" I laughed when Leah and I talked about it. We were on my porch swing. Screams of happy adventure sounded from the backyard and into the woods. "I've never had a church involve itself so closely in the inner workings of a family. Allan *is* tired. But honestly, him being busy has helped our marriage a ton." A year had passed without any physical violence and whether that was due to exhaustion or close quarters or both, I was grateful.

"When Mike needed work, Elder Watson helped him too. Now we're home together every day. I think it keeps Mike accountable through his depression. I guess that's part of what makes us a covenantal congregation. We are accountable to one another in all ways."

"But the pay, Leah . . . they don't pay you guys squat."

"True. They give us enough to get by and they provided the house. There's no way we could save anything up, though, like if we wanted to move away."

"Plus, you have to tithe part of it back to them," I said. "The only job Watson recommended is with Deacon Sands, way out in the Cumberland Mountains."

"Would Allan commute so you can stay here?"

"That's what I want. It would be an hour each way. That's pretty typical in Jacksonville, and he's been driving all day everywhere, so he should be used to it. But Watson said we should work with Deacon Sands's father, who's a Realtor, and try to find a place up there."

"Then, it would be an hour to church?"

"Yes, and an hour anytime I wanted to come into town for a homeschool co-op or to shop or anything we do now."

We rocked for a few minutes, processing the swap and isolation. Then, Leah turned and looked me hard in the eye. "Promise me you won't move off-grid, Tia. We tried that once. It's break-you hard and there's no one coming in an emergency." Her directness felt like she'd just broken the fourth wall, the way an actor on stage breaks away from the dream of the story to address the audience. Years later I'd look back on this moment and count it as one of the times women looked out for each other, going along with the patriarchal game to a point, but breaking rank in hours of real danger. I'd seen Jo and Tina both do it as midwives.

I promised, remembering the near-move to the Canadian Rockies, to echoes and rattlesnakes and isolation. Friends didn't let friends go die off-grid. *Stay where I can see you.*

But even if the location was safe, I didn't want to move again—none of us did. I told Allan, and the kids told Allan, and none of it mattered. Allan and the elders decided for us. So, Leah watched my children, and Allan and I piled into the Realtor's Buick for the drive out to the tiny coal-mining town named for the Reformation itself: Lutherville, Tennessee.

Lutherville had two stoplights, a courthouse with a clock tower, and a boarded-up Main Street. There were two fast-food restaurants, a school, and the state prison. I counted eleven small churches. The largest of them was the Lutheran church, brick and old looking. The trees seemed to hang with shadows.

The Realtor said, "Now watch. Someday a body will emerge from the bushes. It'll just walk on out, and you'll have no idea where it comes from. Take a look at their hands, how the palms and the backs of their hands are the same color. Mullunjians, they're called. Mullatoes and Indians, mixed up like." The dignified Realtor had slipped into a backwoods accent. "They come down off the mountain a few times a year for supplies. Then they disappear again into the trees and mist. No one even knows how many of 'em are up there."

The properties he had to show us were all very different, because there wasn't much for sale. Million-dollar farms and decades-old trailers flanked split-level ranch homes and the occasional brick bungalow. People didn't move here often, the Realtor said, and they left here even less.

We toured a brand-new loft-style house with two bedrooms and a red metal roof, built as someone's vacation rental, never occupied.

An old derelict brick house that looked blown out by a meth explosion and covered in blackberry brambles. There weren't even steps from the front door on that one; once you opened the door, it was straight down into a hole. Allan, who'd gone first, nearly fell in.

And then, the Blue House. Over a hundred years old near the abandoned rail station. It stood on the corner across from a white church with a steeple, with a white picket fence, a wide front porch, and a stately maple in the yard. It looked like a dollhouse I'd once built as a child.

Allan wanted it immediately.

"But it only has two bedrooms," I argued.

"We can fix that. Look at the setting."

The church had once purchased the house as its parsonage. We wouldn't be allowed to attend there because even though it was Presbyterian, it was USA Presbyterian and had a woman preacher the locals suspected was a lesbian.

"We can restore it," Allan insisted. "She's a beauty. And look at the property."

The half-acre yard was a sloping hill nearly straight up, with black walnut trees and a gravel road circling up to homes hidden behind the trees. "We can get you goats," he said with excitement. "I'll build you a fence. Chickens too. There's room for your garden. This will be much better, Tia. I'm giving you the house of your dreams. You'll have almost no need to ever go back into town again."

There was no talking him out of it.

We moved on a rainy Saturday and the elders were right. The smaller radius of our lives solved all of Allan's problems. He no longer struggled with driving all over the state, attempting to sell scraps of hose, or being up at 3 A.M. to unload UPS planes. He had a five-minute drive to work. He could be home almost as quickly as he decided to be.

We had breakfast, lunch, and dinner together at the table.

"I want you to use the McGuffey Readers," he said.

I stopped dishing up plates of mashed potatoes, gravy, and pot roast for lunch and stared at him. "What? You mean the small books from *Little House on the Prairie*? From the 1800s?"

"They're still relevant today. They actually contain more intellectual content than that drivel you've been spending so much money on. They don't need modern books."

"McGuffey Readers are tiny, un-colorful, and dull," I said.

"You'll get used to them," he said.

He ordered the collection and left them on the table for me the following week. Each one held tiny, serious text that was above the reading level of my late-to-read children. I was bored just flipping through them. This was not the homeschool I imagined for my children.

But arguing was pointless. I tried applying my creativity and romantic, pioneer spirit instead. If children in a sod-covered lean-to on the prairie could use them, couldn't I make this appealing?

I tried. But after enough frustrated tears on the sofa, I gave up and sent the kids outside. I gave them copy work for handwriting and we reused old math books. I kept reading *The Boxcar Children* and *A Wrinkle in Time* out loud. William listened to *The Story of the World* on repeat; he couldn't get enough history. I worked the areas that felt good, that made learning come easily and naturally, all the while worried I'd get in trouble.

But instead of pressing me, Allan decided to read the McGuffey Readers with them himself. He used his extra time to get more involved in their homeschool, sometimes taking over whole subjects like math. Within weeks, he put himself in charge of their catechism, grammar, Latin, and math.

I took them hiking in the mountains and swimming in the Obed River. We put in our garden, got chickens, and acclimated to country life. Two days a week I drove them into Maryville for co-op, Scouts, American Heritage Girls, and groceries. As I wound the van through the narrow mountain roads, the views opened around us, the hills dappled with sun and the shadows of clouds. *A harmonized life,* I thought. *We're figuring it out.* The kids had an artsy parent and a serious parent—maybe two lights *could* shine.

A little dog showed up. He was red, like a fox, and didn't look like he belonged to any one breed. He assumed guard over me, standing next to me while I hung diapers on the clothesline or planted rows of potatoes. When William started Rollerblading laps on the old Main Street loop, Red Fox ran behind him, like a little friend.

After Red Fox came other hounds and feral cats, dumped on the corner of our street by country people who didn't want them. The county had no animal control, and I had nowhere to take them, so I added discount dog and cat food to my grocery list, and we started to feed them all. It wasn't long before four cats became twenty and three dogs became bitches full of puppies.

"You went over your mileage today," Allan said.

"What do you mean? I just did the groceries and co-op," I mumbled. I was in bed next to him, reading a magazine. I'd started reading *People* magazine again, to keep an eye on the outside world, and to see what movies Michael might be watching.

"I've been tracking how much that trip takes. It's fifty-one miles to Maryville. You say you go to the market in Knoxville and stop at the Kroger in Oak Ridge. But you went fifteen over. Where else did you go?"

My heart pounded, skin and bone remembering the feel of corners and floors. I slowly closed the magazine, trying to look as natural and calm as possible. "I tried a new farmers' market, and we went to the library."

"Do you swear that's all?"

"Of course. I have four children. Where do you imagine I went?"

"Don't take that tone with me, woman."

I swallowed. "I'm sorry. I'm not trying to have a tone. I didn't go anywhere else."

He glared at me. I hoped the kids were asleep and braced myself, calculating with a rapid pulse how thick the walls were in this house.

But Allan took a breath and didn't raise his arm. "See that you don't. I'm watching, even when you don't think I am. I have spies all over these hills. And there will be hell to pay if I catch you disobeying me."

"I understand."

"No, it's 'yes, my lord.' You've been getting lazy. We're going back to regular discipline and training."

I blinked and swallowed. "Yes, my lord."

As the winter progressed, the barren trees on the hills surrounding the house provided a fishbowl view of our little plot. Outside at the clothesline, I looked up to the golden squares of window light from uphill houses and realized how easily they could see me, when I could barely see them at all.

Spring freezes without firewood brought a bone chill to the house that sweaters couldn't shake. Allan didn't know how to get firewood and he wouldn't ask anyone either. I served the kids oatmeal for breakfast, soup for lunch, and hot tea with dinner. When Leah came over with her kids, I told them to layer up. She brought us a bag of extra quilts for our beds.

"There's no cold like Appalachian mountain cold," she said.

I thought about the snows Mom faced in Michigan, alone with me and Monica out on eighty acres in the deep woods. How Dad plowed his way out to the road with his tractor, ice clinging to his beard, brows, and lashes. They always said the best thing about Florida was the winters.

Maybe that's how life ground you down, one winter, one hungry moment, one tight paycheck at a time. My parents came to Florida relieved. I came crying. But at ten, what had I known about bankruptcy, blizzards, and brittle family ties? I suddenly wanted to call my mom. I wanted my dad to see this house and how we were living and come save me.

I tried praying. I logged on to Trapdoor and tried writing. I posted on the blog about our Dave Ramsey Total Money Makeover and how determined we were to pay down the debt that had risen when the savings from the Florida house ran out. Nothing brought relief or warmed the day.

The doorbell rang. Red Fox barked. William yelled from downstairs, "Mama, a man's here!"

An old farmer in a red plaid woolen coat stood on the stoop shooing cats. Clouds from his breath and smoke from his cigarette surrounded his head. I opened the door, blocking the gap with my leg so kittens couldn't dart inside. I felt embarrassed that the yard smelled like a litter box.

"Ma'am, I noticed you ain't had a plume o' smoke outta that chimney since you moved here. Ain't right for you and those babies to be so cold. I brought you some. Okay if I unload it?"

I nodded my head, dumbstruck. The pile he left seemed enormous.

"That's two full cords of dry-aged wood, ma'am: sixteen inches long, each piece. Oughta take you into late spring. If your husband wants more, tell him to ask for Muffy at work. I got friends there who know how to find me."

As William and I stacked the wood into neat rows against the shed, I thought how much my life seemed centuries old, and that it wasn't 2006 at all but actually 1886, and how in all our churches, *Little House on the Prairie* life had been the plan all along. When William asked, "Why you crying, Mama?"

I couldn't find words for the kindness of strangers, for a timeline that felt as though it moved in reverse. It seemed cruel to raise children against progress and capability, to stunt them out of the chance to live on their own terms.

If Allan was surprised to come home to a house warmed by a stove full of wood, he didn't say. He ate his plate of beans and rice, took a shower, and sat down with his pipe in the living room to read the Bible to Katie, William, and Liam while I bathed and nursed Gavin.

As I rocked my snuggly warm baby, I mulled the day and what it meant to be provided for, and what it meant to play a part in that provision. I knew I wanted more—more for me, more for my children. It felt less like discontentment and more like a call to action. But what was I willing to risk for it? And what would happen if I did? As Dad said, "Failing to plan is planning to fail." I wasn't a new graduate trying to land a husband. I was a wife experienced with biblical marriage and heartache. And I'd learned a lesson I didn't understand how to use: waiting for God wasn't just boring, it was dangerous.

Vessel

I'D STARTED TO WRESTLE. *HOW YOU LIVE YOUR DAYS IS HOW YOU live your life.* If God could see me, the way the neighbors in the hills could, what did He think about women? If all we were to do was cook, clean, and have babies, why did He go through the bother of making us smart and capable of doing so much? Why did we have names? Why couldn't I turn off my thoughts and ideas? Why couldn't I be content and simple, a blank face of utility and function? My days were all the same, rinse and repeat, and I had too much mind for the way they were spent.

"It's the curse," Leah told me one Sunday. Our kids were running over the greening spring hills dotted with early yellow daffodils, and we stood nearby, watching them and talking. "It's because of Eve's sin, and the enmity the woman has with men, the pain she has in childbirth. We're too tempted by knowledge, Tia. You have to submit yourself. You have to learn to turn away from temptation and focus on your mission in life, those babies."

"But it's not like I don't want to be a wife and mother. I'm not trying to get out of my role. I want to feel there's some value in my unique contribution, some reason why it's *me* they have and not some other mom."

"Well, I never thought of it that way," she said.

"It's almost as if I could be swapped out, Leah. Anyone could mother my children according to His wishes. Anyone could clean the house. Anyone could be me because everything that is uniquely me is choked off and shamed away."

But Leah didn't break the dream this time, she leaned into it. "You scare me when you talk like that. I hear what you're saying but trying to stand out is only going to get you in trouble. We aren't called to be individuals."

That conversation was the last one I had with her, and neither of us knew it.

"We need a closer church," Allan said. "Driving so far is unnecessary."

"But there's not a covenant church out here," I said, panicking and suddenly defensive of something I'd tried to minimize and leave. The kids had friends there. We'd adjusted to the routine of Psalm sings and Reformation Days. I dreaded more change, even if it meant getting away from the pastor's weird manners and Watson's barely bridled rage.

Nevertheless, we began visiting country churches. We started with the old brick Lutheran church in town, the largest congregation for thirty miles. Allan had an issue with the rector. "I think he's gay," he said. "I can tell that man is hiding his sexuality. He probably preys on little kids."

"Being gay doesn't mean he's a molester," I said. "They aren't the same thing."

"Bull," he said.

We tried the small Presbyterian church across from the house just because we could walk over. It was exactly like walking into the church on the *Little House* set, built at the same time and with the original wood floors and wooden pews that creaked when we filed in and sat down. The handful of white-haired congregants salivated over the hope of new members and at the sight of children.

"We might have to reinstitute Sunday School just for your family," they laughed. But a service led by a female lasted precisely one time, and Allan said we'd never darken their door again.

I blogged about our wanderings, waxing poetic about the charm of country churches, careful to wash doubts and questions with enthusiasm. I'd become the family's reporter, a sort of brand manager, and I wanted us to look good. Between the lines, in the white spaces between words, thoughts niggled at me the way an itchy tag scratches, but it would be years later in therapy before I realized the discomfort was called complicity. By spinning a pretty image, I was becoming guilty of selling the very dream I longed to escape from.

The elders called Allan after reading my posts.

"Go ahead and find a Bible-believing fellowship in keeping with our teachings, Allan," they said. "We're more than happy to transfer your name from our rolls to that of another, provided they are in alignment with our views."

But there was the rub. There was no other congregation in keeping with the views of Covenant Reformed Presbyterian, except those other Reformed churches scattered across the country. One in East Tennessee. Wilson's in Idaho. The list was growing, but it was small. They said they would tolerate a PCA congregation if that pastor would permit us all to take Communion together as a family.

There were no PCA Presbyterian churches anywhere closer than Knoxville, and to them, giving babies Communion was heresy. We had no choice but to drive in and carry on, Allan stewing all the way. The scarcity of "right" churches snagged in my mind, a gnawing whisper of blood-sugar hunger.

What was I getting from this faith? Peace, love, joy? No—that's not how I felt at church.

Reassurance of eternal security? No—I still begged God to save me anytime the intersection of death felt close.

A sense of belonging with Special Christians doing life right?

I belonged alright. I belonged too much. But what if we weren't "doing it right"?

Routine crafted a container for my doubt. I tried to diminish the importance of Sunday. "We have so much going on here at home," I said.

And that was true. The cats multiplied. New litters hit their first heat and inbred. Red Fox corralled them like a stout colonel with a monocle and declared to the other hounds that this was his territory. Most of the dogs shoved off after a day or two. But the cats remained and overran our porch, and as the spring warmed, so came fleas and the starving mews of wormy felines badly in need of a vet. One of my blog readers donated supplies. The stench of urine rose with the morning dew.

William spent hours skating in circles. Katie played dolls or forced Liam and the baby to be her pupils for her version of school. I couldn't bring myself to force her into housework and childcare or to practice being a keeper of the home. They built a treehouse at the top of our hill and gathered eggs and dressed new kittens in doll clothes.

But a shadow fell over my mind. I saw everything as through a screen that obscured clarity and beauty and light, the way my bridal veil once had. On the outside I looked the same; on the inside I was melting. Evaporating. I was becoming an interchangeable, invisible female, with no specific purpose or value except perhaps to these four children, and I'd seen enough of the world to know that if I died or went away, in time, they'd adjust to a new mother. I felt ashamed for being, for existing, for taking up air in a room better used by someone else. Was God watching? Or was this what I was to have learned all along? That dying to self required surrender to the point of being hollowed out and empty?

On rainy days, I leaned against the window and watched rivulets of water stream down the glass, reflecting fragments of the world outside—brown grass and silver skies.

Allan didn't take well to being forced into attendance. He put his foot down about the driving into town and said we wouldn't go. "We're going to home church," he announced, and the elders didn't argue. No one could dispute a father's right to worship with his family at home.

I would've felt relieved, but along with refusing to drive in for church, Allan said we had to quit Scouts, American Heritage Girls, and co-op too. "You can go out for groceries and the occasional hiking trip," he said. "Otherwise, your place is here at home and I expect you to stay here."

Here. I looked at the walls of the Blue House. Out the window at our little half acre of hill. Being commanded to stay here felt like prison, but as soon as I had the thought, I scolded myself for being ungrateful. Real prison is bars and concrete cells.

I hoped his assertiveness with the elders would help him in time. He didn't like them telling him what to do and being angry increased his rule over me. But I could see his exhaustion. Allan wasn't doing well, and it felt like for every step we took forward, we took at least three back.

One day a postcard came from Michael. He said he'd asked my parents for my address because he was moving to Massachusetts. He included his phone number. I'd only spoken to him one other time since the wedding—right after 9/11, because he lived in New York when the towers fell and, panicked he was dead, I'd gotten his number from his mom.

"I'm getting married," he said. "It's legal in Massachusetts and I hope you'll come."

It would be in October. I tried to imagine it—getting permission, traveling with four children. I dodged the question to avoid the pain. "Maybe," I said. "I'll certainly try."

We re-established a habit of talking a few times a week at nap time. Our secret felt like the first light spring clothes after a heavy-coat winter. Our friendship had been in another life, but he remembered that other Tia, the one I used to be. With him, I was her again, even if it was just for a little while on the phone. That part of me still existed because I existed in his memory.

One day he said, "You know, I reached out to you because of that photo on your blog."

I knew which one he meant. My header image was a family picture I'd taken with black-and-white film for our cards last year. I was proud of it because it showed the closest we'd come to the ideal Vision Forum family. I had on a navy jumper with a white shirt and the children wore coordinating clothes. Allan, with his beard and his arm around us, exuded authority. We matched in every way, serene and calm smiles plastered on our faces, like the Duggars. "Yeah?" I asked.

"You fucking didn't look like yourself," he said, suddenly hot as a struck match. "That look on your face. It's so robotic. So dead inside. You didn't look anything like the real you, Tia, and I wondered what the fuck you were doing."

I remembered that other day on the phone, the one so long ago. Michael saw through me. He saw through the bullshit around me too. He'd always know in a glance that I wasn't as happy as I pretended to be. *Tell me what's wrong,* he'd wonder. And he'd know if I was lying.

But this time, I didn't back away and cut him off. Being seen felt like coming up for breath.

I had a dream around that time about a snake eating its tail. I was walking from room to room in my house. An enormous snake wove through every room, slithering in a circle to swallow its tail with its hungry mouth. Even full, the snake, like Nagini in Harry Potter, could speak. In the dream, I heard a voice say, "If man and woman were created in His image, why are women so invisssssssssible?"

I woke up sweating and panting. Allan slept with his back to me, as usual, and I stared at the blue moonlight falling across our bed from the window. If I had to believe in God, did God believe in me?

Was it even worth believing in a God that said that because I was a woman, I didn't really matter except in relation to my husband? He could believe *for* me in that case. Personal belief was irrelevant. I was a utensil, a hollowed vessel valued for her shell, not even what she contained.

What would happen if I didn't believe? And why was Eve's hunger for knowledge considered sin? Wasn't it good to know the difference between good and evil? Good to shatter the dream?

There was life outside of Eden. There was reality. And once Eve knew it, there was no going back.

Suddenly I realized that if no one else wanted me, I knew that *I* still wanted me. I didn't want the sleepy daze of a dream that left me dead inside. I wanted to awaken as one Tia, a woman with a name.

I needed to find a different way to be a Christian.

I turned to the library in Oak Ridge for help. If the Covenanters, Presbyterians, and Baptists were wrong, maybe there was a faith that was right. BethSC on Trapdoor explored Catholicism. Several were reading *The Dance of the Dissident Daughter* by Sue Monk Kidd. Clearly, there were options.

I checked out a book on every major world religion. The one on top was the smallest—it was called *At the Corner of East and Now,* by Frederica Mathewes-Green, a writer whose name I recognized from film reviews. And just like the elders predicted, what I wrote about became an undoing.

Frederica was something called Eastern Orthodox, a term I knew only from one of Frankie Schaeffer's lectures I'd attended years before because I loved his mother's *The Hidden Art of Homemaking* and his father's *How Should We Then Live?*

There was a little diagram I found online of the early church. It was a straight line until the Catholics branched off to follow the pope, and the Reformation broke into a forest of Protestant trees from there. But the Orthodox said they'd stayed the same all these years. There are Greek Orthodox and Russian Orthodox, Coptics and Egyptians—worldwide, it's the same church expressed in various cultural traditions. And now, because a group of Episcopalians in Tennessee mass-converted, there were American Orthodox churches who followed those same traditions in English.

The word "Theotokos" means *God-bearer*. It's used to refer to Mary, the mother of Jesus, the daughter of Joachim and Anne. I had never heard the names of Mary's parents before—never considered Mary had a mother. Jesus had a grandma. In order to send His son to earth, God needed a human woman. She was a vessel but a named and needed one.

I couldn't shake that thought. Men needed women too. They couldn't accomplish what they wanted without women. I'd spent a lifetime hearing that woman utterly depended on man, but now it felt flipped on its head. What if men insisted we needed them so much because they really needed us?

I wrote my thoughts on the blog with an image of the Theotokos. The phone calls started that night.

I stood in the kitchen scrubbing pans when Allan took Watson's call. I glanced over my shoulder afraid he'd be angry and was surprised to see he listened with a twinkle in his eye.

"I'll talk to her," he promised, smiling.

"I'd better see this book you're reading," he said to me after he'd hung up the phone. "Anything that makes them that hot requires my attention," he said. But he wasn't angry—he was enlivened. I remembered his charm over winning at chess when we met and realized he *wanted* this fight with the elders.

As it turned out, there was a small Orthodox parish named for the mother of Mary, St. Anne, in Oak Ridge, and Allan invited the priest over for a meal. Father Stephen arrived in a simple black cassock with a silver cross around his neck. Over bowls of soup and coffee, he answered our questions.

He showed us the branches of Protestant churches and explained this was why it was impossible to do as the elders required and find another church that taught what they did. Protestants argued, and then took their toys and went home. They started new churches. Every one of them would be different.

He talked about time. God was beyond linear time—qualitative Kairos instead of chronological Chronos. "You *were* saved, you *are being* saved, you *will be* saved," he said. "The Bible was written for people living in those times. It was relevant to them. It's relevant to us now. But we also have the saints and creation and the church. There's a great cloud of witnesses surrounding us every day. Asking them to pray for you is like reaching for a friend."

When Allan accepted saints instead of *sola scriptura,* the belief that Scripture alone is authoritative, I knew the petals of TULIP had fallen. His mind was open. He was listening to a man who venerated a woman, serving a parish named for a woman, and he was opening his mind to mystery and metaphor.

It astonished me to see that men who venerated women, instead of relegating them to merely functional vessels to be filled and fucked and fiddled with, were different kinds of men. Father Stephen didn't speak of women as if they were objects. They were important enough to name. They had identities and faces, stories and, sometimes, voices.

I felt like I was finally taking a drink of water. Someone had found a knife and cut my veil, and I was finally unbound, able to drink. "God is a good God, who loves mankind," the priest said. "That includes women."

About theological arguments and endless debates over who was the "most right," he offered suggestions to remember God is a mystery. "How powerful is a God you can figure out?" He shone like a gentle and patient parent. "You can spend your entire life focusing only on trying to love God and love people. It will never get harder or easier than that."

I blogged about that too.

Allan submitted to three meetings with the elders. They met at a bar-and-grill restaurant on Tuesday evenings.

The first was primarily an inquiry into what was happening:

What was I reading?

Did you know about it, Allan, and do you agree with it?

Why haven't you been censoring your wife's writing?

Why do you allow her to continue writing, and do you realize how dangerous it is to allow your wife to be a public spokesperson for your family, Allan?

Allan's spoil for a fight wavered. The passionate questioning with so much love and concern jarred him. He'd forgotten we were a covenant family. He told them maybe he'd been wrong, that they made a strong argument for fidelity and faith.

When he told me about it at home, I trembled in airless anxiety. Trusting that Allan's curiosity for a fresh ideology could win over his drive for belonging terrified me the way it would to follow him out onto thin ice. It wouldn't hold both of us. One would cross, one would drown.

But the following Lord's Day, he chose Oak Ridge over Knoxville. We stood in candlelight, incense, and chanted music. Father Stephen remembered Clara in the liturgical prayers and I finally felt validated that yes, she was here with me, she'd been here as a witness all along. She was the hand reaching to me from heaven so I wouldn't drown.

The second elder meeting was a response. This included litanies of researched and Bible-backed explanations of how Orthodoxy was heresy. Hyde made theological appeals to Allan's intellect and ability to see reason and pressed him to schedule appointments for more study and again I trembled. Allan craved the attention of a small and heady discussion group, like J. R. R. Tolkien and C. S. Lewis's Inklings.

But then they offered to compromise on certain church tenets, so that we could be safely released to the membership of another church. To Allan, it reminded him the offer was a token. "It's all about them," he said to me conspiratorially. "They're worried about what it means for their own standing if they just let us go. They sound ready to consider anything but the Catholics and the Orthodox."

Allan retold these meetings in a lather, clearly getting off on this debate. He liked having the power to make them squirm. "They are so worried about our souls," he laughed. "They're concerned about their culpability and what it says about them if they simply let us go do what we want."

I breathed a sigh of relief at his use of the word "we." *We* were doing this together, not one of us more than the other. It felt like a significant settling, the way a heavy peg finds the right notch and fits its way in. Maybe this was what we'd been working toward all along, this maturation of our relationship. Neither one in charge, neither one overly burdened in service. Pulling as a team.

Restrictions loosened. The closer he got to Orthodoxy and Father Stephen, the more he relaxed some of my restrictions. In the St. Anne's parish, most of the children went to school, and some of the women had jobs. They wore pants. There were a few homeschoolers who did it for educational and not religious reasons. The men were kind and looked women in the eye, even if they "belonged" in marriage to someone else. They had co-ed conversations. The women got together for coffee and lunch dates. They had fellowship groups.

Orthodox Christians celebrated holidays, like Christmas and Easter, and a bunch of feast days I'd never heard of before. Halloween wasn't a big deal, and I realized the kids would be able to trick-or-treat like normal kids. I knew none of those women were spanked. They'd all be horrified to know such a thing ever happened. Visibility resulted in safety. *Stay where I can see you.*

And secretly, I realized I'd done this. I'd gone to the library, found the books, and recognized Frederica Mathewes-Green's name. Allan only knew about Orthodoxy because I'd been willing to take the risk and try.

And now we were about to be free, in a parish that focused on love, and I was the one who'd led us here. If I could trigger this much positive change, I wondered what else I could do. Proud of myself, I blogged about how I'd helped my husband by growing into who I was supposed to be.

The third meeting was formal church discipline. We were being excommunicated and formally shunned. They had the letter printed, ready to sign, when they came to the restaurant. "We'll mail you a copy," they told Allan. "Don't expect to hear from us ever again, until such time you are ready to submit and repent. Likewise, no one in the congregation will recognize you, even if they pass you at Scouts or the store."

But their words blew right past me. The plan to move us out here to control me had backfired. Allan had defended us and now we were a team. I told myself happiness and heaven were on the way. Memory merged with rekindled optimism and hope. There was even a skip in my step as I wiped counters and runny noses. With a kinder religion and a unified goal, I knew we were on the right path to better days.

Erased

EVEN THOUGH I WAS RELIEVED TO BE FREE OF THEM, MY HAND still shook when the envelope came. Dudley La Touche had mailed it to Allan at work, to be sure he read it before me. These were the consequences of our choices.

> 27 December 2006
>
> *Dear Allan,*
>
> *Greetings in the name of our Lord Jesus Christ.*
>
> *It has been over two months since your family was last in attendance on the Lord's Day at Covenant Reformed; as you will recall, when we met with you in Lutherville, we encouraged you, due to the distance to which you have removed your family, to transfer your family's membership to another like-minded, Bible-believing, Protestant church closer to your new home.*

I snorted. This reminded me of how young girls wrote the right thing to say in their diaries, knowing their moms were going to read it. There was no such thing as a like-minded CRPC church around here and La Touche and his buddies knew it.

> *We also warned you, Allan, that a move towards Eastern Orthodoxy was not acceptable. In fact, we would fear for your family's very souls. More than anything else, two reasons stand out.*

First, as we made very clear when we met with you, **Eastern Orthodoxy rejects** **the pure, apostolic doctrine of salvation by grace alone received through faith** **alone in the once-and-for-all propitiatory sacrifice of our Lord Jesus Christ** **alone.** *Like Roman Catholicism, Orthodoxy teaches a* **faith + works** *doctrine of justification.*

The letter continued for three typed and single-spaced pages, debating salvation and works, and the ancient error of the people in Ephesians who needed correction from the apostle Paul. It explained that Orthodox church taught damnable heresy. There was a long section on the cannibalism of Orthodox Communion and the Catholic's view of transubstantiation—the mystical conversion of bread and wine into body and blood—and what it meant that the Brown children often spilled during Communion. Did we now believe they were defiling the actual blood of Christ? And another long section on how venerating Mary and the saints was polytheism more in line with the Olympic heroes in ancient Greece, and thoroughly corrupt.

But then, they got to the point. Their real issue was that they believed Allan had abdicated his authority over me and that I was leading my family into damnation, because he was too worried about conflict in his household to make me stop.

Allan, you are allowing your family to be led into destruction **and you know better.** *You understand these issues, but you are not being the man in your home, the spiritual leader in your household. It's not enough just to win a paycheck, Allan. You must protect your wife and young ones—even if that means causing a ruckus in your household.*

If your brother, the son of your mother, your son or your daughter, **the wife** **of your bosom,** *or your friend who is as your own soul, secretly entices you, saying, "Let us go and serve other gods . . . you shall not consent to him or listen to him, nor shall your eye pity him, nor shall you spare him or conceal him . . ." (Deut. 13:6–18). Allan, if you do not act now and protect your family, then you are abdicating your responsibility and leading them into apostasy by default. And the Lord will hold you accountable for William, Katie, Liam, and Gavin.*

*"Whoever receives one little child like this in my name receives Me. But whoever causes one of these little ones who believe in Me to sin, **it would be better for him if a millstone were hung around his neck, and he were drowned in the depth of the sea.**" (Matthew 18:5 & 6)*

This time, I gasped, and my hands shook, holding the ivory papers. Was this pastor, this "shepherd," actually suggesting that my children were better off drowned? But I kept reading. The real concern wasn't about our children—it was about them. They were still reading my blog, still mad over it, and didn't want to be held responsible for "our souls."

Allan, we cannot simply release you and your family to nowhere, and we certainly cannot release you to Eastern Orthodoxy. According to Tia's blog, not only has she herself accepted the idea of offering prayers to Mary and "venerating" the deceased "saints" of Orthodoxy, but your entire family has been participating in the corrupt worship of an Orthodox congregation in Oak Ridge and has undertaken preparation for membership as catechumens. We as your elders, who are to give an account for your souls, cannot idly stand by as you destroy yourselves. As we warned you; and as you and Tia took membership vows in our congregation, swearing ". . . in the name of God to support the ministry of this church and in its worship and work, submitting to its government and discipline, while pursuing its purity and peace," we have erased your names from our membership rolls.

Allan, in separating yourselves from the Lord's people, His body, and giving yourself over to the errors of the East, you have in effect excommunicated yourself. And you may well have passed the point of no return.

Heck yes, we did, I thought. We'd given ourselves over to another faith—but it was one where women held personal value. Not to my destruction, as La Touche insisted, but to my survival and salvation.

Allan, come back to your senses, not only for your own sake, but for the sake of your wife and kids. Come back to the Lord's people and be restored through repentance

and faith. We want to see you and your family restored and would gladly transfer
your family elsewhere with our blessing.

In Christ,
The Session of Covenant Reformed Presbyterian Church

I folded the letter and stuffed it back into the manila envelope. Fear tore
at me as if I'd run into brambles and thorns, scratching and snagging me as
I fought to get away. Hate. Vitriol. Control. To be a woman so reviled by
a pastor. Years later, on Instagram, I'd read a meme that read, "Why were
we taught to fear the witches instead of the men who burned them?" And
who were witches, anyway, but women with knowledge, skills, and names?

The next day I got a letter at home, this one from Leah. Four handwritten
pages front and back, addressed to "Allan and Tia," and I knew that was her
signal that this had been read and approved by the elders. She apologized for
not speaking up as I shared my thoughts and experiences. She sought now to
admonish me in love as a "baby Reformed Presbyterian" and asked the pastor to speak for her.

She said Pastor La Touche had begun a Bible study on the Byzantine
Empire, the seven churches in Revelation, and the sins of idolatry and mys-
ticism that had been very helpful to her in understanding why I'd fallen to
this temptation. *Damage control,* I thought. We'd be his object lesson. Leah
urged me to reach out to the membership for love and support, because they'd
welcome me with open arms, as long as I repented and chose a church other
than Orthodoxy.

Allan wrote the session back thanking them for their time, kindness, and
charity.

Our decision to move our membership was simply due to our leaving the area.
The reason for our research into Orthodoxy is more complex. You would have to
be privy (and you were not) to my growing dissatisfaction with Protestantism in
general . . .

Allan's efforts at restraint paid off. This reply was polite, well-written, and
most of all brief. It made La Touche's elegant "packet" seem like a pillow in

contrast. But he reasserted his headship with the last line. No longer was he going to submit to a Tennessee theobro telling him what to do.

The implication that my wife has steered me or that I am not being the head of my home has caused much laughter among the knowledgeable adults. It was a risky joke you made, however. One might actually think you meant it.

> Cordially,
> Allan Brown

Ironically, because Allan hadn't let up on my rules, the shunning went down easier than I expected. Forbiddance to attend Scouts, where Watson was a leader, or field trips I'd once gone on with Leah sort of served me. We'd been erased from their rolls and memory and the rejection of it might've hurt more. But his rules offered a mercy in helping my heart cut ties, the way First Baptist's social provision had once made skipping prom easier.

Gently, I stepped from the black-and-white world of rigid Calvinism and Reformed theology into the tapestry of ancient Christianity, and for a while it held me in safety, the way beeswax holds a flickering flame. For all my life, I'll hold the fragrance of this space in my heart as a sacred healing. It was a tender first step met with love, a holy unction and anointing that soothed so many hidden wounds.

I decided to devote myself to our new life with my whole heart the way a saint would. Father Stephen called women like Juliana of Lazarevo, the name I chose for my chrismation, "living saints," venerated not for a martyr's death but for how they lived their lives. Like chords in a sacred chant, I wove threads I loved from Thoreau and Annie Dillard and motherhood into my new story.

Juliana lived deliberately, not by withdrawing from the world to a monastic cell, but within a family, amid the cares for her children, husband, and household. She was known for her kindness and respect to others—even those her culture deemed beneath her. She had thirteen children and six of them died in childhood, but through all that loss, she'd carried on. Juliana so believed in love and mercy that she left a legacy of healing in her wake.

I'd never heard of a woman who'd succeeded at a hard life so well. From her I took hope it could be done. Love could win so powerfully it impacted centuries. I knew now I was more than a vessel. God's love, not God's rules, would get us through.

The domino of becoming Orthodox happened April 1, 2007. I'd discovered how to help my marriage, family, and myself thrive. By remaining steadfast to Allan, we'd made it to this landing on the stairs, this union of souls. In turn, that protected my family. And without the patriarchy and the hierarchy that held women down, I'd discovered space for my words, art, and self. I was sure all that was left was to thrive. I dried my face and turned toward the dawn.

Shatter

LIFE OPENED LIKE AN EARLY SUMMER WINDOW. WITHOUT THE RE-strictive bindings of Federalist marriage wrapped around us, Allan and I both relaxed. He, into his new history and teachings, me into concocting a career from scratch, as if it were the morning biscuits.

My blog was regularly getting over a hundred thousand hits a week. Like my brother-in-law had predicted, my knack for keywords and content paid off. I started adding interviews with homesteaders and other folks who had blogs aligned with a living-deliberately ethos. As my site traffic continued to climb, the attention led to opportunity. I tipped my chin with a smile now.

There was a public speaker I'd known in the homeschool co-op who read my blog and he wanted to learn how to use blogging in his business. I couldn't believe it, but he offered to pay me to teach him how. Tim Richardson be-came my first "client," a word as new to my vocabulary as to my consciousness.

I didn't understand the back end of what I was doing. So, late at night af-ter the kids were in bed, I spent hours on the phone with Jake, learning code and how to customize websites. I learned how search engine optimization worked and why my content had resulted in such high numbers. Tim told his friends and they became my clients too. Suddenly, I had clients and an income of my own.

I went to the bank and opened an account in my own name, without even talking to Allan about it, let alone asking permission. I didn't know it then, but I was tapping into a freedom the patriarchy didn't want women to have. Women couldn't open their own bank accounts until 1960. They couldn't get a credit card until 1974, the year I was born. And while both of these facts predated my marriage, the attitudes around them persisted in our communities. Submissive wives don't need their own bank accounts and credit cards. In the parade of "why doesn't she just leave" comments, outsiders had no idea the historic obstacles and outdated ideas we had to confront first.

Allan was so excited about Orthodoxy that he stopped watching my mileage or picking at the budget. He forgot to monitor my every move and I remembered to save almost every dollar. Part of me wished old Pastor La Touche could see me now, not only writing in my own name, but making money at it too. I thought about him every time I made a deposit.

This happiness was the reward for hanging in there, I was sure of it. I just knew we'd finally be okay, and I forgot the days of the silver-white rain of our cold season in the Blue House. I created a vision board using magazine clippings of our future together—color schemes for our home, a prayer garden, and the words, "I'm married to my best friend." It wasn't true yet, but I claimed it for the years ahead like a pictorial prayer.

We went to church on Wednesdays now, for Vespers, and sometimes Saturday nights as well. Sunday morning was full of Sunday School, Great Liturgy, and coffee hour. Where my Baptist upbringing had blank walls, Orthodoxy had icons. I stood in the beeswax candlelight and incense, lifting prayers toward heaven. We sang the same words and creeds used two thousand years ago in the early church. Nothing was performative; there were no "special soloists" or praise and worship choruses. We learned a new vocabulary from the ancient world: Akathist. Liturgy. Prokeimenon in the third tone, *let us attend the Holy Gospel*. Bells rang.

We learned about Great Lent and Pasca, the Eastern Easter. We sang Memory Eternal for Clara and commemorated our dead. Orthodox Christians didn't shy from their torment or loss. They accepted it.

It felt like the most honest and tangible Christianity I could have ever imagined. It was as if time was and is and would be. I felt Clara with us in spirit in church. We were finally all together, the unified family I'd prayed for, hurt for, and bled for. I didn't wrestle with theological questions anymore and Allan didn't debate. I rested.

In the space and freedom of not having to solve for God or having to proselytize strangers, I felt my nerves begin to settle. I wondered if the calm that came was part of the acceptance ushered in with my early thirties. I hadn't been a girl for a long time. But I'd only just begun to feel like a woman. When I looked in the mirror, I saw an adult woman, red hair to her waist in a braid. I saw a mother. I saw "a good man in a storm." I saw someone who smiled most when looking at her children. Someone smart. Someone I might like to know.

I let her guard down.

One Wednesday night, when I was in a hurry to get us all to church, I made a mistake.

I'd baked bread to contribute to the common meal and had to carefully coordinate the dash to the van, dodging the mewling mouths and quick leaps of so many kittens. More than once, we'd driven all the way into Oak Ridge and discovered a kitten hiding under the car seat. So, in my urgent rush to get everyone loaded, I tried to ignore the dog.

Red Fox barked, upset and crazed, for a reason I couldn't make out. I wondered if I should put him in the house while we were gone. But we were late, and the kids were in the car. I started the van and pulled out of the driveway.

As I turned onto the highway, Liam shouted, "Red Fox is following us!"

Sure enough, a little red blur sped behind my van, barreling toward the highway. Before I could pull over to send him home, a car came from behind me, slamming into Red Fox hard and launching him into the air, a rusty streak against the gray sky.

He landed with a thud onto the shoulder of the road, narrowly missing the guardrail that would have dropped him far below, onto the railroad tracks.

The kids all screamed. I pulled over. William jumped out of the car and ran over to Red Fox's heaving body. The dog's eyes were bright and startled. I could tell he didn't know what had happened to him, or why he suddenly couldn't move. Tenderly, I scooped him into my arms and William and I walked back to the van. I lay Red Fox in William's lap and ran around to the driver's side.

Pink foam bubbled from Red Fox's nostrils onto William's lap. The dog labored to breathe, gasping and wheezing as William sobbed into his fur. "Please don't die, Red Fox! Please don't die!"

I sped through the woods, taking the curves as fast as I dared, racing us toward the only vet in town, knowing it was past six and begging God for them to be open. We hit both lights at green, and the wheels skidded on the gravel in the parking lot of the vet. They were closed.

I got out and pounded on the door, hoping someone was in there, maybe with animals who were boarding or who had stayed over from surgery.

A young girl opened the door. She wore scrubs. "Can I help you?"

"Our dog has just been hit by a car. He's aspirating blood. I think he's going to die. Please, can I bring him in? Please, can you help him not be in pain?"

"We're not open, ma'am. The doctor isn't here."

"Please. I have four crying children in the car who just saw their dog get hit. Please, can I bring him in, so he doesn't die in front of them too?" My throat ached from holding in sobs. She had to let me in. She had to help.

"Okay, you can bring him into an exam room. Let's at least take a look."

I told the kids to sit in the waiting room, and the tech and I went into an exam room, where I laid Red Fox's broken and limp body onto the table. He tried to cry out, but the congested sound of blood in his lungs muffled his voice. The tech said there was nothing she could do because it was apparent how much internal bleeding he had.

I begged her to please put him down. "I know you have the medication here. Please, just put him out of his misery."

She got a syringe and gave him a shot, and in a few jerky moments, it was over.

Red Fox dying ushered in a series of struggles that anyone I asked attributed to "life out in the country," but secretly, I knew were happening because I lacked the courage to make them stop. Any calm confidence I'd felt before was officially gone. I spent the days worrying and reacting to a hemorrhage I couldn't staunch.

Such as the lump in William's leg. Hang Judith's old warnings about doctors—I took him to the only doctor in town, terrified it was a tumor.

"Do you have cats?" asked the doctor. "Particularly un-vetted cats?"

We were overrun with the cats by now. Today's count was thirty-eight, and just this morning, in my hurry, I'd popped the head of a kitten when I backed out the van. I'd scraped the little body into a bag, careful not to let the kids see, and choked back my tears because I didn't want them to see me cry either.

"I think your son has cat-scratch fever, not cancer. Here's a prescription. Get rid of the cats," he said, tearing a paper for antibiotics off his pad.

Next came the intestinal symptoms that ravaged little Liam's gut. We went to Children's Hospital for that, in Knoxville, because he needed a colonoscopy and eventually a PICC line.

The doctor said stress and bacteria were the likely culprits, and could I please tell him what life was like at home.

Next up, the fact that Gavin wasn't talking. At almost two he had only a handful of words and was delayed in his motor skills too. A pediatrician-directed evaluation revealed he had a 25 percent speech delay. It was enough to be a concern but not enough to qualify for state-provided therapies.

"Get out more," the doctor suggested. "A playgroup, instead of being carried around by older siblings, will go a long way."

Katie discovered a cat who'd snuck into the house, delivered a litter of kittens beneath her bed. She cried over having watched the cat eat the afterbirth, sure the bloody licking would soon include the mewing kittens.

I asked the vet about adoption options or a shelter in another county.

"That's not how it's done here," he said, obviously irritated by outsiders. "Around here we use the countryfolk solution, if you get my drift?"

But I didn't tell Allan about what the vet had said. The calm and clear season of peace had begun to shadow. His eyes were red and glassy, his pupils large and dark, and I wasn't sure why. He looked different than he used to. I didn't want him to remember we owned a gun, let alone encourage him to use it.

For all my hope and optimism, we weren't thriving, any of us. So, I dug in harder. Cheered harder. I refined meal plans and school schedules, taking out Steve and Teri Maxwell's *Managers of Their Homes* again and dividing our days into fifteen-minute increments. More, more. The tone of the home is set by the mother, I remembered. *The Excellent Wife* had scriptural options to do better. "We can do it!" I wrote on the blog.

My scrimping and earning paid off. When we sent in our last credit card payment, I threw a "Beans and Rice" Total Money Makeover party and we made it onto Dave Ramsey's blog. All our Maryville friends came. I missed Leah, because she'd been part of that goal, but I knew that lesson so well. At church, friends are friends forever "if." I kept my attention on the credit card cake and the beans and rice taco spread and refused to think about the past.

"Tia, I have a very, very big idea!" Tim said.

"Oh yeah?" I smiled wide because Tim's big ideas usually meant work plus money for me. His big ideas launched miracles like a new career and a savings account in my own name.

"The World's Biggest Blog Party," he said. "Forty-eight hours of live blogging. We'll interview major charities and ask for donations. We'll raise a ton! You build the website and I'll run the show. What do you think?"

I jumped in because I wanted to, again without asking permission. This was my job, my new career, and shadows or not, the old discipline lifestyle was far behind us now. "Third weekend in October, right before Halloween? Let's do it!" I gave Tim a high five.

Life split again, offering me two lives, two different stages on which to perform. At home, I was a homeschooling mom to a busy crew of creative kids, a small-scale urban homesteader, and a wife to a man increasingly walking an emotional dark night of the soul. A few hours a day, I was a blogging consultant, taking client calls and teaching professionals how to use keywords and create content their audiences would search for. As long as I kept both of them straight, the lines were clean, and I didn't have to choose between them. I could curl my toes around each tightrope and keep going.

Michael called. His mother was having a hard time accepting his marriage to Mark. "Would you talk to her?"

I sat on the porch with the cordless phone in my hand, eager to reconnect with her. I loved Michael's mom. Her severance from me had been collateral damage from Allan's orders, another casualty I'd counted. I listened to her tearful confession that she'd hoped all these years that being gay was a phase Michael would eventually get over. She didn't know how as a

Christian she could attend his wedding. Yet, as a mother, she didn't know how she could not.

"I don't know, Tia. I guess part of me always thought the two of you had something together, and that one day he'd tell me he was in love with you."

"Oh," I said sadly. I wanted Michael to be fully accepted for who he was, not just tolerated while his family hoped he'd change his mind. "We aren't like that. We haven't ever been like that. He's as close as a brother as I'll ever get. I know he's gay and always has been, and I know he loves Mark with all his heart."

"But what about what the church says about homosexuality?"

"'God is a good God who loves mankind,'" I quoted Father Stephen. "We're just supposed to love people. You love him. Love means you celebrate his joys alongside him. Being there for him is what God wants, I'm sure, and I would be there too if I could get there."

"And can't you?"

"No," I breathed, my voice cracking. I knew Allan hadn't changed enough to let me say Michael's name, let alone travel to his gay wedding. "I can't make it, and I'm so very sad and sorry about that."

She didn't ask why, and I was relieved not to have to lie.

By high summer, the leaves on the trees were so dense I couldn't see the houses on the hills anymore, though I knew they could still see me, the small woman who lived in the Blue House. I picked bowls of purple blackberries along the train tracks to can jam, pretending I couldn't feel the eyes watching. I felt like I pretended more than I didn't. *Fake it till you make it.*

Confirmation that Allan's reprieve was over started with a fight at work.

"They put this woman over Tommy," he said. "She doesn't know what she's doing. She shouldn't be telling me what to do."

Twice, he'd been called in for disciplinary meetings for his communication style. She said he talked down to her and refused to give her work because he "had his reasons."

I knew Allan's reasons the way I knew the silvered scars on my temple. I had flashbacks to when he lost his job in Jacksonville, forcing the move. It was happening again; this was a bad sign. There were no other jobs out here other than the prison.

Tommy was his supervisor and the woman wasn't really over him or Tommy— she was just knowledgeable and sometimes contributed to operations decisions. Allan wanted her job.

I thought he should be grateful he even had a job, because after our excommunication, Deacon Sands could've fired him.

"She's a man-hater, and she needs to quit telling me what to do."

I wanted him to be cautious. Stay in line. Stay employed.

It seemed like a good thing when he was invited on an overnight coon hunt with the guys from work. Having friends might help. He took William with him and the gun. They ran through the woods all night, and someone's dog treed a raccoon, but William said no one shot it because all of them were laughing their silly heads off and missed. He was too young to realize what drunk was and I assumed Allan was the sober one, because we only had the occasional glass of wine. Allan left his gun at the office the next day. He said one of his friends planned to paint it.

But watching Allan descend into darkness this time felt different. I worried he was depressed, but we weren't allowed to say that. Maybe in Orthodoxy we could, but some of the old Baptist and Covenant thoughts died hard. Words like "lunatic" and "deranged" came to mind when I saw the frantic gleam of his eyes at night, new words I'd never thought about him before.

On Trapdoor, my friends talked about their marriage problems. Is that what I had? A run-of-the-mill marriage problem that every wife faces? I learned our men didn't have to define us. Allan's instability didn't have to mean I joined the ride. I turned my focus toward being the one who kept us steady. Maybe he was going crazy. But maybe it was a storm that would pass.

I started facing each day as if he were just another factor in the day—not the determining one. With a job and an income, I started changing in ways I liked, just because I liked them. A queue on Netflix. The Sunday edition of *The New York Times*. I took the kids to the library again and we watched TV. I'd reinstituted everything Judith warned against: doctors, science, toys, snacks, pants, friends, barbers, dentists. I scheduled a gynecologist appointment and read about the upcoming presidential race, because I decided I wanted to vote. Orthodox women voted—Allan couldn't object. And when the subject of bedrooms came up, I spoke up boldly with a plan.

Four children in a single bedroom wasn't working. Puberty was coming, and Katie needed privacy.

"Move the kids down into the living room," Allan said. "I'll build a wall in their room and divide it into two. We'll cut a door for Katie. It will be fine."

But Allan didn't know how to build a wall and we both knew it. "I'm going to call my dad," I said. "They have a camper. They could stay in it while they help us build the rooms."

"We don't have the money for the kind of improvement your dad will want to do," Allan said.

"Yes, I do," I said. "I've been saving my blog money. I want to invest it in our home."

I didn't flinch or breathe as he stared at me, sizing up what I'd just said. He didn't ask how much I'd saved. I couldn't tell if he didn't care or if knowing scared him. Finally, he said, "Get the family rate. And see if he'll handle these damn cats while he's at it."

I exhaled.

Dad had been a country man once. He'd put down dogs, cats, and rabbits they'd raised for meat. He'd remodeled and adapted countless houses. I knew he could help me get my house in order. And when I called them, both Mom and Dad jumped at the chance to come help. "We're overdue to see you," they said. The isolation impacted them too.

I was surprised to realize this. My life was chaotic but separate. I hadn't spent any time thinking about what it must be like to be a helpless family member watching our choices go down. Or how hard it was to wait on a call that never comes. To see family traditions come undone. To see the light fade from my eyes or see their grandchildren get sick.

Allan's mother complained about it. But he called her even less for it. My parents were trying not to interfere. I'd incorrectly interpreted their silence as approval. What else had I been wrong about?

As the summer weeks passed before their visit, Allan worsened rapidly. We had so much freedom now without a high-control authority telling us what to do and how to live. It was as if his system couldn't function, like a released prisoner who flails his way back to crime and the comfort of his cell. Allan needed rules to know where the lines were, and now there weren't any. As if his heart had been replumbed and his body couldn't handle the surgical gift of flexibility and grace.

He started pacing at night, pulling his hair and scratching his skin. His eyes were wild and black, glinting like moonlight on water, like a rabid deer chased by a hunter no one else could see.

"Why don't you see a doctor?" I urged.

"No. No doctors. No psycho medications. This is spiritual warfare." And then he'd pull and pinch at the skin on his arm, at the tattoo that had once earned him the nickname "Psycho Eyes," trying to scratch it off.

He'd pace some more and then turn on me.

"You fucking bitch. You whore. You're sleeping with him, aren't you? That's why you're gone with this damn blog party. It's a farce. It's a lie so you can leave me."

"No," I answered calmly. "It's just what I said it is. You can see the website for yourself."

"Liar. You're a lying bitch. The pastor was right. You're a Jezebel. You're better off drowned than as the mother of these kids. Do you know what I should do?"

He charged across the room toward me, spewing hot, rancid air in my face. "I should take them. I should take them away from you when you're not here. I can make sure you never see them again; do you know that? Do you realize?"

He abruptly left the room. This scene rewound and played itself back several times a week. I found it harder to breathe, harder to allow my footsteps to make sound.

I kept my hands busy. Folded laundry. Picked up laundry. Refolded laundry. Dusted the furniture. Anything to keep moving in an ordinary, steady way.

Eventually, he'd wear out. Go lie down and fall asleep. The next morning he'd get up and fill his cheek with fresh tobacco and leave for work without a word. I couldn't put my finger on why this darkness felt so different than the times before, but it did. Allan seemed perpetually disoriented, hounded and hunted from within. And he smelled different too, like a pickle left in the sun.

The blog party plans progressed seamlessly. Tim secured a venue, an old theater in Maryville. And charities lined up for interviews and exposure. Blog Talk Radio would broadcast all forty-eight hours. I was nervously excited about all of it: the live stream posts we'd publish, the radio interviews, the weekend spent being professional. I tried to stay focused on what I now called "my work."

But the mounting pressure was never far from my mind. Mary Winkler shot her husband that summer. I read about it in *People* magazine. She'd shot him with a hunting rifle in the chest, buckshot sprinkling him on the wall, and threw her kids in the van to head for the coast. He was a pastor in a small town in Tennessee not far from here. *A good man,* the community said. The authorities chased her down and arrested her for murder.

"Silly Mary," I said to myself while folding clothes after one of Allan's episodes. "What made you think you could get away?" I matched the seams of sleeves and folded stacks of little boy shirts and overalls, wishing life could be as sweet as clean clothes from the clothesline.

My parents drove up in August. They'd be in town long enough to watch the kids while I went to blog party prep meetings. They didn't understand what it was I'd be doing, but Dad was impressed with the money I'd saved.

"You've got enough for the build-out, new floors, a new toilet, beds for the kids, and some secondhand furniture. All the paint and incidentals too. I'm proud of you," he said. The project would take all the money I'd saved, but if it restored harmony to the house and got us back to our good place, it was worth it. What was I earning money for, anyway, if not to help my family find stability?

I thought about our old chats in his woodshop. *Yagottawanna. Have a plan,* my dad would say. I felt connected to the Midwestern resourcefulness we'd had on the farm, the birthright I'd hungered to inherit. When I kept my head in this space, I was sure of it, sure of myself. I could fix this. Handle it. Control it. Manage it. I knew how to balance two lives and keep us all from crashing down. I knew how to keep up appearances. But I also knew how to survive.

In the Letters to the Editor section in *People* magazine, someone wondered, "Hadn't Mary Winkler thought of divorce?"

In confession, I told Father Stephen I'd started to imagine Allan dying on the side of the road. The visions came in dreams after Allan's episodes. His car twisted around a tree. His taillights hidden in the underbrush. I felt relief, not grief. The priest said the dreams made sense—in a certain context.

"It's often easier for Christian women to fantasize about their spouse's death. That's because widowhood is less shameful than divorce. Death is easier, albeit sadder. It's one of the key indications of abuse, though, if I'm honest with you. Are there any problems like that at home?"

I couldn't tell him. Old memories of the First Baptist counselor shrouded around me like gray smoke, sealing my throat. "Things are fine," I said.

I wondered what it said about me that I lied in confession.

"I make sure they never feel a thing," Dad told William. The two of them were sitting side by side on the porch and Dad was explaining to William what was about to happen to the cats.

Mom and I were in the kitchen. She stitched a set of curtains that were to hang in Katie's new room soon. Her nose was red from crying. "Putting animals down humanely never gets easier," she said. "It's a shame this county can't get its act together and build a real shelter or animal control program."

I heard William say, with all the manly bluster his little chest could produce, "I'll help you, Papa. I can handle it."

I stiffened, reflexively reaching out the way a parent catches a wobbly toddler. The way my arm sprang across the passenger side when I had to hit the brakes. No. No way was he ready for that. Not so young. Not so soon after Red Fox. I was on my way to the door when I heard Dad say, "No, you won't be helping. Let Papa take care of this. You're a little young yet."

I exhaled. My parents were safe. Allan wouldn't cry in hysterics or call me horrible names in the night while they were here. I still had to be careful—still had to be the last one to sleep, the first one awake. But with oversight, skill, and experience, my parents were fixing more than they knew.

It helped too that the hours were limited. Allan was at work all day and my parents slept in their camper in the yard. That meant we only had to get through dinner all together. I only had to hold my breath for that one meal, hoping they wouldn't notice something was wrong with Allan.

Dad created built-in bunks for the boys, each one with a bank of drawers beneath the beds and a privacy curtain pulled across. The bays were like berths, on a ship. He installed a light for each one and a little bookshelf for their treasures. Katie's room had a small slanted door at the top of the stairs. I painted her walls pink and she hung her horse posters. Together, we created order out of chaos.

But when the day came, I felt a tugging temptation: I could load the kids up and leave. The idea materialized like an apparition coming to life, like the holograms I'd once seen on *Star Trek*.

Allan had already left for work, after offering what he called "a cordial farewell." Dad rolled his eyes and muttered something about ten-dollar words.

Just for a second, I felt myself wanting to call out to them. Dad had given me that *are you sure you want to do this* look.

And, just as suddenly, I tipped my chin and smiled, betrayed by habit. They'd done so much for me. I was no longer overrun with shitting, disease-carrying cats. I no longer had four children in a single room. I'd had a whole month away from the worst of Allan's outbursts. And I had a job to do because this weekend was the blog party, and after that, the kids' first Halloween. Was I just going to leave after all that relief? I tucked the longing inside. Snapped off the hologram. I was doing all of this so I could make things better, not so I could leave.

I raised my hand to wave goodbye.

On a cold morning a month later, I woke up to a high-pitched crying. It wasn't coming from any of the kids, but it seemed to be in the house with me. Invisible cries and wails or . . . yips? I followed the sound to the kitchen, then the kitchen floor. I got down on my hands and knees and pressed my ear against the green linoleum. Puppies. The hound had delivered in the crawl space beneath the kitchen floor.

I didn't get up right away. I lay on the floor, cheek to linoleum, counting my pulse in my ears. Whoosh, whoosh, whoosh. Life had become a piece of repeating music, never finding release to the coda. If a tear burned, I blinked it away before it had a chance to gather on my lashes.

A little while later, Allan crawled under with William, and together they pulled the pups out, their worried post-birth mother moaning as she dragged herself out after them. Six puppies and a mother hound and suddenly, we had seven dogs.

"Shit," Allan said, not even careful not to curse in front of the kids.

And then it was the World's Biggest Blog Party time and I needed to go to work. This was survival. This was how it was done.

Keep doing the next right thing. I packed a weekend's clothes and curled my hair. The weekend away would probably complete Gavin's weaning. I left meals in the fridge and a stack of books and movies from the library. It was two days and I had to hope on hope that they'd get by.

Allan let me borrow his cell phone, so I could reach him if I had car trouble on the way. I drove up to the theater in his little gray sedan, instead of my mini-van full of toys and finger streaks on the glass. The mountain roads helped me see the boundary between my two lives and I felt excited that Tim and I were pulling off what we thought might be the world's first ever live blogging event.

Tim was on fire—dynamic and energetic. He had a news crew at the reception. Music thumped between sessions with various charities. The theater was crowded at the kickoff event, drinks in hand and smiles on faces. Some danced. I felt like I'd stepped through a portal into another world, one wholly unrelated to anything I'd known before. The donations rolled in.

Sometime after midnight, the crowd slowly went home, and we were down to the core crew to blog and talk through the night. Tim did the radio interviews, and I paid close attention because tomorrow, I would do the same. Even though I'd only conducted interviews for my blog, at home in my closet office, I'd soon be chatting with the chairmen of major charities and nonprofits.

The night passed, and Keith, one of the volunteers, brought me breakfast at dawn. It was a plastic tray from the Waffle House—a yellow waffle with two eggs sunny side up, and two links of sausage. But I'd never had Waffle House before, and somehow, it tasted like a great feast. When had anyone ever brought me breakfast?

I sat in the glow of my laptop in the dim room. Keith said I looked beautiful, serious, and smart. The words swam in the caverns of my ear canals, unfamiliar and strange, until they floated out again. I was unaccustomed to flattery. I couldn't process the syllables, let alone the kindness behind them.

Saturday passed by on coffee, and then Saturday night did as well. On Sunday morning, I conducted two interviews: one with the nonprofit To Write Love on Her Arms, and the second with Millard Fuller, the cofounder of Habitat for Humanity. During the third interview, I passed out, falling flat on the chewed-gum theater floor.

I woke up in the emergency room. "You have an elevated heart rate," Keith said. "The doctor assumes I'm your husband, so he let me come back here with you."

I tried to sit up, instantly afraid, and a beeping monitor sped up. "You can't! My actual husband is going to find out! You can't be here!"

"Shh. It's okay, lie back, you need to rest. I spoke with your actual husband. I called him."

"You did?" This made me tremble, my hands shaking uncontrollably.

"He's on his way. He's going to drop your children off with some friends at a pumpkin party in Maryville? Anyway, he didn't seem too worried, not like I'd be if my wife was all of a sudden in the hospital."

Three hours later, Allan came in, hiccupping and red-faced. *Drunk?* Had he driven the kids all the way here, drunk? My mouth hung open. I'd never seen him like this before—had I? We didn't get drunk . . . ever. This wasn't the wine of Cana. This was sloppy and slurred and dangerous.

And then, just as suddenly as a puzzle piece pops into place, I realized I *had* seen him like this before. Many times. The pickle smells. The delirious eyes. The words that slid from his lips like he had a mouthful of peanut butter.

"Your wife is very exhausted, sir," the doctor said. "What she needs is rest. I'm recommending she stay in town, in a sequestered environment, and sleep for as many hours as her body requires. It's what we'd do at the hospital, but now that her heart rate is coming down, I don't feel admitting her is necessary."

Then, he looked down at me. "You get some rest, young lady. You're tired beyond your years."

The plan was that I'd stay in Tim and Adele's guest room. It was separate from their home, so none of their five children would wake me. Allan would take the children home after he sobered up in town first. I had no choice but to trust him; I could hardly hold my head up.

Tim took me to his house and Adele tucked me in. I turned off the cell phone and sank my head into a cloud of pillows. I didn't dream and I didn't cry, and I didn't measure time as it passed in the night.

The phone rang sometime the next afternoon. It was Tim's office phone. The late daylight slanted through the blinds across the bed. I'd been asleep for over twenty-four hours. I reached for the cell phone and turned it on.

A text: Tia, where are you? We are so worried. It was from Mom.

Another: Tia, please let us know you're okay. It was from Monica.

From Allan: I don't know where you are. The children are worried that their mom isn't coming home.

Right away, I called home. "Allan, what's going on? What are these texts?"

"Well, I didn't know where you were, Tia."

"Yes, you did. You were there. I'm at Tim and Adele's. You heard the doctor."

"That was so long ago. You've been gone a lot longer than I expected."

"Allan. The doctor said to sleep until I woke naturally. I'm sorry it took so long, but I'm right here. I'm not even out of bed yet. It hasn't even been longer than a day."

"The children are afraid for you, Tia. Don't you realize that?"

His voice was cold and finite, like a skilled scientist dissecting a chilled frog, slicing the membrane with a #10 blade.

"Why is my mother worried?"

"Wouldn't you be worried if your child went missing, Tia?"

I sped home thinking of Mary Winkler in her van, driving toward the coast, except Mary had had her daughters with her. What had he done to them? Told them? What would I find when I got home?

I was over an hour away. I tried to stay in my lane and not speed, the car sometimes careening around a mountain curve.

I called Mom on the way. "I'm fine, Mom. He was wrong to make you worry. I was never missing. He knew where I was; he agreed to it."

"I'm frightened for you, Tia," she said. "There's more going on, I'm sure of it."

"I'll tell you about it later, I promise," I said. "I need to get home and re-assure the kids."

Relief flooded me when they ran out of the house to meet my car. Allan wasn't home. His text said he'd gone to the store. I didn't leave them home alone yet. The sight of them washed over the azure blue and the swords and shields I'd felt when they were born. *This is a threshold,* I heard my heart say. *This is near the margin.*

"We were scared for you, Mommy," Katie wailed, pressing wet cheeks into my stomach as I held her. Liam and Gavin clung to my legs.

"Mommy was just really tired, honey. I got sick at the event and needed to sleep. But I'm fine. See? I'm fine." My arms strained to hold the three of them. William stood off to the side, in the shadows from the house in the sun. But also covered in shadow, not the same little boy I'd left on Friday.

I'm here, I thought repeatedly. *I'm here, and I'll keep us steady. I'm here. I'll fix it. Mommy will fix it.* But I was so mad at myself. This was not the kind of mother I promised them I'd be. This was not being their shield.

William was pale and silent. He wouldn't let me hug him.

"William, what's wrong?" He clenched his fists and glared.

"It's the dogs," Katie whispered.

"What dogs? The puppies?"

"He made William kill them," she said, her lip sticking out and weighted tears streaking down her face.

William turned and ran upstairs.

Ashen and horrified, I chased him.

At the top of the landing, I caught his right sleeve. When he spun around, his forearm cuffed my cheek. The force knocked me to the wood floor, shocked and dizzy. The bedroom door slammed behind him.

"Go away!" he yelled.

Like a wounded reptile, I crawled over the threshold on the cold vinyl floor of the bathroom, kicking the door shut. Katie's words sliced through time. Then and Now. Before and After. *He made William kill them.*

My little boy was on the other side of the door, out of reach in every way. He was as tall as I was now. Judith would've called him a man. So would've

Doug Wilson and Doug Phillips and Bill Gothard and every patriarch I
knew. Boys William's age aren't taught by their mothers anymore, let alone
protected by them. They're young men assuming leadership in their homes,
molded by their fathers.

I didn't know then what I know now: that as traumatic as it is to put an
animal down, William's shock was more about the visceral step into manhood
he thought he was taking, and he didn't think his dad made him do it out of
violence or abuse. I didn't know how important perception is when it comes
to traumatic experiences and how they're stored in the brain. The same event
can happen to two people and one will be traumatized, and one won't, because of how they perceived it in the moment. I didn't know anything except
one concrete, glaringly harsh truth:

I could not live like this anymore.

Out of breath, I let the cold concrete of reality settle in my blood. Allan
was right—I was a shit wife, a shit housekeeper, and a shit mother—because
I'd stayed here too long. Seeds of strength began to assemble in my body. I
felt cells replicate and develop mass.

All along, I thought I was protecting the kids. Shielding them from realities behind closed doors. Sacrificing to maintain a two-parent Christian
home. Making hard, better choices for their faith, family, and education than
I made for myself, trying to safeguard them from pain.

But they saw. That was obvious now. And staying meant raising sons who
hit women. Staying meant raising a daughter who stayed with the man who
hit her. And that would be my fault: the woman who perpetuated the cycle.
I'd be the one who taught them life like this was okay. I didn't just let erratic
violence continue happening—I helped by refusing to leave. I sanctioned it
with my tolerance.

Good mothers don't let this happen to their kids, I thought. But this time,
the realization that I'd played a part in this dynamic didn't plunge me into a
puddle of self-pity. Complicity is a choice.

The mass of courage building within me quickened with intelligence. I remembered reading the signs of partner violence that led to murder. His rapid
increase in drinking was a sign. Reporting me missing to my family was a sign.
And shooting animals was another sign. Allan was escalating and there was only

one other human on the planet who could do something about it. Me. I was the one who saw, and I was the one with the agency to do something about it.

My children didn't have no one. They had a mother.

Sometimes awareness rises like the dawn, a gradual warmth that lightens the day. But sometimes it's the interrogator's spotlight. Glaring, harsh, and utterly definite. There was darkness, there was light. There was not a space between.

Just as my spirit knew the hour to give up Clara's body, and just as how she'd so indelibly changed me that I couldn't go back to what was, I now knew with precision that I had to get my kids out of here, even if we were damaged in the leaving. It was more than not being the mother I wanted to be. Living there would ruin them. And might even kill them.

I had no idea what Allan might do. He'd already done so much more than I feared. What else was he capable of?

Whatever was out there or whatever price we paid in leaving, it had to be better than this voluntary hell. How many close calls did I think heaven would grant me?

It was time for me to reckon with reality.

No hoping for a better day.

No tucking the feelings down inside.

No balancing a precarious double life with lies.

No special God-rules to help us escape our pain.

I grounded myself in time: *today is Sunday, October 28, 2007.*

I finally didn't care if it resulted in eternal damnation or public, humiliating shame, or endless poverty and financial ruin. I didn't care that I'd just remodeled the house or spent all my money. The time for excuses was over.

This time, it hit me when he hit me—reflexively today but with intention in the inevitable future. This life was a cycle. Little boys lose their laughs. They grow up hurting, and then they hurt other people. And that's if we even made it that far.

Truth came in a sequence.

My children would not survive here.

There wasn't a savior coming.

It was up to me to save us.

I pushed my hands flat to the floor and rose to make a plan.

Part
Five

AND WHEN
SHE IS FREE

Run

TO MAKE A PLAN, I NEEDED A BEAT. I KNEW I'D ONLY GET ONE chance and if I screwed it up, that would be it. I was too afraid to imagine the consequences. There was a pressure at my back, an invisible force urging me away, away. I counted items to take with me. The scrapbooks, the baby clothes. What else?

Halloween. Mom had made the kids costumes while she was here: Elvis, Pippi Longstocking, George Washington. Gavin would wear William's old bunny costume from our fall festival days. The kids were looking forward to it with so much fervor, I hoped something happy would distract them from what they'd just been through. We'd leave the day after. November 1, while Allan was at work.

I needed to tiptoe careful. Allan couldn't know what I was thinking. This meant staying steady. There could be no changes to the routine at all. Meals needed to be ordinary and on time. Bedtimes strictly enforced. School needed to resume. I could not crack. I could not lose my shit. I could not even fully recover from the exhaustion I'd suffered at the end of the blog event.

The silence hurt my ears, but so did sound. I couldn't swallow food. Water in the shower offended and then enveloped me. I proceeded robotically, afraid the walls were listening to my thoughts, afraid I'd be found out.

Details sharpened, like the grain of the warm wood floors when the sunlight hit them and the scent of lemon in the bedsheets when I tucked Katie in. I heard a ticking clock when we had no clock and time crawled by, tethering my feet to the floor.

As soon as Allan left for work on the twenty-ninth, I called Father Justin, who worked as a sub priest at St. Anne's and who'd adopted one of the kitchen puppies the week before.

I gave him the rundown of all that had happened since my last confession. Speaking the words out loud felt like someone else was saying them. My ears heard my mouth tell the truth about the puppies and Allan reporting me missing to my family and of his seeing demons in the walls at night. I kept my voice low and even, because I knew the time for skirting and wishing and allowing cracks in the plan was gone. This could not go the way it had years before when I told Mom I couldn't stay here. We wouldn't live if it did.

"You have to get out of there," he said.

I exhaled and kept pacing. "Yes, but how? I don't know how."

"I'll help you. Can you pack some things?"

"I can, but we need to be careful, Father. I'm afraid for our lives. I can't make sudden movements. That will only make Allan worse."

"When were you planning to leave?"

"In two days. After the kids do Halloween, it's their first."

"You're going to take them trick-or-treating before telling Allan you want a divorce?"

"I know it sounds ridiculous. But they're children. They won't understand divorce. They *will* understand they've missed their costumes and candy on top of everything else. And Allan doesn't know."

"That's for the best," he said. "In my experience, when men like Allan think their world is about to change, they go crazy. It's the stuff that makes news headlines. We don't want that to happen. Okay, I support the Halloween plan. Pack what you can. Take your kids trick-or-treating. Write Allan a letter, and when he goes to work, bring the children to the church. We'll go from there. Nothing will happen once you are in town."

I put the phone down. The plan felt so clear and sequential, like an algebra equation. A + B = C. Could it have been that easy all along?

From what I could tell, Allan was barely sleeping and barely eating. He constantly paced, irritated and itching, thinking. He cried in the bathroom but wouldn't unlock the door. He screamed in the night about the demons, which he now said were the old ladies who used to live here and died in these rooms.

Allan came home after work gray and silent, unchanged by leaving the house.

I washed all the clothes and folded them in piles on the table, same as always, and worked out the plan in my mind. Pack. Letter. Costumes. Sleep. Church. *Stay where I can see you.*

I figured we'd go to the church, and Father Justin would call Allan and facilitate a conversation about a separation. He'd finally go to therapy. Take medication and stop drinking. After a while, he'd have visitation and we'd keep things reasonably intact for the kids. As I folded baby shirts sleeve to sleeve, I realized this softening was the danger of time. I'd been here before, in Clara's death room.

I'd held out for the good man I knew was inside. The one playing chess, the one good with a colicky baby. Wiping the clean counters again, I started crying. What had wishing gotten me? What had putting up with so much pain done to bring the good Allan back? I dried my tears with the back of my hand and straightened my spine. I needed to stay steady and avoid sadness before safety softened my resolve.

Twenty-four long hours later, it was finally Halloween.

Our small town designed a sort of loose route for trick-or-treaters and the kids bounded and leaped with their plastic pumpkins, collecting candy like normal kids. I wondered if next fall they might attend school here. A small-town school wouldn't be so bad, and I could use the hours to work. The night was picture-perfect and sentimentally ideal, with a deep purple night sky and a yellow-white full moon gleaming down on myriad little witches and ghosts and Power Rangers and superheroes.

Allan and I didn't speak. He walked next to me but felt miles away. I panicked and then forced myself to compartmentalize. I thought about what we looked like to the others around us: the weird couple who wasn't from here, with the gloomy, moody husband and the skittish, nervous wife, and their odd but cute kids. No one else in town had dressed up like George Washington.

We let the kids fill their pumpkins and then steered them toward the van and home.

I stowed the pumpkins on top of the refrigerator, like Mom had done with mine, and then gave the kids baths with lavender to calm the sugar highs. Clean pajamas. One extra story because they were a little hyper. Tuck ins. Doors closed. I stood in the hallway holding my secret that this was our last night here, at least for a while. I walked down the stairs to clean the kitchen again, anxious for tomorrow.

Allan came in from wherever he'd been. All through the bedtime routine, I hadn't known where he was. In our room, downstairs, outside. The night suddenly felt wicked and pregnant with dread. I counted the knives in the drawer, hoping it looked like I was searching for something.

Allan was riled up, animated, his black eyes bright with rage. He paced the living room, snorting like an angered bull, drawing his hooves against the dusty arena, ready to do battle with one clearly undermatched. Consequences were coming for me.

The oven clock read it was nine. I kept my body moving, making no perceptible wind-down toward the bed, because he was pacing in front of the staircase, between the steps and the woodstove. What if I climbed the stairs and he pulled me down? What if he grabbed my braid and dragged me around? The kids would hear in this house. They'd wake up.

"Go to bed, go to hell. Go to bed, go to hell," he chanted.

I saw him reach for a length of firewood, the last of what Muffy had delivered. I knew it was sixteen inches exactly, aged, and splintered. As his pacing moved into the kitchen where I was, I willed my body not to flinch, not to run in case I was chased.

"You fucking bitch. You whore. I know why you were in town. I know what you're going to do. I ought to take you out there and smear your face in dog shit. You reek. You stink of other men. I always knew you'd leave me."

He spit on me.

I refused to flinch. I reached for the dishcloth and wiped it off, keeping my head down and making my movements as slow and ordinary as a tired woman usually moves at the end of a long, hard day. Dish towel. Casserole pan. Dry it even though it's dry.

The clock read ten, then eleven. He continued to pace and spew and spit. I was a Jezebel; I would ruin him; I *had* ruined him. He should kill me; he should kill all of us; he should send us to our maker. La Touche was right, he knew it then, and he knew it now. He should drown me; he should get rid of me tonight, he should, he should, he should.

The firewood waved the air, slicing like a pointer, reminding me that at any moment he could bludgeon me, and it would be over.

I dusted and then oiled the wooden furniture. Sorted the markers from the crayons. Moving but never quickly. I scoured the sink and wiped the surfaces of the washer and dryer, digging my towel-covered finger into the cracks around the lid. I took meat from the freezer for tomorrow's dinner, an ordinary motion.

We danced like this, the two of us, always moving, Allan fueled on insults and hatred, and me on prescient fear and watching.

I finally had to go upstairs because I'd run out of things to touch downstairs. I climbed the stairs slowly yet quickly enough to remain out of reach in case he decided to pull me down.

What happens to a man that causes him to harm the flesh of his flesh intentionally? What happens inside of a good person that turns them into this? How was I staying so calm? How many hours were there until the dawn?

In our bedroom, I went to my desk and organized. He seemed to struggle with the habit of preparing for bed, going to the bathroom, and going through the motions. He was stalling.

I moved my new L.L.Bean boots from one side of the closet to another, a blog-earnings treat. He erupted in fresh jeers, this time a poisoned blessing.

"Those boots! Oh, so nice! You bought them with your money, didn't you, Tia. You bought yourself nice new boots while I suffered with my old ones. Well, guess what? *I want new boots too!* I want nice things. I'm sick of being your husband. I'm sick and tired of living this hard life with you. I'm sick of being slammed with animals and living in this dump and always-always-always having something responsible to do. You're so bright and talented? Well, guess what, Tia?! You ARE. You *are* bright and talented. And I'm nothing. I'm uneducated and stupid and exhausted. I hate this life and I hate you. You have no idea how much I hate you. I hate how successful you're going to be. I hate how bright you're going to shine because people love you and want to hire you, and of course, our children will choose you because even the damn dogs choose you. You're a fucking talented Jezebel whore who always wanted to outshine me and damn you, I'm . . . I'm . . ."

He turned and walked out of the room.

I blinked, unsure I'd just seen him leave. He'd never left in a fight. Ever.

His feet shuffled down the stairs. I heard his tread cross the kitchen and the door slam.

For several seconds, I stood absolutely still, astonished at what just happened. Then I stood and stared at the black square of the window. Two red taillights traced a line from our corner to the highway.

I heard a voice say, *"RUN."*

The plan executed prematurely but in a fluid wave, washing us out. I loaded sleepy kids into the van along with my laptop, the laundry on the table, Allan's cell phone from the counter, and their two favorite kittens. I backed out and drove.

Desperate. But calm. Like I'd gone above when Clara died, I was above again, up in the stars, watching as my minivan traveled through the hills, like a little green Monopoly car moving across a game board. There were no other cars this late—just the high white moon and the listening mountains and trees watching me go. Around the curves. Up the hills. Down the hills. It's something to be seen by the moon.

There were no lights on in town except for the clockface of the courthouse tower, and the traffic light that flashed yellow on my face as I approached.

"Mommy, are you and Daddy getting divorced?" Liam asked.

His voice startled me. My mind returned to the car. How did Liam know that word? I caught his glance in the rearview mirror and lied to him, to avoid upsetting them all. "No, honey." *Separated,* I thought. He'll get therapy. Medication. Visitation. Restoration.

I held the cell phone in my lap, ready to call 911 if he found and chased me, but I had no idea where he'd gone or when he'd come back or what he'd do when I eventually saw him again.

By the second traffic light, by the courthouse, there was a car coming toward me as I approached it. I kept the wheel steady, on course, with no sudden movements. When the glare of the headlights passed, and I could see the car, I saw it was Allan, but that he hadn't seen me.

His eyes were focused straight ahead, and he looked delirious, like a madman. He came from the direction of the office, and that's when I remembered the gun. He'd left to get the gun.

Hours later, the children asleep on pallets of blankets made by Jodie, Father Justin's wife, I sat looking out at the lowering moon. Jodie was the first witness to the shame of my failure, but she listened with love, and poured hot tea in a blue mug while I poured out words. Kenai, the kitchen-floor puppy, slept on her lap.

I felt hollow, like a blown-out egg. A fragile shell that couldn't hold my life, let alone keep the five of us safe. I'd given it all that I had. Secrets make you hate yourself, but they proliferate and entangle others, and that's your life, a series of secrets and lies and ugly truths. Detangling a web is nothing easy, but I was grateful that night for a midwife of a different kind. A friend who didn't offer platitudes, just a witness. I didn't have to tell every secret that night—just one.

As the sun broke over the trees, I sat in stunned silence near their picture window on the first day of my free life.

This would be the first day I'd told the truth.

Late that afternoon, Father Justin arranged a meeting with Allan, to say a brief goodbye to the kids. This would protect me, he said, because if Allan said goodbye, then he could not accuse me of kidnapping when I drove them home to Florida.

Allan was sweaty, unbathed, and exhausted. He never looked at me. "See you soon," he said to the kids.

Father Justin promised to watch over him. I got in the car, and he handed me a cup of coffee for the road. "Look up Father Ted when you get there," he said. "He can help."

I drove out of Oak Ridge, down I-40 toward highway 95 S. I called my parents on the way and told them the whole truth, all fourteen years of it, while the kids were sleeping.

"Just come home," Mom said.

And that's what I did.

Drive

FIVE HUNDRED AND SIXTY-ONE MILES FROM THE CUMBERLAND Mountains. One hundred and eighty-six thousand miles on my van. One mother, three little boys, a little girl, and two kittens. Guided down 95 S by the light of the hunter's moon. Cell phone in my lap, all of our belongings left behind.

I drove the van pursued by more than fear. I traveled over asphalt and highways, past the old farms and pecan groves of southern Georgia, every mile underscoring a truth, a dividing line too vast to ever cross again.

I knew I was near the ocean by the flatness of the land. Stoic rows of pine crowded out the sky, but I could see it in glimpses, high and blue, reflecting the sea even this far inland. The flatness yielded to the breadth of the sky, and the open sky meant now I could breathe. I was almost home. And if I needed to scream my sorrows, I knew the vessel of tears and sea would receive me.

I came to Jacksonville relieved, too hypervigilant for crying. I pulled into the small town on the outskirts where my parents were building a farm, sure I'd just left the fires of hell.

This is what it was to leave, to tear the veil from top to bottom, to constantly count their heads in my rearview mirror and know—to the hollow echo of my soul—that life would never be the same. There was no *back*. No *I'm sorry*. No *let's try again*. I'd sworn to pay any price for survival and now I would, without knowing if survival meant freedom or flame. All I could pray was *away, away, away*.

My brain reached, then failed, to comprehend the pathways and events that led us here. My sizzled nerves couldn't keep still. I was exhausted, sleep deprived, and devastated. A sweaty nervous chill kept spreading over my chest and upper arms that felt like I might vomit up the clots of my broken heart. My children were confused, trying to do the math of Halloween, a slumber party at the priest's house, and saying goodbye to their father for a sudden trip to Grandma's. Their candy was still on top of the fridge.

All I knew were these truths happened and led to one another. The dominoes had fallen. Somehow, I felt held, sustained by angels or the mystical cloud of witness or God—but only in the moment. Held like a spotlight and if I stepped a toe beyond, I'd be cast in darkness. I had no idea what the rules were, or who would still love me when they heard my story. What did "we got away" even mean? Where was I? *Who* was I?

I wanted to lie down and sleep for a thousand years. Nothing within me knew how to let go. In the days that followed, my disembodied brain told me we were safe now. But it would be years before my body—organs, cartilage, muscles, tissues—trusted this was true. I flinched and jumped when startled, even by a bird on a branch or a ringing phone breaking the silence. I couldn't set down my cell phone, ever. Well-meaning friends said I needed to make peace with the peace, but my body didn't know how. I could see we were safe, but my system didn't believe it.

The new farm was only partially constructed when we arrived. Dad set up the camper for me and built bunk beds for the kids inside the main house. I slept fitfully, drowning in terror and sweaty, twisted sheets. I woke grateful the kids couldn't hear my screams. Mom made them regular meals and organized art projects. Numb, I took long walks under the pines trying to sort out how this had happened and where I was supposed to go from here. Sometimes I trembled for no reason.

A week after arriving in Florida, Allan called on Mom's office line. He said he wanted to speak to the kids, but he was so slurred I could hardly understand him.

"Thank you, Tia. Thank you." He was crying, moaning in between his words. "You did what I couldn't. You blew up our fam-i-ly. You blew it up."

I clutched the receiver of the phone, as breathless as I'd felt that night in the kitchen. "Allan. Listen to me. Are you okay?"

"I'm about to be!"

"What does that mean?" The line was silent except for his jagged breathing. "Allan, what does that mean?"

"It means, silly woman, that in a few minutes, I'm gonna be in heaven. You
see I've got this gun here—"

"Mom!" I yelled to the other room. And then into the phone, "Allan, Allan
listen to me. Please do not hurt yourself, please, for the kids."

I was crying and shaking. Mom came in wide-eyed. I put my hand over
the phone and told her to call the police in Tennessee because Allan might
shoot himself.

I slumped to the floor and tried to keep Allan talking. "We'll be back up
there soon," I said. "You'll get visits with the kids and we'll figure out an ar-
rangement."

"Good thing, where have you gone," Allan slur-sang. "She left me here
with the demons."

"Allan, just stay here. Keep talking. Please, Allan."

He wasn't talking, but I heard shuffling.

Then, POP! POP-POP!!

Gunshots????

Time went quiet, as if sounds evaporated. I held the receiver in my hand,
still as a statue created from volcanic ash. Mom took it from my hands and
hung up the phone.

An hour passed. And then an officer called to explain.

"Mrs. Brown, I arrived at your home to find your husband stumbling on
the porch. He threatened to shoot me, but I was able to engage with him because he didn't seem to be armed. After threatening the other officer on the call
with me, your husband fell face-first off the porch. He was quite intoxicated,
ma'am, and was placed in custody. I then conducted a search of your home
and found a Ruger pistol on the bed in the master bedroom. Your husband
will remain in custody and be evaluated by a mobile crisis team. I would ad-
vise you, ma'am, to remain in Florida and keep your children safe."

Allan's attempted suicide resulted in an involuntary week-long hospital
stay. I wondered what he'd said to the officers to specifically flag a warning
toward me and the kids. But I did as they directed and filed for an Order of

Protection. I started searching online for an attorney. Monica and Jake said they'd help pay.

Now that it was clear we'd be in Florida for the foreseeable future, I planned a road trip back to Tennessee to pack my things. I used practical matters and crossing items off my list to distract myself from the dread and regret that Florida had caught me again. A neighbor had been feeding the pets and needed supplies. I'd make a quick trip, there and back, and go to the house while Allan was at work.

When I got there, the house had a vacant, winter's bone look to it, as if no one had been there in a long time. I walked through the front room gathering a few books and toys into a basket. Then I went upstairs. Except for our torn-up bedroom, everything else was as we'd left it. The only thing I could see that was missing was my vision board. The spot next to my bed where it had hung was blank and empty, too new to have even left a shadow on the wall.

I packed a few boxes, loaded the van, and remembered to grab the kids' candy. I backed out of the driveway but then decided to pull into the church parking lot across the street to get my shit together. I was crying, bits of transient loss and failure hitting my consciousness like dandelion seeds in the wind.

That's when I saw Allan's car.

He sped around the corner and screeched into our driveway, bursting out of the car and tearing into the house, screaming my name.

Frantically, I locked my doors and dialed his work. "Why isn't Allan at work?" I asked the woman who answered.

"He is," she said. "He's in the warehouse."

"No, he's not. He's at our house! And now the police are here!"

A patrol car pulled in behind Allan and then a second one. I got out of the van, waving frantically where they could see me. One of them approached.

"Ma'am, we got a call about an intruder."

"I'm not an intruder, this is my house!"

Allan threw open the front door, jumped off the porch, and headed toward us.

I scrambled behind the policeman, to hide behind him and keep Allan between us. "I have an OP! He can't come near me!" Desperately, I ripped the paperwork from my purse and held it in the air.

The officer stood between us and made Allan back up. The other officer came over and looked at my document.

"Well, he done called the cops on himself," he laughed. "Let's take him in. He's clearly violating this OP."

They loaded Allan into the back of one of the patrol cars and I looked up shakily at the hills. Someone up there had seen me, called Allan at work, and told him I was in our house. What if the police had shot me, thinking I was an intruder?

I trembled the whole drive back to my hotel. I hired an attorney I'd found online, a ruddy Irishman who specialized in car accident claims. His office contained piles of court files and sort of confidential records but no furniture and was dimly lit by desk lamps sitting on the carpet instead of actual side tables.

"Here," he said, handing me a book after I'd given him the high points. The front cover showed half of a woman's face, bruised. Red slanted letters read *The Battered Woman*.

"I wasn't battered," I said, confused. "Allan never once punched me in the face."

"You were abused. Read it. You'll see your story in the pages."

My empty stomach heaved, and I could feel the pulsing of my carotid artery against the muscles in my starving core. I stared at the cover, recognizing the living-dead gaze of her eyeball. I knew that feeling—but my brain resisted matching my experience to ugly words like "battered" and "abusive."

When I got back to the camper in Florida, I read about cycles of abuse and invisible wounds. About rage and misplaced eroticism. Triggers. Remorse. Repentance. Patterns that played out in predictable sequences from the first few months of my relationship with Allan.

I repeated the words in my mouth, trying to force them to have meaning in my body. "Battered." "Abusive." My mind understood. My heart failed to comprehend how a good Christian girl who chose what God wanted ended up this way. My body held its breath in suspension, wondering if heart or mind would win. Hadn't I prayed? Hadn't I obeyed? Wasn't God bigger than all of this?

Later that month the judge made my temporary Order of Protection permanent and ordered a forensic investigation to determine stability and custody. I drove back to Tennessee to meet the doctor.

Dr. W was silver and grandfatherly, his office decorated like an old western. In the first meeting he took my entire history, all the way through the scene with the police at the house. "Tomorrow, I'll meet your husband, Tia, and then I'll call you to set up a time to meet the children."

But his plan wasn't what happened. When he called me the next day, I was just leaving the Starbucks drive-through before the long drive back to Jax. "Go get your children, Tia. I want you to take them and hide. Don't tell your parents where you're going, don't tell anyone but your priest."

I spilled my latte as I asked the doctor to repeat himself. The gray sky covered us all, mountains, highway, small broken woman in an old minivan. Where could I go that he wouldn't find us? Where does a single mom with four children hide?

She finds a Trapdoor.

Having a network of online friends that Allan had no clue about turned out to be salvation. I tried framing it as a giant field trip, a mammoth-sized homeschool adventure up the East Coast, but even with support, it was a farce that was hard to hold up. The kids were smart enough and old enough to know Mommy didn't usually just take them on long road trips through the snowy north.

BethSC had a giant trampoline in Greenville. In DC we saw all the monuments and had bowls of hot soup in Chinatown. Dali made blueberry pancakes in Philly. Michael took them sledding in Massachusetts. Anna taught them how to feed hogs in New York. But I also got lost on the New Jersey Turnpike, slid on the ice in New York, and cried while cleaning up puke that spread from the backseat to my steering wheel when Liam got carsick. An elderly couple stopped and asked me if I was okay and I, with vomit freezing on my fingers and no idea where to go next, lied and said I was, because I was too overwhelmed and humiliated to tell the truth.

We were gone for four months. Sometimes I flew back to see the doctor or see my attorney, trusting my children would be loved with my friends. While away, I connected with my clients or used the alone hours to grieve.

I thought it would help if I could pin down *what* I was grieving, because I wasn't sorry. As hard as it was to be out, not once did I wish I was back. I took long runs and pounded the pavement with questions I didn't have answers to, questions I was afraid to ask out loud.

Was I grieving him? Was I allowed to? Could I feel sadness for someone I'd run away from, who'd held me under threat?

Was it the loss of couple-hood that hurt? Debriefing and comparing notes on something cute the kids had done? Was it safe to let myself go there? Missing the good parts could lead to weakness. I couldn't afford to be soft during the legal wrangling, and he was not letting me go without a fight.

I couldn't let myself imagine the day in Clara's death room or his fierce blue eyes when I'd met him. Those moments were an elusive wave I tried to hold back until the tide pulled it from my fingers. Grieving was like trying to hug a vapor, a ghost.

In loneliness I realized I grieved the idealized dream.

The dream of all I'd been promised so many years before. *Stay pure and wait for God's best to find you,* they'd said. *These rules lead to happiness and heaven.* I'd never been enough. Never submissive enough, never sweet enough, never serving enough. I grieved failure and the years I'd lost. I grieved the magic God who blessed rule keepers. I grieved who I might have been. I grieved that in saving my children, so much was hard for them here.

The migraines began and I lost weight, at first a little, and then a lot.

In confession, Father Ted recommended nights out with friends and also a therapist. "You're still a young woman," he said. "You'll get through this."

He gave me Stephanie's name and number, the counselor he referred parishioners to, and I scheduled an appointment.

A few days later, she sat across from me in a paisley chair near the window in her office. I sat on a couch across from her, trying to hold it together. I was here because I was cracking under the pressure of running from him, and keeping us safe and steady, while trying to get on my feet. A nap seemed more attractive.

Like the doctor, she too began with my history.

"What happened to you was rape. It was abuse. It was control. It was trauma. It's important you learn to call these situations what they actually are, and that you learn to stop relying on wishful thinking to get you through."

I stared at the horizontal window blinds over her shoulder. This felt like a floor of new eggshells. How do you call what happened to you "rape" and at the same time support the reputation of the one who raped you? How do you come to terms with an abuser you also loved, who sometimes did kind things and made some of your dreams come true? How do you come to comprehend that someone is sick, and navigate around their symptoms, when those symptoms threaten to harm you and strip you of all native compassion? How do you represent both sides of that person to your children?

I didn't know how to do it.

"Tia, tell me the first time you remember feeling abandoned," Stephanie said, and that took us back to the beginning, to further back than I expected. It took me back to church and realizing how I was too much and I'd be left behind.

"There's a reason why you married him and blew past the red flags," she said. "What did you learn about marriage, growing up at church?"

I used the drive back to the kids to process her questions, not knowing that Stephanie had put her finger on the religious trauma I'd spend the next decade processing. Sensations stuck in my memory the way burrs once clung to my crimson mittens in the snow, the way old brown blood will stain white sheets forever. I felt filthy. Ruined for life. I'd blown past red flags for so many reasons. My obedience was supposed to lead to beauty, not ashes.

But in the months ahead, Allan and the marriage I'd hoped we'd find haunted me.

I couldn't remember the last time we'd had sex—but I could remember the taste of his tongue in my mouth when we were dating.

I couldn't remember any holiday gift he'd given me—but I was triggered by the scent of wintergreen mints, which smelled like the snuff he kept in his car.

It was as if Allan was in my veins. Inside of me. Part of me. Unsheddable. Indelible ink that stained my cells.

Who had I been before him and who was I with him? When I cried about it, I couldn't tell if I meant my husband or God. It was an interesting question that once spoken, I couldn't un-ask. Who was I before I heard about God?

Who was I before they told me I needed Him, and that if I didn't satisfy, I'd be abandoned to burn in eternal flames?

Who was I without that?

Who was I when I sat down in the dirt without any qualifiers and without any faith and without any definitions? When I was just *me* in the dirt under the trees and in the wind?

What was my purpose here? Why did I matter? *Did* I matter? Beyond my family and their love for me, did my being have any purpose at all? Questions ate my days and swallowed my nights until I felt like I walked through a hall of distorted mirrors and blurred realities.

Love. It's such a small word. God, Allan, love, faith, loss—none of these were simple. The ground undulated beneath me always. I spun, the world spun.

I didn't know who or what to trust.

Like I had before when I was grieving Clara and disoriented by a life that went on without her, I went to the ocean to scream. I screamed at GOD. I screamed at MEN. I screamed at VIRGINITY and PURITY and SUBMIS- SION and SPANKINGS. I screamed about my dead baby and my sad, suf- fering children, and I screamed at my failure. I screamed until my salted voice was hoarse and my eyes swelled as red as my sunburned skin.

In Tennessee, the doctor urged me to talk to the kids about how to love a sick parent who may not be able to care for them. The kids were beginning to unspool and ask questions. They missed their father. They didn't under- stand divorce.

"Tia, you were in charge of your family's public relations for years," said Dr. W. "And you still are. The reputation of the absent parent is the respon- sibility of the present one. Your children will direct all their anger at him to- ward you, because you are here and safe and they can trust you not to leave when they get emotional. You must hold space for them to be able to do that."

I remembered how mothers contain and grow life within their hollows. There was space for their feelings within me there. But I also sat in the tension of learning to call what happened to me using correct language, while simultaneously holding that named trauma far enough to the side to remember he was still their dad. Where would he face accountability? Why did mothers have to support the reputations of men who weren't there? It was as if the support resources—the therapists and investigators and judges—all understood that parental alienation was terrible. But they'd swung so far the other way that there wasn't a healthy way to hold absent men responsible for their own reputations. Somehow, I had to spread my arms wider and hold it all.

On May 21, 2008, the judge finalized our divorce. I startled as he tapped his gavel, listening like a cardinal on the branch as he granted me the Blue House. It wasn't safe to live there, and I'd have to fly away, but what a thing to hear it called mine. Allan had been fired and, without an income, child support would be calculated after custody. Dr. W determined Allan was stable enough for me to stop hiding, take the kids back to Florida, and establish residency, and for Allan to have supervised visitation at a facility.

I quivered, hearing these men use words like "safe," and "yours," and "it's over now." New skin burned in the light, but that day, I took tentative, dancing new steps, walking on sunshine, so grateful to be *divorced*. I'd spent a lifetime hearing divorce was the ultimate loss. I said I didn't believe in it. But my spirit unlocked, free like the birds in the late spring trees in downtown Knoxville. And I believed, now, in freedom.

I walked through Market Square downtown, wanting to notice every detail, like the patina of peeling paint on a store's front door and the delicate scrollwork on the gate to a courtyard. I thought maybe I spotted Reese Witherspoon wearing a hat and carrying a yoga mat. Maybe it wasn't her. But daylight glitter and fireflies and celebrity sightings all suddenly seemed possible! I couldn't help but wonder . . . what else had they said was horrible that might actually feel like bliss?

That afternoon, Tim offered me a trip to New York City in exchange for some work on his website—a chance to network my skills at the National Speakers Convention—and I took it, excited to step forward into this mysterious future.

When I got to New York, I blogged that "I went to the city to live deliberately." Central Park and street bagels and John Lennon's Imagine covered in flowers bolstered me the same way a retreat in an isolated wood might've Thoreau. The city pulsed with second chances. At the keynote with Tim Ferriss, I met speakers and some of my clients, handing out business cards with genuine smiles, and attended panels. At the end, I had drinks at a table that included a man introduced to me as K.

I didn't take much notice of him at the time. I was laughing with Marsha, a favorite client known for her tenacity and wit. There were four or five of us there and K stayed quiet, down at the end, silently sipping wine. All these years later, I'm still not sure we spoke that day.

So, when I got home to Florida, I wasn't expecting the two things that were waiting for me along with the kids. One was a manila envelope with a letter from Dr. W recommending full legal and physical custody be mine. The second was a message from K. He worked for Business Breakthroughs with Chet Holmes and Tony Robbins, and he wanted to offer me a job.

I walked into Dad's woodshop and sat down in the sawdust, not caring I'd get covered in it. This—these lustrous opportunities and surprises—had to be what it felt like for the universe to catch me, for a village of support to come around and hold me. Maybe healing was possible after all, and maybe I *could* still reclaim the years ahead.

Something strong rose in me then. An ember, a part of me, a hope—a cheetah woman or lioness—I didn't know. I could only feel her burn, feel her sudden hunger to see beyond what the collective *they* said I had to be. I could be Mother. Friend. Daughter. Maybe even Wife again. I could cook and grow and read and serve. But there was also the word I'd put away like a box of photographs, stuffed into the back of the closet. I held the word now, watching it materialize as my finger traced it into the sawdust on the floor.

I could be *more*.

I called K back and accepted the job.

Learn

claim my life, which looked very different from *Little House on the Prairie* or Covenant Reformed anything. I chased the *more,* sometimes like a puma and sometimes like a hawk and sometimes like a sloth. Now I was free to be the mother I wanted to be. Now I'd be an SEO writer and help clients grow their businesses online. Now I'd train for a sprint triathlon and become a physically fit mother of five. Now I'd feel thirty-three instead of fifty-three. Now I was free, the heroine of my own story, and I'd sleep in peace. I'd be an artist writer mother hiker friend.

Rediscovering optimism felt like the morning after a hurricane. I bounced when I walked and squinted with a smile into the sun. Youth pulsed in my veins again. I didn't expect that.

I posted a farewell on Living Deliberately and deactivated the blog. Posting in a place dedicated to my old life felt out of alignment—more like walking through the empty rooms of the Blue House, searching the shadows for answers. I started painting again, pressing my brush into pigment. My friends Julie, Beth, and Susan from Trapdoor were also divorcing and the four of us processed our experiences together. And I joined a domestic violence support group called Micah's House, sitting in a circle with suburban women I could've passed in the grocery store and never suspected their *battered, abused* realities any more than they suspected mine.

Something I learned quickly from them: my kids needed emotional space from these memories the same way I did. So, swallowing my fear they'd be bullied or harmed or taught scary things, I enrolled the kids in public school—the small county school in my parents' new town.

I told them their only job was to learn how to "do" school—to get used to schedules and homework and having to raise your hand to use the bathroom. They did so well it hurt my throat to hold back happy, relieved tears as they bounded up the driveway with their backpacks and smiles.

The emotional space, and the success of it, burst a blistered bubble I realized I'd been protecting for years: the idea that the world was inherently dangerous. That my trauma would replicate as theirs. That I could solve for the pain of the human experience. I didn't know then that my bubble was shared by so many other evangelicals, that we'd been guided to make these decisions as part of a wider cultural movement. In our fear, we'd lived inside a bubble of our own making, only to choke on fumes. And like any infected blister, the burst hurt. But it also revealed that the world wasn't what we thought it was, not at all—and eventually, that blister healed.

I struggled to trust a phenomenon that repeated itself over and over again: when I had a need, the universe rose to meet it. I wasn't alone out here. I was held—by angels, a cloud of witnesses, God—I wasn't sure who or what to call it. But it manifested in the form of caring teachers who helped my children acclimate from homeschool. And neighbors who noticed my van broken down on the side of the road and stopped to help. And friends of my parents who donated furniture. And new friends at our new church, St. Justin the Martyr, for me and the kids. Every day it was as if the more I made choices that saved me, the more others showed up to help save me too. The world, actually, was beautiful.

Julie, Beth, Susan, and I started reading Elizabeth Gilbert's *Eat, Pray, Love.* Like I had with *The Battered Woman,* I found myself in these pages. I felt awed at her honest realization of *I don't want to be married anymore,* right before she blew up a perfectly ordinary and nice life.

She left it—the nice man and the nice marriage and the nice life. I stared at the words on the page as a wave of debris washed over me. Disbelief. Jealousy. Curiosity. Wonder. Horror. Guilt. Courage. Self. Choice. More.

Could a woman do that? Get divorced to choose herself? Even churches that allowed divorce always said it should be for a big bad reason like adultery or abuse. The sermons always said people who got divorced without a big bad reason simply didn't value marriage. But I listened beyond sermons now.

Here was a woman who seemed to value marriage very much, and even loved the man she wanted to leave. But she couldn't stay with him without abandoning herself, and that had to change.

I sat with those words. I knew I'd spent so many years blaming Allan for our problems that I'd spent very little time exploring my own discontent and complicity. And I'd never considered all the ways I'd forced myself to shift, adapt, and change to meet so many expectations. What would it be like to choose myself? Or hell, just *be* my Self?

It was as if that cheetah (or lioness or puma . . . I didn't know) paced outside the camper. She was hungry. She wanted me to get it, to *understand*. She was strong enough to wait.

My hands shook when I read the pages, as if I held freedom porn that I'd get in trouble for reading. Gilbert presented a very freeing way to think of God. The divine wasn't the damning wrathful patriarch that misused women or pummeled us with a list of rules. And he/she/they wasn't a collection of vague and mysterious names like the ones I'd resorted to—universe, mystery, God-thing. Gilbert acknowledged Jesus as a great teacher of peace, but she had enough world experience to know that Jesus wasn't the only path to the divine in many cultures. Gilbert described God as an experience of supreme *love*. She said, "I believe in a magnificent God."

Magnificence. The word reminded me of the first time I met God—in the trees, not at church. On our eighty acres in Michigan, I often wandered the fields and woods alone while my parents were working.

There was a cluster of aspen and birch trees in the western field—a favorite of mine because the cluster felt like a magic circle and familial, imbued with belonging. It called to me as if a magnet, and I trekked beneath the high blue sky as a lone figure across the fields, small and out of place. Looking back and able to do the math, I must have been five in this memory, because I hadn't yet heard of hell. Five is too young to wander so far and yet, I always knew where I was.

The leaves on the trees were *magnificently* aflame, the color of school buses, sunflowers, and honey. When I arrived, I stood in the midst and looked up. A beam of white sunshine pierced the golden canopy. Warmth flooded through me and I heard a breeze—but more than that, I heard the trees breathing, the leaves laughing like pillow-soft aunties who pull you into a hug. I felt love kiss my nose. I felt love make me warm. I knew in my bones this was God.

For years I counted this experience as a pretty memory. I told myself I was mistaken to feel the divine. Given to a wild imagination. That was before I knew how aspen trees connected underground. How, beneath the surface, the roots of birch and aspen trees resemble the human nervous system, networked together in communication, memory, and learning.

Harvard scientists studied the symbiotic relationship between the trees' roots and the fungal microbes in the soil. The mycorrhizal network between them creates families they utilize for protection against harmful threats and stress.

What was happening that day as I stood in their midst was that the trees identified me as friend, not foe. Unified underground, they offered me belonging. We were kindred beings, reflections and fractals of one another—souls who breathe, communicate, learn, and remember.

Now in the camper I understood the difference between religion and the divine. The cat in the shadows sat on her haunches, curling her long tail around. I felt her waiting, but calmer now. *Understand.*

Never had I ever had that same feeling in church. There were no rules in the woods—only an experience of supreme love. I didn't want to bury that love in rules ever again. My doubts and questions either. Love exceeded belief. Curiosity conveyed love more than any litany of principles and answers, because to be curious is to be free.

In the pages of *Eat, Pray, Love* I found inspiration to live independently and confidently explore my world. And I uncovered the seed of a secret prayer I was afraid to breathe to love or heaven or even the trees: Maybe I still had a chance at romantic love. Maybe someday, there would still be for me a partner lover friend.

Stephanie and I continued working in therapy. She used cognitive behavioral therapy to support me in finding the language to name my experiences and talk it out. But our sessions often remained in story and I didn't feel relief for having gone there. Talking it out didn't feel good. I sat in her paisley office clunkily making excuses, embarrassed I couldn't satisfy the teacher.

I churned inside, as though liquefied by venom. Even though I went to the gym most days and ran for miles to pound it out, horror and helplessness still hounded me. My night rages continued; my brittle flinches remained. I woke up sobbing and without words and went whole days feeling numb and unable to eat. When I was in Jacksonville for therapy or church or an errand, a simple road sign or landmark related to my marriage with Allan could set off heaving panic and a feeling I was being followed. Ghosts were everywhere.

This was not entirely only in my head. The few times Allan came into town for a supervised visit with the kids, he violated the OP and followed me, pranking my cell phone repeatedly. One time, my tires were slashed. The visits themselves went okay but there were always small infractions included in the reports, digging insults about me he said to the kids in front of the facilitator. The danger never felt far.

I wanted a tidy end to the struggle. An *over*. Stephanie said healing would be hard as long as an active threat remained. I needed to do it anyway. "You may be tied to him until your youngest is eighteen," she said. "You deserve to live an abundant, healed life in the meantime."

What was that? I could've tripped right over abundance. Not only was I doubtful I deserved it, but I also wasn't sure I'd recognize healing if it came. I decided to look for clues.

Sleuthing started with naming good deeds. On Sundays I drove into town with the kids, an hour each way, for church. Father Ted picked up where Father Stephen had left off, becoming my confessor. Parishioners paid for my children to attend summer camps that were nothing like the ones I'd grown up with, and when gas prices spiked, I found random twenty-dollar bills in my church mailbox. These were kind people extending generosity to us at a time when I most needed it and I understood now what it meant for God to work through people.

Mr. Fred Rogers had said, after disasters, "Look for the helpers," and he was right. Helpers were the source of hope. Hope was not born from following a list of rules. The truth was life was full of hurt. But the truth was also we were surrounded by help and hope.

One Sunday, in the line for coffee hour, my friend Noel tugged on my arm and said, "Tia, there's someone I want you to meet. This is Cary Grant."

My heart skipped.

His name wasn't really Cary Grant. But he reminded me of my favorite film hero in an instant, electric jolt of *he smells good* and *look at that posture* and *oh my god is he a dancer* and then he spoke and he was all smiles and warm mahogany and asked for a hug and of course I hugged him and felt his firm shoulders and muscular back and then we let go and I stood there gobsmacked and astonished this man existed. He was like a walking Eternity cologne ad. I swooned and tried to hold the swoon in and ended up smiling really big instead, a leaky transparent goof who'd never felt chemical attraction before.

Noel introduced him to my children, who quickly ran off to play, and we went through the coffee hour line for plates of sandwiches. We sat on the front bench and talked.

Cary Grant wasn't a dancer—he was a black belt in karate. He had three older children out of the house, worked in banking, and wore crisply ironed shirts with creases he'd placed himself. I asked him if he liked to read and he told me his favorite book was called *Neither Wolf Nor Dog* by Kent Nerburn and asked me if I'd ever heard of *The Soul of an Indian* by Ohiyesa. When I said I hadn't, he offered to send me a copy and asked for my phone number and email address.

What kind of a man reads about Mother Earth and talks about her at church? I was more than dazed by this man—I floated several hundred feet above the ground like a dizzy hot-air balloon.

I drove home trying to process what had just happened. Is this what it felt like to be attracted to someone at first sight? That afternoon it stormed, and I left the camper to walk and dance in the rain. Warm water from heaven felt like grace and healing to me, as if this earthly baptism replaced the contrived one in a chlorinated pool with red lights to represent the blood of Christ. This baptism refreshed and enlivened. The *more* came over me.

What to make of a man who attended an Orthodox church but spoke openly about Native American spirituality? He sent me an email and signed it, "Life can be hard, but God is good." He sent me a copy of Ohiyesa's book with an invitation to get together soon over a bottled water. This became a running joke as my schedule hardly allowed to meet up for coffee or water. Instead, we relied on email.

I found it profoundly comforting that *The Soul of an Indian*, as well as my new friendship with C. G., allowed room for mystery and nature. *The religion of the Indian is the last thing about him,* Ohiyesa wrote. *Worship of the "Great Mystery" was silent, solitary, free from all self-seeking. Our faith might not be formulated in creeds, nor forced upon any who were unwilling to receive it; hence there was no preaching, proselytizing, nor persecution, neither were there any scoffers or atheists.*

C. G. asked me if I knew of a place called Wallowa. I did, because nearby Joseph, Oregon, was known for fly-fishing, which I'd learned after seeing *A River Runs Through It*. He emailed, I don't like artificial heat. I get the fire going, throw some blankets on the ground and imagine it's a cold night in a teepee. I like the natural warmth of a fire, the sound of the wood burning and the smell. Remember that scene in *Dances with Wolves* when Kevin Costner is sitting by the fire and telling his concerns to Ten Bears? He's told to forget his concerns and to just enjoy the fire. There's comfort in simplicity.

His emails left me breathless and burning in a way my body didn't recognize. Here was a man responsible and professional, experienced with the world, with grown children and a deep affinity for the natural world. We could discuss books and films. I started looking forward to Sundays for reasons that had nothing to do with church. When he hugged me, I wanted to melt into his body, to climb into his clothes with him and share his food, share his shower, share his bed.

We finally had a first date—a double on the water at sunset with Noel and his girlfriend. We continued sending each other novel-long emails and texting late into the night. In August, I let him kiss me—a perfect rose-petal explosion of fire and chemical reaction and safety. I kissed him back. I participated—something at thirty-three and five children in, I'd never done with abandon before.

Here was *more*.

My dreams changed. My entire body came alive. Desire wasn't a word I'd known. But now I felt a rising inside and a division within. A curvaceous, gloriously seductive version of myself stood up and declared to Cary Grant that she *wanted*. Oh, how she wanted! I felt pulled forward by my hips. My body issued an invitation, followed by my mind and spirit. The invitation was accepted with tenderness and the wisdom of a man who knows how to take his precious, sweet time.

I hadn't realized my great reckoning with reality would include pleasure. That I would discover and unlock rooms with names like JOY and POWER and LOVE and DELICIOUSLY DELIRIOUS SATISFACTION. Being alive meant feeling all of it. It meant letting my guard down and trusting the hand I held as we danced together in the summer rain. It meant biting into decadent chocolate and juicy berries warm from the sun. It meant the scent of roses in the morning dew. It meant *let me grill you a steak* and *let's put on a good movie*. It meant eating when I was hungry and sleeping when I was tired. It meant fat, juicy goblets of miraculous, marvelous wine.

These rooms were every bit as real as the strain of single motherhood, driving with a broken AC in the Florida summer sun, with an ex-husband who couldn't stay sober long enough to see his kids. Real wasn't always difficult. Sometimes it was interstellar wonder and amazement at how many ways a generous lover could make a human body feel good.

But that's the thing about puritanical high-control religion. All those God-rules had numbed the entire human experience. The good and the bad, the joy and the pain. The rules said there wasn't *more* and I was wrong to thirst for it. Now here was reality, offering me drink.

I remembered my reflex of counting the good. I wasn't using it anymore as a way to bear the unbearable. I wasn't gaslighting myself, as I'd learn to call it years later. Simple gratitude for the good helped me identify what wasn't good, flower from weed.

I'd begun keeping a count of the teachings that had turned out to be wrong. I noted them in a little purple book I kept by my bed, finding hope in reality instead of dangling promises. I tucked my tiny diary of truth in the drawer the way I once did my little pink book with the padlock when I was thirteen, embarrassed and protective. I made lists, this time not about boys I liked but about the lies and what they'd cost me.

Purity culture hadn't prepared me for healthy sexuality. Keeping sweet hadn't equipped me to speak up about abuse. Waiting for touch to happen all at once hadn't allowed my nervous system to acclimate to intimacy. Doctors weren't evil agents of a New World Order. Scaring me with hell hadn't led to loving Jesus. Cutting off gay friends didn't make them straight. What else was wrong? Every day I found new things, old beliefs to pick apart and sort through.

Later that year, C. G. and Dad came with me back to the Blue House to pack up and retrieve my things. While the judge had granted me the house, it was in Allan's name and he refused to transfer the deed. The mortgage company refused to acknowledge my payments. It was time to let it go.

I'd left here a thin whisper. Now I was strong, alive and changed. As my feet treaded across the worn floorboards and I stood by the empty cold wood-stove, I realized the rooms didn't want me here. They felt rested and closed.

I cried, letting my fingers trace imprints in the drywall from the violence, remembering how I'd scrubbed and painted and planned for a life that stayed. I saw the shabby furniture with new perspective, my body aching to realize the poverty I'd held back like a hoary beast always threatening to swallow us whole. I stood in the closet office and wept with gratitude for the career that had been born in such a humble place. I cleaned up the ruined bedroom and gave most of the furniture to the neighbors. I built a fire in the yard and burned my clothes—bras, panties, dresses—anything I'd worn in that previous lifetime.

I looked up at the hills and let the ones watching know I was still standing.

As Dad and C. G. waited in the truck with my boxes, I stood in the empty Blue House alone, one last time. I'd left it clean. I laid the house key on the counter and said a prayer of gratitude to the experience of supreme love that had helped me survive. To the magic night when snow fell, and I'd gotten the kids out of bed to come see. To the blackberries by the train tracks warmed by the mountain sun. To Red Fox who ran with William while he skated laps. To the garden and the walnut tree and the woods where my children played. To the stove that burned cords of Muffy's firewood and kept my babies warm. To the spirits who saw what was happening and told me at that critical hour to *RUN*.

I turned and closed the door. Red leaves from the maple tree fell and scattered across the porch. I left it all behind as best I could.

When the new school year began, I moved into town to my own apartment with the kids and enrolled them in schools in Jacksonville. I turned the key in my own door and stepped over the threshold to a home I knew would be safe and sound. Only I wasn't a Christian princess cloistered away from reality, at someone else's mercy this time. I was an actualized grown woman with agency and autonomy providing her children a nurturing home.

And while I didn't always believe those words, I knew I was on my way to them. I was ready to be whole.

Part Six

———

SHE WILL DEPART FROM IT

Clear

GROWTH CAME IN LAYERS, AND THE COURAGE TO BE FULLY ALIVE
rose in increments. Registering experiences with awareness often felt harsh—
sometimes exciting. I thought I was free—and then a situation would trigger a slip into old patterns of wishful thinking and people-pleasing as I
searched for a rule framework that would make life feel less like swimming
in open water. A lot of times I chickened out. Many more times I reverted
into old patterns.

Dating C. G. was often a source of relief. He adored me—I, so unaccustomed to adoration. He brought roses and cooked meals and often kept the
house quiet so I could nap. C. G. bonded with each of my children and he
wanted a second-chance family. He proved the corny love songs were true. Cary
Grant helped me believe in love again, and I loved both him and the experience
of falling in love with him. We dated three years this way.

In therapy I fretted I didn't know how to choose my own partner, folding
and refolding my hands as I worked it out. Holding boundaries, so different
from setting them, was unfamiliar and I could be easily talked out of an opinion or preference in order to support harmony, or his older wisdom, or male
logic. As someone who loved spreadsheets and organization, he also loved systems and rules of convention. I tucked away some of my bold ideas of what
freedom looked like and rested in the illusion of safety that came from *this is
how it's done.* Insecure, I taught my kids to go along with what he wanted, a
fawning people-pleaser yet uncured.

Looking back, I can see that season in 2011 as a fracture inside of me. I can see that my muscles weakened, and I gave in. An older voice who'd done it all before outweighed my fledgling efforts to soar with my children. And even though he meant well, and I tried to go along with it, I was doing what I'd spent my life doing: conforming to someone else's vision so they'd keep me. *No one will love you unless you obey their rules.* I swirled in conflicted feelings and then shamed myself for having them. Ungrateful. Dramatic. Weak.

The day came when he rounded the corner to my door with a dozen roses and a box. *Will you marry me, my Tia?* I said yes, focusing on cologne and magic hours, pushing down the resistance of traumatized children and age gaps and the traditionalism that came with carefully ironed creases.

Our wedding heralded the return of love. We had herbs—basil, rosemary, and thyme—and olive trees for the flowers. Mom sewed a linen dress. We "jumped the broomstick" and I danced barefoot, laughing, delirious with joy. We honeymooned in Wallowa. When we arrived, I sat down on the earth and grounded, so thankful I'd pushed past the bright shock of morning.

But, the body does, in fact, keep the score.

One day I woke up and couldn't see anything white—it had been replaced with a pale shade of bubble gum. Clouds, sheets, paper—all pink. Migraines stretched from hours into days, the pressure intensifying until it felt like my skull cracked like an egg so a green-horned alien could birth itself out of my brain. I cried in the darkness with an ice pack pressed to my eyes, dreading the computer screen for work or driving in the Florida glare.

The doctors commenced chain pharmaceuticals, trying every migraine medication and then antidepressant on their list. They either didn't work or caused side effects worse than the symptoms in the first place. Weeks became months. The doctors added tests and hospital stays, ruling out strokes, heart attacks, tumors, blood clots. Debilitating nausea joined the party, then joint pain. Then my peripheral vision clouded.

It wasn't fair I'd be blind and immobile after fighting so hard to be free. I raged inside but held it in. I cried inside and held that in too. I kept going to the doctor, feeling like a failure, furious I'd worked so hard to be *more* only to end up in bed, useless to anyone, including the children I'd tried so hard to save.

My third neurologist's office was dark paneled and dim. Even though migraine patients are often light-sensitive, the doctors test neurological symptoms with a bright light right to the eyeball. I flinched in pain. *Assholes,* I seethed silently.

"We have your MRI results back," he said. "You have a few lesions. I believe you might have multiple sclerosis."

OH HELL NO. The second the words left his lips my entire body recoiled. The idea that I'd survived so much only to develop a debilitating condition rebounded off me like a racquetball. My system rejected these words. YOU WILL NOT CURSE ME.

"We don't have a test for it," he said. "We have our best guess. Only time will tell if your episodes continue or not."

If dissociation and wishful thinking and delaying earthly happiness for heavenly hope had taught me anything, it was that bad news could be compartmentalized. With a crack, an inch of hope, I had a chance. I didn't have to end up in a wheelchair because this man wasn't sure. A crack was enough to seize the day.

I knew I still had a little fight in me yet. Only this time the bully wasn't outside of me. It was within. I wanted to fight to prove the doctors wrong. *Fuckers.* But the battleground was between my ears. If I wanted sanity, safety, and surety . . . I needed to get real about what was wrong with me.

It was like how the Sunday School teachers talked about the Holy Spirit. The still small voice that was supposed to steer you the right way. Only instead of keeping me out of Blockbuster or keeping my boobs covered, this time the still small voice prodded me to go back to therapy. She sounded so reasonable about it too. If I was going to be wheelchair bound, a therapist would help me deal. But if I could somehow solve the symptoms in the first place, that would happen in therapy too.

But I already knew talk therapy alone wasn't enough. Talk therapy left me feeling drained, on edge, and reeling from triggers that intensified my migraines and brain fog like a hangover that lasted for days. There's nothing like a migraine to make a woman google solutions.

I found Bette, a tiny gray-haired woman with nerves of steel whose website said she specialized in *trauma* therapy. I booked an appointment, ready to quit banging my head against the metaphorical wall of doing the same thing over and over but expecting a different result.

Bette's office was lit primarily with natural light from large windows and she decorated with books and houseplants, no pink paisley in sight.

"CBT works well for many," she said from her chair. "But what you have, Tia, is trauma. Rehashing your experiences may be re-traumatizing you, rather than repairing the damage from the first time around, because you're reliving them when you tell the story. You have post-traumatic stress disorder, and because your traumatic experiences happened in an extended, repetitive way, I think it's CPTSD, or complex PTSD. There's a difference between the narrative story you tell about your trauma and the actual traumatic memory. I think if we can resolve those memories, you'll begin to heal from them. You might even begin to physically improve."

We started noting how being sick was impacting me and the feelings of shame around not being able to get out of bed as an otherwise healthy thirty-seven-year-old woman. Or, on the days I did, how challenging it was to work full-time and raise four kids, who by then were also in four different schools. And how having a second husband was radically different than having a lover with my own apartment. Asserting my own will required effort I couldn't carry, but the consequences of constantly acquiescing to his will took a toll on my psyche.

I knew I was pissed. Angry and hurt and confused. It wasn't fair that the trauma of the past would devour my future as well. I refused to accept it. But everything I was going through presently was tied to experiences I'd had in the past—experiences I'd either denied or dissociated from. Bette said my anger could help me fight but not if I held it inside. I didn't know what she meant. Christian girls don't get angry. Even though I wasn't sure I was one of those anymore, I knew my rage had to be controlled or everyone would leave me.

I lived in a state of high alert that bad things would happen to me, while simultaneously pushing away the memory of the bad things that had already happened. I was trapped in trauma responses such as freeze or flight, as evidenced by my body completely focused on suppressing inner chaos the way autoimmune diseases do. It wasn't even conscious. Bette said my nervous system did this for me, in order to protect me.

"We're going to try Eye Movement Desensitization and Reprocessing," she said. "EMDR. It's going to help us access the memories you may not even have words for. By stimulating both sides of the brain, memories can be transformed from traumatic to empowering."

It sounded like hypnotic hoodoo to me at first. The plan was that I'd sit on Bette's sofa and she'd wave her finger from side to side in front of my face while I thought about one of my traumas. We wouldn't talk about it in depth; I'd just go there in my mind while tracking her finger. Supposedly, my locked memories would loosen up, the emotional charge around them would decrease, and I'd be able to put them into perspective. I wouldn't be controlled by them anymore.

Skeptical as I was, she said I didn't have to believe it could work, or even trust her, for it to be successful. This was encouraging news, since I had a hard time trusting anyone. But I started to tremble when she suggested we start with the biggest one: the night I left the Blue House.

"Let the images come back as much as you're able and only that far," she said, and moved into place in front of me. "Emotions will rise. That's perfectly okay—let your feelings help you access the moments of that night."

Effortlessly, I was back in the kitchen, counting the knives, folding the clothes. Terror moved through me with a chill. I felt Allan at my back, waving the firewood, and the fear that he'd bludgeon me with it. I started to sob but kept my eyes on Bette's finger. I knew I was ugly crying in front of someone and should be embarrassed, but the scene was so vivid that I didn't care. In my mind, I could smell the old house and the lingering scent of fresh paint. I heard my footsteps on the stairs, remembered the round knob of the banister in my palm.

But I also saw myself moving through the rooms calmly, the children sleeping undisturbed. I watched as my younger self entered the bedroom, how she seemed almost indifferent to the swearing madman pacing around her. How steady she was, how strong and brave to manage such fear. I watched as Allan left and I sprang into action to gather the kids because I listened to intuition and had a plan in place to follow. I marveled at how smart my younger self had been!

Bette called me back and stopped moving her finger. "I want you to take some nice long cleansing breaths, Tia."

The Blue House didn't feel as intense and precarious anymore. In fact, I now saw that night as resilience. I exhaled and noticed how clear my head felt, how my physical pain had diminished.

EMDR became a weekly practice that excavated every heavy traumatic experience in my marriage to Allan. I left Bette's office red and splotchy from crying, wads of snotty tissues in her trash can, but also clear minded and stronger. I started to see white again. Then my headaches faded.

That year I also began Al-Anon. We met in a classroom at a Methodist church and sat at a round table and I learned new vocabulary there too. Words like "detachment," "co-dependent," and "enabling."

Working the steps helped me access a higher power outside of high-control religion. But it also helped me delineate between what was "on my yoga mat"—my interpretation of the serenity prayer. Not everything was under my control—hard words for the hypervigilant. Not everything was my fault. "You're not powerful enough to be responsible for everything," my sponsor said. Learning the difference helped me set a few things down, and I made amends for my side of the street, terrified of rejection the whole time.

For example, I enabled. I fought a tendency to do for others what they could do themselves. I covered up Allan's offenses and put a pretty spin on pain, so we'd blend in. And by refusing to stand up for myself, I allowed others to tread upon me—an unhealthy situation for both parties. I desperately needed boundaries and to unpack the shame I'd developed around having any, but I was scared to set them and even more scared to hold them.

"But isn't it mean to tell someone no?" I asked my sponsor. "I hate disappointing them."

"That's People-Pleasing 101," she said. "If you're only saying yes so they'll like you then you're abandoning yourself and operating from a place of shame and extremely low self-worth."

My stomach clenched. Saying the right thing to be liked and wanted ranked among my earliest memories. The right thing was whatever the listener wanted to hear. What I wanted didn't factor into it.

After meetings I'd treat myself to a coffee at the bookstore. One day I wandered into the poetry section and picked up Mary Oliver.

You do not have to be good, I read. I sat down on the carpet in Barnes & Noble and read *Wild Geese* while my hands shook, and tears streaked my face. *Whoever you are, no matter how lonely . . .*

Sometimes you don't know you are a thing until someone points it out.

Many aspects of life "out here" had culminated in a deep desert of loneliness. Severe trauma will do that, Bette had told me. But it was more than "just" trauma. Migraines were an invisible illness. Depression was too. My experiences in religion didn't match the happy-clappy faith and hymns that seemed to bring so many others comfort. I *was* lonely, but who would believe that of a woman with a loving husband and four dynamic kids, a job, vacations, and friends?

Deserts are in-between spaces. *How far until the next water?* I could see the expanse of sweltering heat without rain or ocean as comfort was a purgatory of loneliness. But the poles were extremes I felt torn by. Allan as abuser on one side, Allan as my children's father on the other. Cary Grant as friend and lover on one side, Cary Grant as high-control stepparent on the other. God as patriarchal authoritarian on one side, God as magnificent She-Tree of love on the other. I wandered in between, sunburned and dry.

I can tell you it's profoundly difficult to both reckon with the past and live in the present at the same time. And it wasn't fair to my children that their mother had to heal and put herself back together in the same time span that they grew up.

William, my first high school graduate, set out into the world in freedom. He had options—scholarships and opportunities. I dizzied to remember how my world narrowed at his age. As my children explored and expressed, the contrast of how I'd shrunken my world in *adolescence* intensified. It turned out teenagers didn't go right or wrong. Sometimes they went left. Up. Out. Over. Under. Into. Life was so much bigger than they taught us at church.

As I struggled with depression, unaware depression was anger turned inward, my migraines suddenly intensified too, becoming three- and four-day-long events with my bedroom door closed. And then one day I couldn't raise my head. It was too exhausting to move.

This time I saw a migraine specialist at the Mayo Clinic. He cleared me of what he called "the big stuff"—cancer, tumors, pathologies—and diagnosed me with adrenal fatigue. "And possibly," he said, in a clipped Italian accent, "complicated grief." His prescriptions included an anti-inflammatory diet, a list of supplements, and rest. "What you need more than anything is rest. I think cannabis would go a long way in treating your anxiety and migraines. And please continue your trauma therapy."

I sat on the beach and thought about what he said, my many griefs reverberating in my brain the way the sunlight sparkled on the water. A specialist at the most famous hospital in the world had pretty much told me to chill out and process my feelings. And instead of getting angry with him for suggesting this pain was "all in my head," I considered that maybe it was. Maybe the stress, trauma, and internalized messages I'd learned to carry had manifested in physical symptoms. Maybe my body was attempting to force me to do what it seemed I would not surrender to: stop people-pleasing and rest. Say no. Take time out. Let them deal with their feelings of disappointment without trying to assuage their pain by compounding my own.

A tantrum technique I used in early childhood came to mind. I'd simply sit on the floor and refuse to move. If they tried to move me, I kicked and screamed. I didn't get up until I was ready. Now, I could look back and trace how overloaded my senses felt and how sometimes, sitting down and making like a heavy rock was all I knew to do, until all the noises and colors and lights calmed down.

What if I did that again? What if I sat my ass on the ground, literally and metaphorically, and left them to it all—the chores and their choices and his rules and all those loaded expectations—and just . . . made like a rock?

When I got home that day, I got a call from K. Business Breakthroughs was reorganizing and I was out of a job. I wasn't even sad. Now there was plenty of time to sit down.

The more I made choices that saved me, the more others showed up to help save me too. Maybe that's an odd perspective for sudden unemployment, but my life had changed a lot in five years. My children were growing up, I'd been to therapy, I had a thriving relationship. With a safety net and a window for peace, losing my job didn't have the same rattle.

C. G. and I shifted things around so that I could take time off. We got a rescued foxhound and named her for our favorite city, Savannah. I sat in the grass a lot, ass on the ground, doing nothing except feeling the earth support me. I started taking gentle serenity walks, made getting enough sleep my highest priority, and said no to stimulating, crowded experiences that jacked up my anxiety. This included church.

The choice to stay home from church coincided with a discovery I'd made online. I first read the words "religious trauma" on Instagram. I found the hashtags people coming out of adverse religious experiences used: #exevangelical #religioustrauma #purityculture. I read *Pure* by Linda Kay Klein and found the work of Dr. Laura Anderson, co-founder of the Religious Trauma Institute. I hadn't realized there was an entire community of others traumatized by church. Suddenly, I didn't feel as alone because I was far from the only one who'd suffered this way.

While my small Orthodox parish and kindly priest were lovely, I couldn't breathe at church, and I knew religious trauma was the reason why.

In therapy with Pat now, a tidy sports fan with a gray bob and a sassy wit, I was increasingly uncovering the harm done to me as a small child through vivid portrayals of the crucifixion, the fires of hell, accusations that my sin killed Jesus, the horrors of abortion so that we'd vote a certain way, the heaping shame around the developing female body, the concept of purity, and the intentional lack of agency girls like me grew up with. I ranted over how incongruous it was to restrict violent movies but then show detailed imagery of hell and crucifixion to a four-year-old. And now, no matter how kind the church, my nervous system couldn't tolerate the reminders. I trembled in resistance to the perceived threat, shaking with angry protection over my sensitive little child self if I so much as pulled into a church parking lot.

Pat urged me to slow down, breathe, count four things I could see, three things I could touch, two things I could smell, one thing I could taste. This is how she brought me back into the room when I dissociated, but I was still a long way from coming back into my body.

Like all trauma, religious trauma is not about the event itself, but rather, how our nervous system interprets what happened. This is why I felt traumatized by my experiences growing up, but my sister, Monica, for example, had a different association with the same teachings. Sometimes the messages went over her head, because she wasn't as visual as I was. Where I felt terror I'd be left behind, others were able to think critically and keep rapture doctrine in perspective. For them, the rapture didn't crinkle secure attachment.

Curiosity over how we all ended up hounded me. Who was traumatized by their faith and who found comfort in it? Who among us was "okay"? I reconnected with old names on Facebook and looked up school friends, never-forgotten bullies, people I'd known at every church along the way, and the new ones I was meeting now. I studied how everyone turned out, Nancy Drewing the mysteries once more.

Hannah seemed to be thriving. Her children were older like mine now, even though we both had lots of friends in their early thirties just now getting married and having babies. "I feel nineteen again, sometimes, and forty-five at others," she said. I did too. We were old young women, too old for our peers, too young for women in a similar life station. But her "live laugh love," #blessed, boots-and-curls photos triggered me to hold back on reconnecting.

I wondered about Jo and how she was doing. But she barely had a digital footprint at all—just a name page. She didn't accept my friend request. I wrestled with mailing her letters, calling, persisting. I wanted it to be okay, for everything to be okay, because I was out now. The ugly reasons we'd lost touch were over. But Jo, even though she'd been with me in the thinnest air between here and the spirit world, was proof that I couldn't demand that okayness. I couldn't declare "everything's fine" for both of us and just will her hesitations away. She set a boundary I didn't like but still had to respect, and it meant accepting I might never get to tell her I was sorry.

My eyes widened to see April posting about her dissonance regarding faith. She sought authenticity and truth and no longer slaved to keep up appearances.

Charity doubled down; her page flaunted courtship matches with prominent IBLP families and quiverful Scriptures.

At least three of the Miller kids went on to find themselves and live their truth outside of the fundamentalist world built by Bill Gothard and his kind.

I wondered how many other Gothard refugees wandered in search of their souls. With nineteen Duggar kids, the chances someone was going to break rank and tell seemed high.

I found Marci. She'd had some rough years and a daughter. But at some point, she went back to church and met a man who made her dreams come true. They lived in the country now on a farm. In our messages, she thanked me for taking her to church. As I read those words, I realized how grateful I was she'd shown me life *outside* of church.

My wrestling continued as I typed and searched like an itch I couldn't scratch. There were entire blog sites built on the exodus from the institute. Rediscovering Grace, Ex-ATI Girl. Long threads of stories I'd either observed or lived myself.

Like Charity, Judith Small and her family remained hard-core, although sometimes the girls wore pants. Anna Tinker had as many children now as her mother had when I met her.

Ruth Ellen accepted my friend request with a joint "Charles and Ruth Ellen Strickland" because her husband monitored her conversations. Very often I felt caught between my two worlds. Not every woman I knew even wanted to be free. Plenty were content to merely have a window.

Trauma therapy continued, which meant digging into my responses. For some reason I bothered putting on eye makeup before sessions, never learning I was definitely going to cry it all off before I left.

My body buzzed with reactivity. Impact from decisions others made forced me to continually adjust and recalibrate, which kept me on edge. Sometimes I became defensive. I'd spout and vent the way outraged women talked on TV—a sound I quickly learned is tolerated in fictional characters much more often than someone's wife, mom, or daughter. Pat said reactivity was a trauma response.

I was familiar with fight or flight. But less familiar with freeze and fawn. She explained fawning as supercharged people-pleasing. It's engaging in behaviors (often self-betraying behaviors) in an attempt to appease and pacify a traumatic threat.

Fawning placed everyone else's needs over my own, which also, perhaps conveniently, modeled Christian behavior. But as I "did my work" to heal traumatic memories, my self-esteem rose, as did my ability to be assertive. I found I didn't panic anymore when a boundary needed articulation. I didn't tremble when I knew C. G. was disappointed, because my body wasn't confusing him with Allan, whose disappointment could be dangerous.

People preferred to be fawned over more than they liked to hear a woman in fight response, but both responses were my reaction to feeling triggered. Fawning was my attempt to pacify a perceived threat and my relationships were entangled by it.

It seemed like I could sum up my entire childhood as fawning. I felt groomed to fawn. It was in the tone of voice we were taught to use, our smiles and crossed legs, our servant hearts.

Talking about this with Pat, she suggested we try another therapeutic modality.

"EMDR is great for adult traumas. But I've had better results for childhood traumas with Brainspotting."

"Isn't that a movie? A dark comedy about drugs?"

"No," she laughed. "I'll admit it's not a great name. Brainspotting uses your optical cues to identify where you've stored subconscious memories. In other words, where you look points directly to a storage chest of memories in your brain. Whole Rolodexes will rapidly flip-file, if we're lucky."

"So, the eyes really are the windows to the soul?" I laughed. It was the nervous laugh of someone about to board a rickety roller coaster. I fidgeted and wished I'd taken more homeopathic nerve tonic.

"What upset you today?" she asked.

"C. G. left without telling me. He was just gone."

"Good, let's start there. I want you to say that again and let's see where your eyes go."

I stared at a spot on the wall in the upper left corner of my vision. Pat placed earbuds in my ears and turned on a track with undulating sounds: right, left, right, left. My stomach heaved and my heart raced, stuck in the moment where I realized the house was empty and no one had said where they'd gone. I started to cry.

"Good, good . . ." Pat soothed. "Emotion is a key that unlocks your mind. Allow it to open and access what's stored."

My consciousness faded from Pat and her carpeted room. Instead, I saw the pink ceiling of my bedroom as a baby. Then my grandfather's lap and wanting to get down. His wife's collection of glass bells, none of them ringing despite alarm bells going off in my head. Driving away from the farm in Michigan. Speeding through the night from the Blue House. Fragments of memories and images flashed before my inner eye. I sobbed harder, and clutched the upholstery of the couch, desperately racing through big feelings of fear, terror, pain, anger, grief.

But in a few moments, my breathing slowed. My tears stopped the way a summer storm dumps gallons of rain and then, suddenly, the sun comes out. The emotions cleared. I took a deep breath and realized I no longer felt so afraid.

Pat smiled. "See?" She threw out her hands like a magician declaring "TA-DAH!"

The next time, we went to church. "What upset you today?" Pat asked.

"Church. My family is so upset I can't go. They don't understand why it hurts to be there. They think I'm making it up."

"Good, let's start there." We homed in on where my eyes went, and she set up the earbuds and sounds. I felt dizzy, my body protectively resisting what it perceived as dangerous territory. *Throw up,* a voice whispered.

But my mind left Pat's room, the light dimming until I realized I was inside of an empty Sunday School room in the church basement, staring at an illustration of people drowning in the flood. Then *Mommy's getting a spanking* spoken in daylight. My excommunication. Millstones and my children drowning. The dead dogs. The scourge of the whip tearing Jesus's flesh. My hand reaching up to nail a card to the cross. The screaming red faces warning of *Gonga-rhea*. Marci. Troy. Stink-ass campers.

I sobbed so hard this time my shirt was wet. But when I came back to the room, I suddenly felt lighter, cleansed somehow.

The third time, I ran.

We set things up and off I went, my mind ready for it this time. I landed in the middle of my favorite reoccurring dream. I'm flying but it's more like hovering—a few feet over the grass, up the trees, over the house—high but with something solid always in reach. I love this dream because it feels safe and adventurous at the same time.

I'm at the farm in Michigan. I'm nine. I have rainbows pouring out of my chest and I'm run-flying, sparkles and wings and light behind me.

I'm spinning,

I'm dancing,

I'm flying.

I'm FREE!

On the sofa, I laughed and cried simultaneously, like I'd cracked myself open with pure, unbridled emotion. "It's my eternal self I see, Pat! She's my trueness, my light! I so wish you could see her!"

Pat was laughing and crying too. "I can! I can see her! She's all over your face!"

It took days to come down from that high. Pat said reckoning with trauma led to such freedom. That as I healed, I would discover and unlock versions of myself long hidden away—protected so that one day they could emerge into the newness of the open life I built, the spaces where it was safe to show up and *BE*.

I remembered my favorite Nina Simone song. This *was* a new dawn, a new day, a new life for me. And I could finally say, I was feeling good. My vision and strength were returning. I tipped my chin but this time it wasn't to swallow a reaction I was too afraid to show. I tipped it with determination.

New

WHEN DONALD TRUMP RAN FOR PRESIDENT AND TALKED ABOUT grabbing women by the pussy, and then was lauded by Franklin Graham and Jerry Falwell Jr. and called a man of God, and all the Christians of my youth on Facebook applauded him and voted for him, I knew my problem wasn't with spirituality or the divine. It was with the systems and personalities who'd sought to gain control and power in Jesus's name, amen.

That January I did more than just vote—I protested. Itchy and desperate to *do* something, I eagerly agreed when friends invited me to the Women's March. My sign read A NEW COMMANDMENT I GIVE TO YOU THAT YOU LOVE ONE ANOTHER. It's from the book of John, and I made the *O*'s rainbow hearts. A sea of women and men chanted THIS IS WHAT DEMOCRACY LOOKS LIKE. I felt like I got a little piece of my voice back—the freedom to scream on emotional roller coasters, the agency to rage at the outrageous.

I screamed at the top of my lungs to the dirty reverends, the scary pastors, the Puritans and Federalists, the spankers and special Christians more focused on rules than human lives. I felt like a badass in my Chuck Taylors, joining the so-called Nasty Women reviled by toxic misogynists for our refusal to fawn and conform.

But at the end of the day, we had to go home, and the pervs in power remained that way.

When the #MeToo movement happened, my voice joined the voices of others. Me too, *me too*.

In some ways, #MeToo worked, and the men started to fall. It wasn't cool to be a misogynistic dick anymore, and consequences mattered, ironically more in Hollywood than Christendom. Kevin Spacey and Harvey Weinstein faced more accountability than cult leaders.

But, along with scandals of abuse in the Catholic church, the Protestants and fundamentalists slowly reflected the movement.

Gary Ezzo was fired from Grace Community Church and he and Anne Marie were dropped by their publisher after babies parented with their program suffered malnutrition and failure to thrive.

Joshua Harris, author of *I Kissed Dating Goodbye,* recanted his teachings on courtship. He stopped publication of his books and disavowed his position on purity culture and Christianity. I felt like I understood conversion from the inside out—he admitted his complicity without deflection—and I trusted it. To this day, Harris stands out as not only a high-profile ex-evangelical, but also one of the few who's taken tangible action steps to address the harm done by his former work. He's unique in the field that way because the rest of them seem to sneak off and wait for their chance to come back.

Facing legal accusations from a slew of secretaries and students who claimed he'd been inappropriate with them, Bill Gothard was removed from the board of IBLP in 2014. A lawsuit was brought but was voluntarily dismissed by the plaintiffs in 2018 after a lengthy court battle that triggered an emotional re-victimization. The plaintiffs stated that the dismissal did not indicate they'd recanted their stories. The Indianapolis Training Center was sold to a community college and the remaining IBLP focused on Big Sandy, Texas. But TV personality and IBLP biggie Gil Bates took over the board of directors. The IBLP wasn't going away anytime soon.

Like the Duggars' *19 Kids and Counting,* the Bates family had a show on TLC, and were even higher up in the IBLP. But for all the parallels, viewers saw them as less conservative than the Duggars. The Bates girls wore pants sometimes and didn't have a "Josh." But as an IBLP homeschool family, the restrictive curricula and lifestyle practices were likely to be the same, even if they seemed happier and more sincere on TV.

It bothered me how fundamentalism simply flew under the radar for fans, sucking them into the pretty ideals the same way Judith sucked me into the

IBLP. What happened to me was neither sweet nor wholesome. It was fundamentalism in different clothes. And even if the parents chose that lifestyle for themselves, who was checking with the children?

Pastor La Touche faced church discipline himself, for reasons the internet kept silent. But he was defrocked and forced to leave the congregation. I tried to connect with what it felt like to see my excommunicator fall but felt nothing. I didn't care. It wasn't enough. It didn't matter. And anyway, he was soon pastoring another church.

Doug Phillips was caught sexually abusing his children's nanny. She was a girl groomed for that position, a girl trained to never say no. Her story underscored the lack of consent I knew to be true in fundie families, and that when we are not free to say no, we're not free to say yes, either.

Paige Patterson, a fundamentalist former president of the Southern Baptist Convention, was accused of covering a rape charge at Southwestern Baptist Theological Seminary and terminated.

And it wasn't just the Baptists and Presbyterians. Warren Jeffs of the Fundamentalist Mormon church was convicted of child sexual assault, having married underage girls as well as arranging the marriage of children to older men. I knew a heck of a lot of Baptists who thought the Gothard lifestyle wasn't like the fundies out in Utah—but other than polygamy, I knew there were similarities. Viewers of the documentary *Keep Sweet* recognized them too and we talked about it online. Survivors were nervous. Conservative state legislatures debated the marriage age, sometimes using a defense of parental rights.

The mighty were falling, but with fundamentalist leadership rising in Congress, were they falling fast enough?

The thoughts that kept me kicking my sheets at night centered on what I knew deep in my soul: the fundies want to run the country the way they run their homes. What I knew about that world was more valuable than useless trivia. It was insight.

What if life in America became what I'd lived as a fundamentalist wife? Was I willing to just stay silent about what I saw? What I lived? Because even though many men were held accountable, we still had a raging narcissist in the White House who sounded like every power-hungry pastor I'd ever had.

Michael Pearl still taught parents to spank their children. Doug Wilson moved his blog to YouTube. R. C. Sproul Jr. was defrocked but then had a resurgence on Twitter, especially among bearded theobros who love to argue theology. A whole slew of dominionists made it their job to make America a theocracy by running for public office, from top governorships to local school boards. They weren't just evangelical—but also Independent Baptist, traditional Catholics, and Mormons. For now, they voted together, united over abortion and their red wave.

And it wasn't just the men. As the years passed, dominionist theology and Christian fundamentalism congealed with nationalism—often with women who'd benefited from feminism leading the charge and the fundies went along with it for political power. There were enough Marjorie Taylor Greenes and Lauren Boeberts and Kellyanne Conways to remind me that toxic patriarchy needs women to survive. Moms for Liberty hit the PTAs and a fresh wave of evangelical Christian Nationalist influencers rose on social media. This new nationalism had a bunch of followers I used to go to church with—women I used to pray with now flying Trump flags on boat parades on the St. Johns.

Fools, I thought. Not as an indictment against any one woman but because so many of them dallied with this devil, oblivious to what it really looked like behind closed doors. What if they knew what happens when a woman has served her purpose to the people in power and is no longer considered useful?

Once again, I felt lost between the extremes. On one side, a mountain of religious power rose. On the other, accountability took some of that power down. I walked through my days writing, working, and wishing—and none of it felt like enough.

In September of 2019, First Baptist Church listed nine of its ten city blocks for sale. Attendance and tithing had been down for so long, they couldn't pay the bills. Wind blew around me as I sat back and stared at the news on my screen, a lonely howl of useless devotion and wealth reduced to dust and dated upholstery. What had it all been for?

There were notes in my inbox from fellow alumni of the megachurch youth group where we started.

"I heard they're going to tear the buildings down, to sell clean lots. Can you imagine the orchestra room and hallways full of practice rooms just imploding?"

"I have mixed feelings about it. I don't disagree with them. But it was our entire childhood. It was our world." *Colorful dominoes,* I remembered. Good along with the bad.

"The megachurch era is over."

"Somebody tell Mark Driscoll and Joel Osteen."

"Will they even have an orchestra anymore? The Hobson is so small."

"This puts FBC in range of the other downtown churches. Historic. No bigger footprint than one city block."

First Baptist's failure was too sad to gloat about, but also relieving. It hadn't all been bad, growing up in an evangelical megachurch. On the other hand, their negligence to prepare us for the real adult world had nearly cost me my life. I didn't know how to register my feelings, a sensation my therapist called discomfort. She said I needed to sit in it. Let it be.

What did it mean to hold two opposing truths at the same time?

At the beach, sun glinted on the waves like diamonds. Grief now came quietly. I didn't scream with rage in the waves so much as I pondered continuance, crest, trough, endurance. There's no end until we reach the far shore.

I had a book with me that day. *How to Be an Adult* by David Richo. It's one of those books where it was hard not to highlight every line. I sat back under my blue umbrella and read to the sound of waves.

What was missed can never be made up for, only mourned and let go of. Richo wrote that remembering a loss with sadness and anger was the first step in healing memories so we could depart from fear and move into Self. If you were still afraid, it might point to unprocessed grief.

I knew not all of my traumatic memories were buried in my subconscious, accessible only through EMDR and Brainspotting. Many of them were compounded by learned behaviors nurtured by false beliefs, such as passivity, settling for negative excitement and drama, allowing anger to manifest inward as depression, and allowing guilt to make decisions for me. As much as I felt anger toward the perpetrators, deep down I didn't believe I deserved any better. And some of this pain still actively churned, which made processing difficult.

No amount of anger was going to get me my childhood back. Nor my children's childhoods. I needed to grieve the losses. Confronting the beliefs that I'd been betrayed, abandoned, rejected, and isolated would help me move beyond the story of blame and into a healthy, actualized adult Self.

I sniffed and stared at the horizon, absorbing the continuance of grief work and pondering Richo's words. Healthy. Actualized adult. Self.

Wasn't I too messed up to really get there? Wouldn't I always be a little flinchy and scarred? Always be damaged? I wanted a Self. I wanted to heal. To become a non-reactive adult who no longer felt pressured to obey someone's rules in order to be loved.

From behind my sunglasses I watched a dolphin arc in the waves, doing loops just because. Loops in the waves weren't going to gain the dolphin extra fish. No one would applaud. His fellow dolphins weren't testing him to see if he was loopy enough to swim with them. But my conditioning bubbled as acid reflux in my throat. Wasn't wanting a Self *selfish*?

I used a section of my favorite kind of notebook—a college-ruled, spiral-bound, five-subject notebook with dividers. The first section is always for work notes, the second for ideas, the third for therapeutic exercises, and the last two for morning pages—a stream-of-consciousness meditation technique taught in Julia Cameron's *The Artist's Way*.

I started with the facts, followed by Richo's instructions for response. I was learning how to flip the script and reframe the story I told myself, similar to what I'd learned with EMDR. Shame over being selfish would have to wait. Following the format in the book, I made a list.

1. These things happened to me. *It's okay to feel sad and angry about that.*
2. Through those experiences, I learned ways to compensate and cope with the loss and consequences. I learned to adapt, navigate, and survive. *I'm thankful for my resilience.*
3. In therapy, I learned a new perspective of my actions and how I endured. *I am no longer a victim.*
4. I forgive those who should have protected me, but who did not or were not able to, including myself. *We all need compassion.*
5. But I now drop the expectation that others should stand up for me. *I stand up for myself.*

I sat back and looked at those words, feeling the ideas click. *I stand up for myself.* Not a Christian princess waiting for rescue. Not a co-dependent woman attempting to control someone else. A grown-ass adult who'd become her own advocate.

A breeze fluttered my sun hat and I noticed a seagull standing a few feet away, observing me with one round, wide eye. I remembered Children's Egleston Hospital and Amy's lesson about the magic of calling for an advocate. Clara felt as close as that bird.

"Hello, sweetie." I smiled.

The abuses were still wrong. AND I'd grown past feeling locked in time by them. The rules weren't love. AND I deserve love. It was both/and. Not either/or.

Sitting on the ground with my notebook, I inhaled salty air that smelled like fish and sunshine. Authoritarian, high-control religion doesn't allow for both/and. Everything is either/or. Same thing with high-control politics. Having health and balance, then, means being able to hold both. And to do that, one has to be open, willing, curious, kind. *That doesn't sound selfish,* I thought.

Grief work done with consciousness builds self-esteem, since it shows us our courageous faithfulness to the reality of loss, I read.

The reality of loss. Oof. My stomach retracted sharply. *The shadows of finger-like branches on the wall. Room 202. The light of the moon.* I read the words again: . . . *courageous faithfulness to the reality of loss.*

I remembered holding Clara after she died and kissing the cool firmness of her cheek. I was grateful I held her until the truthful weight of her death saturated my heart. It was during those hours I made the decision to share her life by counting her.

"I have five children," I say when someone asks. "Four surviving. My daughter died in infancy and I talk about her all the time." There's a catch as they register meaning. An awkward breath. And then, the opening.

All I'd have to do to save that moment of discomfort is deny Clara's existence and answer four. No one would even question me on it, because I had four teenagers. But every time I told her story, I opened space for someone else to share theirs. Mothers told me of their miscarriages and stillbirths, fathers told me of drowned toddlers and children with cancer. Grown siblings shared their lost brother or sister.

I'd been faithful to the reality of Clara's loss. But what about the other losses? My lost dreams? My lost years? My youth? Everything I was losing now because I had to heal past trauma instead of giving myself fully to the present? That was costing me big-time with my teenagers, as their childhoods rapidly crossed into adulthood, rules mandated by a stepparent instead of their mother.

I swallowed and sighed. My chest felt hollow and open, as if my skinless bare ribs encased a lonely, floating heart muscle, a bird in a cage. I had not been courageously faithful to any of it. I'd bypassed the ache. Rationalized the sorrow. Found the bright side. Focused on the silver lining of the cloud, instead of acknowledging what really hurt with clouds was the loss of so much light.

Bitternesses picked at the edge of my mind. Ordinary teenage development. *Lost.* "One wife for life," tender sexuality, the Proverbs 31 "rise and call her blessed" promise. *Lost.* Virginal wedding night. *Lost.* Ten years birthing and nursing children, literally serving my body and blood—not a regret—but my body was scarred. My vitality drained. *Lost.* I'd buried a baby. Quieted my voice. Skipped a formal education. *Lost.*

As Christians, we didn't want to accept loss—so we focused on eternity. *What a day that will be, when my Jesus I shall see!* Had I ever even admitted these losses out loud, let alone written them down?

We didn't cry at funerals—we celebrated "homegoings." *Hannah's mother is with Jesus now. To God be the glory!* What would happen if I admitted how angry I was, not only that these losses happened, but that we weren't allowed to name them?

I wrote, *What if the key was to not only grieve, but to hold the facts of loss and life at the same time? And if that's true, what about the healing traits, like compassion and resilience and self-advocacy?*

My hand scratched notes in my notebook so fast it cramped. I could see the more I extended compassion to myself, the more I had to offer others. If I'd been doing the best that I could, what if they were too?

I could see now how the majority of Allan's behaviors were trauma responses and fear, mental health issues, and addictive attempts to cope. He faced every day and relationship as a fight—and our religious practices nurtured that paranoia instead of helping him reckon with reality.

I remembered the little boy who'd lost his laugh. The inadequacy of his parents to help rather than hurt—both of them the children of violent alcoholics themselves. The thirst he felt to be better. The betrayal it must have been to turn to what he thought were wise elders and leaders only to be told to toughen up, be a man, lead your home, raise a ruckus, and above all, support the patriarchy.

Men in these systems suffered too.

I tapped my pen against the page. Compassion felt like a brave, difficult step. Reflexes took over. My face tensed and my body braced. To go into a place of softness as I tallied the hard facts of his background still felt vulnerable. *Weak.* The Tia I'd been while married to him still quietly searched for ways to keep her anxious hands busy, afraid of what might come in the calm. She still counted the knives. My heart pounded and my neck flushed in panic to even imagine letting my guard down, even in theory, even a thousand miles away.

Journal in hand, I wrote the facts and clung to them. *You're safe now.*

With the kids older, I rarely had to contend with his fluctuations. They tenderly navigated an on-again/off-again relationship with him, and he seemed to finally be thriving, remarried and living up north. The steadier he could be, the easier it was for them. For all of us, really.

I left the beach that day, trudging through the same sand I'd once walked in that nor'easter storm, determined to keep exploring.

I filled three notebooks. In time, I realized my narrative of blame and victimization landed a different way. I didn't flinch to hear his name. And at William's Navy graduation, I walked right past Allan on the street and didn't even recognize who he was.

That same afternoon, I stood with William on the shore of Lake Michigan, amazed by the cold teal water, amazed at how far we'd all come. We'd all changed, and we were all better off for the escape. As if my collection of losses were a stone of remembrance clutched in my palm, I opened my hand and let it go.

Day

YOU KNOW THAT FEELING WHEN YOU OPEN YOUR MOUTH AND SPEAK without thinking about it first and the words simply pour from you as if they begged to be spoken? That's how it started. I wasn't pouring from an empty cup anymore—I was overflowing, with a completed manuscript and a clear, calm voice that no longer stuttered. All I needed was a nudge to spill the tea.

In November of 2019, federal agents raided the car lot where the oldest Duggar son worked. Josh Duggar had been notably absent from the photo and article I'd seen in *Parents* magazine way back in 2003. He'd already been caught molesting five girls and sent to a Bill Gothard behavioral camp. As an adult, he'd been caught in a massive cheating scandal and accused of a violent rape. Now they had him on child pornography charges. "Torture" is a more accurate word for it—the content agents traced to him is some of the most heinous, violent material in existence.

The fundamentalists and evangelicals, now one and the same since the Trump administration, wanted to cast the fallen son of TLC's *19 Kids and Counting* as a single bad apple. But he wasn't a single bad apple—he was a product of their making. Duggar was the fruit of a high-control system that taught children from infancy to suppress their needs and conform or be beaten. It taught firstborn sons would become eventual patriarchs. It gave young children a premature and inappropriate amount of authority over their younger siblings. It taught males are entitled to gratification and servitude from females who can't say no either to men or to God. Josh Duggar registered no guilt for his crimes because since childhood, he'd grown up with an external moral compass, and a feeling of entitlement to women's bodies.

Remembering that IBLP homeschool groups want to run our country the way they run their homes, I suddenly realized why it mattered so much that I talk about what it's like in those households. I could tell the public what it's really like.

No female vote. No consent. No contraception. No choice. No careers. Courtship marriages. Stay-at-home daughters and parentified older siblings. Closets. Suppression. Book bans. Harsh discipline. Rigid roles. High control. Shame.

As bad as it would be for women, it would be worse for anyone gay. Worse for anyone of color. Bad for anyone except a straight white patriarch . . . and I knew from experience it wasn't really good or healthy for them either. We all deserve better.

I sat in my book-lined office and stared at my phone. It wasn't enough that I'd worked on this telling as part of my personal therapy for the past seven years. As someone who knew this system from the inside out, and whose life was saved through women on the internet, I knew I needed to speak out. As Josh Duggar was tried, convicted, and sentenced to twelve years in federal prison, I began creating social media content to tell my story and show how these practices are connected to our headlines. My nudge was the news.

At first, I was shy and intimidated by social media production values. I didn't want to point at words or lip-sync or hawk brands. The solution came to me in an amalgam of favorites: the honest connection of Trapdoor and the experience/strength/hope sharing of Al-Anon. I decided to throw inhibition to the wind and just say what I wanted to say, my way. Forget following rules to be liked. I'd just be myself.

Within hours I could see I'd struck a nerve. My social media account began growing by thousands of views per day. Fellow survivors and those curious about the religious divide, fundamentalist refugees wandering in search of healing their souls. As quickly as I could, I churned out reels on quiverful realities. The comments were overwhelmingly kind and humbling and viewers asked thought-provoking questions.

At night, I stood beneath the moon and tracked the phases, trying to grasp the enormity of it all. The galaxy, sure, but also how far a soul can come. How did the girl who stuttered too hard to order pizza, almost lost in a mountain house in Tennessee, become an articulate author who spoke, made videos, and took interviews? Very often it was too much to fathom, and I'd tip my wine out in the grass and turn and go inside.

That summer Cary Grant took me back to Upper Michigan. The draw of that place in my heart was indelible. Part of me was scared to have my perfect image shattered. I didn't want to see the trees were gone or the house was small. I didn't want to stand in that space and realize poverty the way I had at the Blue House.

But a sense of place began as soon as we came into Gladstone, the little rail and iron-ore town to the south. I'd been nine when we left—too young to navigate and drive. And yet I found my way to my grandma's old house and my aunt's current one by memory. The bluff to my right, the bay to my left, we drove along the curved highway into Escanaba. Instinct pulled my hand on the wheel into a right-hand turn. I knew before I looked up that we passed my old elementary school. I felt befuddled by time. Was I seven or forty-seven?

C. G. waited in the car while I walked around the empty building. It was a weekend, so not a school day. And I was alone but also not alone, because of the ghost-laughs all around me. *King of snow hill! Marbles! Recess!*

How was it the same swings still rose to the sky? The same monkey bars, the same slides? As I played on each piece of equipment, exactly the same as they'd been in the early 1980s, I felt my selves integrate and overlap. Here was a returning, a re-embodiment after such severing loss. I tipped back in the swing and let sunshine blow through my hair.

But we hadn't come to Michigan for my school. I got back in the car and drove down the country lane. *How can I tell you this felt like a rewind?* Time and dominoes righted themselves. Spirits within me rose like a double image, overlapped, and healed themselves. The crunch of gravel under the wheels reversed time as real as any tesseract L'Engle could dream. We came to the end of my old driveway and I parked where our mailbox used to be.

"I have to walk," I said to Cary Grant.

"Take your time," he said.

The last time my feet walked this path toward home was the last day of school before my parents drove us out of here. Florida was an idea yet, a mystical land my parents described like heaven. I was sad from goodbyes to David Pearson, the Fudalas, and the Berubes. Sad to leave my school and yellow bus. Sad to leave this apple tree, now gnarled and reaching for the ground. Sad to leave this field, now forested in the conifers my parents planted in hopes of salvation.

I rounded the curve where the orange tiger lilies still grew. Glimpsed the grove my mother called The Park. The spruce windbreak still stood tall, stoically watching over it all.

Some things were different, some things the same. The rose garden was gone, and the open fields were overgrown. Tart, sour green apples hung from every tree in the orchard, the trunks surrounded with wire cages to keep the deer off. The new owner had built a landing strip for his private plane in the swamp where I'd once seen a bear. The locust tree still stood near my favorite spot to build a snowman.

I sat on the ground and felt this good earth support me, weaving my fingers through the cool, soft grass as if it were hair. My face was wet from crying. The new owner loved this place, I could tell. He came over and stood beside me, a country man with a moustache and a quiet manner. I listened-watched as he pointed to the new front porch and dormer windows. He'd painted the yellow siding ivory. To love is to see need and meet it. He'd more than done that with care.

We spoke a moment. "For the first few years I was here, I spent part of every day just walking these fields," he said. "There's something to the place. Something almost . . . magical."

I smiled, knowing he knew the trees. I wanted to say I'd buy it, even though I knew it wasn't for sale. I wanted to beg to move here. To have it back. But I knew I had to let it go.

I breathed in with an ache in the middle of my chest and tipped my face up to the clouds. Under the sun in the western sky, I felt invisible stitches sew parts of me back into one another. Younger me and older me, grieving me and hopeful me. Optimistic daydreaming me and resilient pioneering me. The part of me who wandered, curious to explore, but also the part of me ready to turn for home.

A year later, I floated on the edge of a happy dream, trying not to wake up and leave them. Daylight danced over my eyelids. In my dream, I'd traveled to Italy—slowly—to see William, and back again to the States to see Katie, Liam, and Gavin. Somehow, at least in the dream, I could assemble them in the same room. I wasn't ready for it to end.

It was disorienting to open my eyes. Where was I? *When* was I? I did the math of the kids—the oldest three out on their own. Gavin down the hall but gone soon too. I blinked at the blank ceiling, registering the walls were blue, not yellow. This was not our bedroom.

The memory that I slept in the guest room now fluttered over me softly, the way a summer sheet billows in the wind before it lies down.

I ground myself in time. *Today is Sunday, October 30, 2022.*

Like a reflex, I counted the good. My children's faces and the spouses they have now too. The passing years. Changing leaves. Ten years in a stable home. The sound of wind chimes on the porch. My literary agent. Selling the book! A whole month of solitude in Shenandoah Valley this year. Hot coffee. A cat at my feet. Girlfriends who check in. Michael. My parents, young enough to look forward to great-grandchildren. The hush of an empty house on Sunday morning. The day moon and a thin ribbon of incense, rising to the sky.

The reality of loss. Cary Grant had asked for a divorce the month after I signed with my agency. There were many reasons for it, he said, and none of them angry. While I'd been head-down at work on my healing and on my book, he'd felt alone and unhappy. We weren't in the same place anymore. Words and phrases ran through my mind, solidifying the shadow.

I still lived in our home because I'd thrown my energy into parting amicably. I wasn't sure I could handle my love story becoming some guy I used to know. But I was dead-sure I couldn't handle throwing my system into shock again.

I wouldn't risk adrenal fatigue. Migraines. Starvation. Nightmares. No . . . a divorce I hadn't planned on didn't get to have my health. It had taken me a few days to absorb his declaration, but I "eat, pray, loved" that situation. I *could* get divorced in order to choose myself, just like Gilbert did at the beginning of her journey.

Choose you, Mom, Katie had said.

Tomorrow, we'd appear before the judge for the ruling—a divorce the courthouse scheduled on the day that happened to be the anniversary of my escape. I knew I held the feelings around this loss like a carefully balanced snow globe. Fragile glass that could crack, cradled in my hands.

I blinked at the blank ceiling and remembered it all clearly now. One of my post-traumatic superpowers is compartmentalization. I could set the big emotions aside temporarily, but I knew that was a limited option. Sorrow comes for us all, a voluminous octopus of flailing emotions able to whip out of nowhere, and I knew better now than to pretend I could keep it locked beneath the waves forever.

Grief for my marriage, for lost love and loyalty, for unexpected rug-ripping collapse during what should've been a golden champagne year, would sear—but it would sear in solitude, in therapy, and with the support of steadfast friends. I'd grown past talking someone into keeping me. And well past sacrificing my life-points to emotional collapse at someone else's behest. I exhaled, pushing back the sheets and swinging my feet to the floor, aware anger impatiently nipped at my heels.

Failing to plan is planning to fail. Old habits die hard. But remaining emotionally regulated and present, refusing to react, wasn't exactly failing to plan either. I was learning to pace myself. Do one thing at a time.

My phone buzzed on the nightstand and I reached for it. The message was from Jodie, with a picture of Kenai, the dog who lived. Born under my basement in the Blue House and adopted the week before it all fell apart, Kenai has had a good life. He watched over three boys and had room to run and warm sunbeams to nap in—and now he's an old boy with a dog beard and wise eyes.

And with that sweet reminder, I got out of bed and did "the next right thing," my favorite advice from Anne Lamott and Al-Anon. Live in spite of the drama. Gorgeous, juicy, fat, grateful, delighted spite and determination to refuse trauma another win.

Hard things happen. Beautiful things do too. Looking up at the cottony clouds I thought about the plot twists in this year. Signing with my agent on Clara's birthday. Hearing "I want a divorce," by the bathroom sink. Selling my book on the anniversary of meeting C. G. Everything clearing so I could spend a month in solitude to finish the book. My youngest turning eighteen. Hearing about the coming grandbabies. Getting divorced on a traumaversary. Losing my job just as I was about to sign a lease. This year was undoubtedly a corner in my life, a comprehensive and sharp pivot at 90 degrees. But to where?

I opened my phone and checked my bank account; my book had earned an advance I'd hardly touched. What if now was the time?

I breathed softly, almost afraid to let the words come. A very old dream of mine to travel slowly, by land and by sea, rippled up. To take an old-fashioned ocean crossing to England and a train across the countryside. To take a ferry to France and a train across Europe. *That's why I was dreaming it this morning.* And William really did live in Italy. So, what if I did it? Booked a passage on the *Queen Mary 2* and took a gap before looking for another job or starting another book . . .

I loved this plan because it was gentle with my senses. Time to adapt, without high-pressure cabins or turbulence or needing to pee at twenty thousand feet, seemed an entirely different way to travel. Nearly everyone who heard it laughed at me—who wants to take a week getting there? Well, *me.* I do. I want to spend time in the space between. Time seeing what I'm passing through and all that's there. We say "joy is in the journey," but then we truncate the journey!

To me, slow travel sounded like time to decompress. Queen Victoria once said, *"Let time slow down so that one breathes freedom and peace, making one forget the world and its sad turmoil."*

Breathing freedom and peace with time to adjust to time zones and scenery sounded perfect to me.

Within an afternoon, the dream became a plan. Whatever future lay ahead, it would first include this quiet, solo adventure, with libraries and landscapes and bread and chocolate. I would get wherever *there* was, if by sea.

To have a dream-plan is like expecting a baby. And though there'd be tears craving release, I couldn't help but smile at the sky.

I have a new spiritual practice now. One that is fluid and deeply private. There are no gurus or holy books of rules. My mycorrhizal network underground communicates through poetry, gratitude, compassion, reality, and supreme love. I'm a tree rooted to the deep with arms reaching for the sky. I'm a woman. A mother writer artist hiker friend, but more than any role. I am not half of another. Nor the completion of their aching soul. I don't owe anyone my body or service. Training is for dogs. I'm a human soul on a journey home and I belong to me.

There's a verse in the Bible I think of often. Jesus says, *I am the way, the truth, and the light. No one comes to the Father but by me.* It's a farewell to His disciples, before His ascent into heaven. They're confused and want to see God. Jesus reassures them that because they've seen Him, they *have* seen God, and if they want to join Him with the Father, they'll keep His commandment to love.

No one comes to the divine but by love. And if we have truth in us, we will have love.

I know now, trueness can't be quantified, any more than the constancy of the sea, any more than the innocence of childlike wonder, any more than the mystery of God. Trueness is within our soul, the intuition and many-vertebraed spine we're born with that supports our beating hearts, a light guiding us home to ourselves.

I go forward now, a little unsure of what's ahead but with one of my favorite Adrienne Rich poems, "The Spirit of Place," as my North Star.

As it is not as we wish it
As it is not as we work for it
To be.

Acknowledgments

When you leave, and you're actually out there, flailing like a new little fish, there are people who catch you. The universe catches you.

—Tia Levings, *Shiny Happy People*

I WAS ON SET IN SAVANNAH, GEORGIA, FOR *SHINY HAPPY PEOPLE* the day I said these words. One of the documentary's producers had asked me, "What happens when you get out?"

I teared up, staring out the window as names and faces floated through my mind . . . the many helpers, saviors, loved ones, and accidental angels who held my hand so I could find my feet and stand. I chuckled then and offered that line, flapping my hands to demonstrate a struggling fish. That clip became a show promo and my words resonated with fellow survivors. I received letters, essays with quotes, and even original art. We've all had a flailing fish moment; we've all been caught by a friend. I'm grateful for the space and time to say thank you.

But writing a book's acknowledgments brings trepidation. What if I forget someone? *I will forget someone.* What if I leave someone out? *I will inevitably leave someone out.* I must trust that if you're holding this book and you helped catch me along the way, you know who you are and I'm forever grateful you cared.

That said:

Father Justin and Mat. Jodie, who were not only our first safe landing space but the loving family for Kenai, the dog who lived. I'm so glad he grew up with boys, and warm sunbeams to lay in, and long walks through the woods, and for the long life he enjoyed in your family.

Randy and Sarah Small (no relation to the Smalls in the story.) Randy and Sarah took in strangers and later fed me poems; you are beautiful ambassadors of kindness who love community, words, and the mountains. Tim Richardson, for your vision and believing in me, and Adele, for your grace. Ray and Sharon Wall, and the rest of the progressive crew in the Blue Ridge Mountains. Your love and kindness brought sunshine into the darkness of those years. To me, you make the most beautiful place in the world even more lovely. To my opossum whisperer, Sarah Kerr, and Shane and your boys. Thank you for being a friend.

Tamara Howard, who dared befriend the quiet new neighbor in the house down the hill. I still laugh with you whenever I cut pineapple. Thank you for sitting on the porch with me and teaching me how to get up from despair. I love you forever.

Keith Webb, for finding beauty where I no longer could. Daniel Frye, for your kind and tender friendship, and for living art and life after great tragedy. You showed me it was possible.

The teachers who helped catch my children—including the beloved "Mrs. Ski"—thank you for showing us the power of public education, for providing emotional space away from the tumult of trauma recovery, and for getting my brilliant ones back on track. They are engineers and medical professionals and artists today because of you.

The kind souls at St. Justin Martyr Orthodox Church. Father Ted especially, who cared for the broken. The warriors at Micah's House for your shelter and support. William Cremins, Dr. Robert Wahler, Dr. Justin D'Arienzo, Harry Williams, and my therapists over the years. Your dedicated work and attention to nuance kept my children safe, challenged me to challenge myself, and helped me see what it is to be fair.

Elizabeth Ondriezek and Jennifer Boston, for being badass women of supreme organization and skill. Every woman should have advocates like you in their corner.

To Dr. Sara Filmalter, for listening to women. For taking my determination as seriously as my symptoms and helping me turn my medical destiny around. You're an incredible physician and thank you for caring for my family.

In Girl Scouts we had a song: *Make new friends but keep the old. One is silver and the other gold.* Thank you, Jenna, for not only your enduring friendship but also the story that gave me one of my favorite lines in the book: I love your hearts. But to the rest of my amazing friends . . . I do not dare start listing you by name. You know who you are and that undoubtedly, we'll catch up as if no time has passed at all, because that's how we are. You're old and new and all-the-time and I couldn't have sustained the writing of this book without all the tacos, iced wine, chips and queso, kayaking, wonky hikes, lunch dates, movie meetups, and long text threads.

The beloved women of the Trapdoor Society. We grew our artistic wells together and became autodidacts with moxie, humor, fire, and curiosity. *All our knowledge has its origin in our perceptions* (Leonardo da Vinci). Cheers to us, Sister Wendy, wine, chocolate, sad movies as therapy, and the Great Books. I'll always meet you by the lamppost.

The dear friends who wish to remain anonymous for their courageous testimonials of life in quiverful homes, and the power your stories lent to the early drafts of this manuscript. We stood in solidarity when none of us could stand alone. Let's keep flipping on that light switch and flooding these darkened rooms.

My Levings family and to Melanie especially, for claiming me as your sister no matter what. C. G., for years of stability and provision. For sixteen times before and for redeeming so many wounded places.

Betty Joyce Nash and Bill Shobe for foxes, fireflies, and fawns, and for the special quiet place in which I was able to finish this book, walk out my tears in the rain, and hear myself think with clarity and kindness. Happy trails and sunny skies.

The greatest gift I ever gave my writing life was hiring a coach. Jamie Morris took a frustrated, unstructured girl with a big story and sat her down one day in Barnes & Noble. She taught me plot structure, emotional timing, and Tarot. Thank you so much for not only recognizing potential and developing my craft, but our magic. You are art and kitten monkey joy to me always. But you also taught me to use my voice, express my heart, and claim my vision.

One day I was fuming about Josh Duggar's trial and how so many thought the Duggars led a wholesome lifestyle we all should emulate, when I knew the abuses that were hidden behind closed doors in patriarchal homes like ours. A fellow memoirist, Ashleigh Renard, said, "Make a reel about it." So, I made a few reels about it actually, and they all went viral. The rest is author-platform history because within a short time and as a direct result of that growth, I'd been contacted to participate in the Amazon documentary, signed an agent, and sold my book on proposal. *Renard* means "fox," and if you've ever heard me yell "FOX!!!," Ashleigh's clever wisdom is part of the reason why. Thank you.

Lisa Cooper Ellison, for the Dev Edit of the Ages, who taught me how to find the story within the situations, and to say what I mean. And also, for laughing until we peed on that dark street corner in Seattle. *Hell yeah, motherfuckers!*

Trinity McFadden, my incredible advocate, my dream agent come true. You are a true curator of talent as shown in my amazing agent-siblings, and we are lucky to have you in our corner. It's even better that I get to call you friend. You are a true creative partner. Somehow you manage to both ground and inspire me at the same time. To everyone at the Bindery, thank you. I'm so grateful for your representation.

My editor at St Martin's, Eileen Rothschild, who heard my heart and protected my prose, you are the editor I hoped for but couldn't even imagine I'd get. To have such a perfect team in you (looking at you, Lisa Bonvissuto—thank you!) and Trinity championing my work has been validating, affirming, and healing. Thank you for your vision, guidance, and wisdom. To the rest of the enthusiastic team at St. Martin's, including Katie Bassel and Michelle Cashman, who have helped promote and market this book, and to Olga Grlic for my sharp and striking cover, thank you. These colors followed me around everywhere for a year and when I saw your design, I knew it was meant to be.

Julie Sweeney Bogart, who started Trapdoor Society and has been so integral to my writing development from the first essay. *Write Bravely,* she said, and I did. Trapdoor unlocked my hunger to study humanities, but our friendship has helped heal my humanity. I'm so thankful for our courageous journey together—out of binary, fundamentalist thought into forgiveness and freedom. Beth Burgess, who brought the color, art, and laughter—whose open door sheltered my children on the way north, who used the phrase "non-coercive parenting" first, who *will* stop the car to get a better look at that crane. Let's just never bike again, okay?

Laura E. Anderson (Dr. Queen Laura in my phone), with whom every day is like a reality therapy TV show for Enneagram Fours and their feelings, and who (thanks to technology) stands in solidarity as we traverse relationships, breakups, world travel, badass visions, and a minefield of religious trauma triggers. You are more than a cohost, more than a friend, and I'm here for your nonconsensual advice and fire-wit wisdom forever and always. Pass the popcorn, my fellow Jezebel.

My Beloved John, who I am never too much for, who is music to my art, who reads me in more ways than one. You have been the sweetest surprise. You opened my heart when I wanted to close it and showed me everything is coming together exactly as it should. You will be here; you will always be here. The universe conspires in our favor. Thank you for such calm safety and rest.

My parents, whose doors and arms are always open, and who raised me with enough wildness to find my way through a wilderness. Who nurtured resilience, skills, initiative, and *yagottawanna* . . . but most of all, have been constant throughout every up and down. To my sister. Your generosity kept us safe and opened the door to freedom. I'm so glad we still have Orion, car, cold grass, that parallel you and me on the moon. Thank you for being Second Mom to my children. To the best brother-in-law in the world, and to my nieces and favorite nephew. I love you all so very much.

Michael, the family I chose for myself, the friend who breaks every mold church and the world tried to foist on us. Movies and Twizzlers and Nina until we're ninety-five and don't have teeth, okay? Our story was always at the heart of this book. Thank you forever for seeing right through me. Mark and the boys, thanks for just sorta adopting me. I love you and I love being your Tia.

I often say motherhood is what saved me. My babies, my loves. You have been my greatest dream come true, the loves of my life, the core of my heart. I adore you, your spouses (V and K as of this writing), and my sweet grands, who make me a new creation: Oma. I've never regretted a single decision I made when you were at the center. You are kind, amazing humans and I'm honored to be your mother as we grow. I hope you never forget that you can reach for your dreams, things almost always work out, everything looks different in three days, and love will always be our home, no matter what or where life takes us all.

People often ask me how I keep sharing hard stories without breaking down. So much of that is therapy, self-care, and boundaries. But the survivor community is "My Why." Your stories are welcome with me. My Instagram peeps, followers, subscribers, particularly those who signed up for everything and attended every tittie and fox party. To my queer friends and LGBTQ vibrant souls who make this world a more beautiful place . . . thank you for being you. I'd never want a world without you and I will stand in solidarity as you shine.

To anyone who walked alongside me and who I've left out, I know that *you* know it was not intentional. You never thought I'd be perfect.

Dear reader, these names all exist outside of high-control religion. While the fundamentalists, pastors, and perpetuators of patriarchy told me I'd be alone, cut off, and abandoned by the fellowship and God if I left and called out abuse, the opposite was true. Love is served at a bigger table. To quote the book that brought us here:

Love does not delight in evil but rejoices with the truth. It always protects, always trusts, always hopes, always perseveres.

Love wins.

Reader, religious trauma is trauma. You may be feeling memories or emotions rise as you realize a story like mine is not as "fringe" as it may have seemed. I've compiled a list of free resources to help you ground, recenter, and take steps toward processing and healing. Access them at TiaLevings.com/religious -trauma-resources.

About the Author

Hannah Joy Photography

TIA LEVINGS writes about the realities of Christian funda-mentalism, evangelical patriarchy, and religious trauma. She is also a podcaster, speaker, and content strategist. She's been quoted in *Salon, HuffPost,* and *Newsweek,* and appeared in the hit Amazon docuseries *Shiny Happy People.* Based in Jackson-ville, Florida, she is mom to four incredible adults and likes to travel, hike, paint, and daydream. Find her on social media @ TiaLevingsWriter. Based in Jacksonville, Florida, she is mom to four incredible adults and loves to travel, hike, paint, and daydream. *A Well-Trained Wife* is her first book.